Programming 101

Learn to Code with the Processing Language Using a Visual Approach

Second Edition

Jeanine Meyer

Programming 101: Learn to Code with the Processing Language Using a Visual Approach

Jeanine Meyer
Mt Kisco, NY, USA

ISBN-13 (pbk): 978-1-4842-8193-2
https://doi.org/10.1007/978-1-4842-8194-9

ISBN-13 (electronic): 978-1-4842-8194-9

Managing Director, Apress Media LLC: Welmoed Spahr
Acquisitions Editor: James Robinson-Prior
Development Editor: James Markham
Coordinating Editor: Jessica Vakili

Distributed to the book trade worldwide by Springer Science+Business Media New York, 1 NY Plaza, New York, NY 10004. Phone 1-800-SPRINGER, fax (201) 348-4505, e-mail orders-ny@springer-sbm.com, or visit www.springeronline.com. Apress Media, LLC is a California LLC and the sole member (owner) is Springer Science + Business Media Finance Inc (SSBM Finance Inc). SSBM Finance Inc is a **Delaware** corporation.

For information on translations, please e-mail booktranslations@springernature.com; for reprint, paperback, or audio rights, please e-mail bookpermissions@springernature.com.

Apress titles may be purchased in bulk for academic, corporate, or promotional use. eBook versions and licenses are also available for most titles. For more information, reference our Print and eBook Bulk Sales web page at http://www.apress.com/bulk-sales.

Any source code or other supplementary material referenced by the author in this book is available to readers on the Github repository: https://github.com/Apress/Programming-101. For more detailed information, please visit http://www.apress.com/source-code.

Printed on acid-free paper

To my family, who inspire and teach me.

Table of Contents

About the Author

 **Jeanine Meyer** is Professor Emerita at Purchase College/SUNY. Before Purchase, she taught at Pace University and prior to that was a manager and research staff member at IBM Research in robotics and manufacturing. She also worked as a research consultant at IBM for educational grant programs.

She was moved to create this book because of a general wish to make programming less mysterious and more appealing while featuring the challenges. She enjoys spending time with favorite pictures and video clips as well as producing programs. The chance for a new edition provided a reason to explore p5.js, tools for using JavaScript with features from Processing.

She is the author of five books and coauthor of five more on topics ranging from educational uses of multimedia, programming, databases, number theory, and origami. She earned a PhD in computer science at the Courant Institute at New York University, an MA in mathematics at Columbia, and an SB (the college used the Latin form) in mathematics from the University of Chicago. Recently, she has given lectures, in-person and remotely, connecting origami, mathematics, and computer science as well as the use and misuse of math in the news. She is a member of Phi Beta Kappa, Sigma Xi, the Association for Women in Science, and the Association for Computing Machinery. Jeanine is trying but remains a beginner at Spanish and piano.

About the Technical Reviewer

Joseph McKay is an associate professor of new media. He primarily teaches new directions in virtual space, programming for visual artists, intro to physical computing, hacking the everyday, senior seminar, and web development.

Joe's work is focused on interactive art games. He makes games that have their roots in fine art but are also fun and easy to play. He is currently working on a VR art game with innovative locomotion.

Acknowledgments

Much appreciation to the subjects of the illustrations in this book, starting with my father (Joseph) and including my mother (Esther), Aviva, Grant, Liam, and especially Annika. Thanks to my children, Aviva and Daniel, for the photography, video, and computer graphics work.

My students, teaching assistants, and colleagues always provide ideas, stimulation, feedback, and advice. Thanks especially to Irina Shablinsky for her efforts in teaching me Processing and how to teach Processing and introducing me to Takashi Mukoda. Thanks to David Jameson, whose comments and concerns made me produce the "Under the Covers" section for each chapter.

Thanks to the crew at Apress/Springer Nature, including for the second edition James Robinson-Prior, Jessica Vakili, Dulcy Nirmala, Krishnan Sathyamurthy, and others I do not know by name. Much appreciation to the past technical reviewers, Massimo Nardone and Takashi Mukoda, and the technical reviewer for this edition, Joe McKay, who brought his considerable talent and experience to the task.

Introduction

Processing is a programming language built on top of another programming language called Java. To quote from the https://processing.org page, "Processing is a flexible software sketchbook and a language for learning how to code within the context of the visual arts." The term for a program in Processing is *sketch*. However, Processing can be used to create applications that are far more than static sketches. You can use Processing to create dynamic, interactive programs. It is a great tool for learning programming.

Though Processing was created for visual artists, it serves a broad population of people. In particular, at Purchase College/SUNY, Processing has been an excellent first computer programming language for our computer science/mathematics majors and minors. It also serves students across the college, who take our CS I course to satisfy one of the general education requirements. This experience has been reported in other places. Processing and this text also are appropriate for self-study.

The ten chapters in this book share a common design and structure. My goal is to introduce you to programming, focusing on the Processing language. In each chapter, I explain general programming concepts and specific Processing features through the use of one or more specific examples. The code and files such as image files are combined as zip files and available at https://github.com/Apress/Programming-101. I hope the examples are entertaining; the goal, however, is not for you to learn the specific examples but instead understand the concepts and features. The way to learn programming is to make these examples "your own" and to go on to do a lot of programming.

The introduction to each chapter starts with a brief description of the concepts and programming features used and the examples; then you need to be patient while I provide background. Each chapter includes a discussion of general "Programming Concepts" prior to plunging into the details. These are not limited to the Processing language but are present in most programming languages. Presenting the concepts in a general way might help you if you are coming to this book knowing another language *or* you hope to move on to another language someday.

Next, I describe the "Processing Programming Features" that are used to realize those concepts and produce the examples. This section will have actual code in it and maybe short examples. This is a spiral approach, going from the general to the specific.

A section called "Under the Covers" describes what Processing is doing for us behind the scenes and the relationship between Processing and Java. This section appears in different places in each chapter. It might be of more interest for readers who know something or want to know something about Java, but I urge everyone to give it at least a quick scan.

I then provide an overview of each example, with screenshots showing the operation of the program. Please note that in some cases, I have modified the programs to obtain the screenshots. I then go on to describe the implementation of the example, which contains a "Planning" and a "Program" section. The "Planning" section is where I describe my thought process. Programs do not spring into existence—at least for me— not like Mozart composing a symphony, which was said to emerge all at once from his mind. It is an iterative process for most of us. This section contains a table indicating the relationship of the functions. The "Program" section includes a table with one column for code and another column with an explanation of that line of code. These tables are long and are not meant to be read as poetry or fine literature. Instead, skip around. Use the function relationship table. If you download the code and try it out, you can use this section to improve your understanding of the program. The most critical step is to make changes, and I provide suggestions in the "How to Make This Your Own" section. This set of sections is repeated for each example.

A section titled "Things to Look Up" will contain a list of Processing features related to the ones described in the chapter. Processing is a large language, and it is growing. I can show you only a small subset of the features, and each feature is used in one way, perhaps using default values. You can and should consult other references to learn more. You can look things up in multiple ways. For example, you can go to the website at `https://processing.org/reference/` and just keep that open. Alternatively, if you want to look up how to draw a rectangle in Processing, it can be efficient to enter "processing.org rectangle" into Google (or another search engine) or the address field of browsers such as Chrome to retrieve a list of possible sites. It is best to use "processing.org" because "processing" is a common English word. You can try "Processing rectangle," but you will need to skip over some sites that have nothing to do with the Processing language.

Remember that the goal of this book is not to teach you how to make my examples, from peanut-shaped bald men to my versions of certain games to rotating 3D cubes with photos of my grandchild, but to help you understand how to make your own programs! Make small changes and then large changes. Make your own programs! Chapters will close with two more sections: a brief review, "What You Learned," and "What's Next."

The book also has an Appendix describing what is called p5.js. This is a way to produce programs for the Web by providing a Processing Library to use with JavaScript. The Processing organization also supplies an online editor.

You are welcome to look at the chapters in any order, but later examples do depend on an understanding of concepts introduced earlier. Moreover, because one of the main techniques of programming is to reuse code, there are many instances of later examples copying parts of earlier examples. Do not be concerned: the tables in the "Implementation" section contain complete programs. It is beneficial for your learning process to recognize the repetition.

Please do take a pause in reading to explore, experiment, and, I repeat, make your own programs. Learning how to program is critical for understanding how we function in today's world and the requirements and challenges of devising algorithms using logic and data. Learning to program might help you get a job. However, the main thing that drives me, and I hope will drive you, is that it is fun.

Enjoy,
Jeanine

CHAPTER 1

Basics

Abstract

The goal of this chapter is to get you started. The programming example will be a static drawing of two cartoonish figures, as shown in Figure 1-1. Be aware that the examples in subsequent chapters will increase in complexity, as we will be producing programs that are highly interactive and, possibly, involving random effects, reading files, and exhibiting behavior based on various conditions.

© Jeanine Meyer 2022
J. Meyer, *Programming 101*, https://doi.org/10.1007/978-1-4842-8194-9_1

Figure 1-1. *Fat and skinny Daddy logos*

The Daddy logo is a version of a drawing my father would make, often as his signature on a letter or note or artwork. I hope that you will design or recall a drawing or symbol that has meaning to you and makes you happy the same way this cartoonish peanut-shaped, bald guy makes me.

We will need to do some work to start us off and get to the point that the coding is clear, but it is not too difficult. The traditional first task in using any programming language is to get the program to display the phrase "Hello, world." This works well in demonstrating several important concepts, including what happens if the programmer makes certain types of errors. Because of the features built into Processing, you can produce a pretty fancy version of "Hello, world."

Be patient with me and with yourself. At the end of the chapter, you will be able to implement your own Daddy logo.

Programming Concepts

This section, included in each chapter, is to provide a general introduction to concepts. I begin with comparing and contrasting programming languages with natural languages.

Programming Languages and Natural Languages

Programming languages have some similarities with natural languages, but they also have significant differences. Programming languages are defined by rules just as a natural language's grammar defines what is proper English, Spanish, or other language. A program contains statements of different types just as we find in English (or Spanish, etc.), and there also are ways to construct compound statements. Statements in programming languages contain terms and expressions involving terms. In programming languages, programmers often come up with our own names for things. The names must follow certain rules, but these are not unduly restrictive. This is a difference from natural languages, in which we mainly use the official words of the language, whereas in programming, we are extending the language all the time.

A more significant difference between programming languages and natural languages is that the rules must be obeyed at all times when using programming languages! Consider that we all frequently utter grammatically incorrect statements when we speak and yet generally are understood. This is not the situation in programming. The good news in the case of Processing, and certain other languages, is that the Processing system generally indicates where an error occurs. The development environments for Processing and other computer languages are themselves computer programs, and they do not exhibit any impatience while we fix errors and try the program again. I will give some examples of statements, right after I introduce the concept of values and variables.

Values and Variables

Programming involves containers or buckets where we can store specific types of things (values). These kinds (types) of things are called *data types*. The following are some examples of data:

Int   integer (e.g., 10)
float   decimal value (e.g., 5.3)

Boolean   logical values (e.g., true/false)
Char   single character (e.g., 'a')
String   a string of characters (e.g., "hello world")

String should start with a capitalized "S". The B in Boolean can be upper or lowercase. The data type is named for George Boole, an English mathematician credited with originating symbolic algebra.

Our programs can include literal values such as 5, 100.345, and "Hello" in the code. In addition, a feature in all programming languages is what is termed *variables*. A variable is a construct for associating a name of our choosing with a value. We can initialize the variable, change it, and use it in an expression; that is, the value associated, often termed *in* the variable, can vary, that is, change. Using variables makes our programs less mysterious. Moreover, we can define one variable in terms of another, making relationships explicit and preventing certain errors. In Processing, Java, and some, but not all, programming languages, variables need to be declared, or set up before use. One characteristic of variables is termed *scope,* which indicates what code has access (e.g., global variables vs. local variables), but that is best explained later.

The following are examples of Processing statements. Explanation is given in comments and later.

```
int classSize;  // this declares, that is, sets up classSize to
                // be a variable.
classSize = 21; //assigns the value 21 to the variable classSize.
classSize = classSize + 5; //takes whatever is the current value held in
                // the variable classSize
                // and adds 5 to it and resets classSize to the new value
float score = 0; //declares the variable score AND
                // assigns it a value. This is called initialization.
if (score == 0) {
    text("You did not score anything.", 100,100);
    text("Try again.", 100,300);
}
```

The // indicates that the rest of the line is a comment, meaning that Processing ignores it. It is intended for readers of the code, including you, to make things clear. You also can use the delimiters /* and */ for long comments.

Note

My examples, because they are surrounded by explanations, tend not to have as many comments as I would use outside of teaching and writing books.

There are rules for variable and function names in all programming languages. Generally, they must start with a letter, uppercase or lowercase, and cannot contain spaces. The most important guidance for naming is that the names should have meaning for you. The programming language will accept single character names or names with no apparent meaning, but these will not be helpful when you are trying to recall what you were trying to do. So-called camel casing, as in `classSize`, can be helpful.

A single equal sign (=) means assignment and is used in what are called, naturally enough, *assignment* statements and *initialization* statements. The statement

```
classSize = classSize + 5;
```

will seem less illogical if you read it as

classSize is assigned or gets the total of the current value of classSize plus 5.

A double equal sign (==) is a comparison operator and often appears in an `if` statement. Think of it as like < or <=.

The `if` statement is an example of a compound statement. The expression `score == 0` is interpreted as a comparison. If the value of the variable `score` is equal to zero, then the statement within the brackets is executed. If the value of `score` is greater than zero or less than zero, nothing happens. Again, you will see many more statements in the context of examples.

Functions

Programming work in any language is structured into units. One important way of structuring code comes with different names: *function, procedure, subroutine, method.* These are ways of packaging one or more statements into one unit. You will read about functions in the "Processing Programming Features" section and methods in the "Under the Covers" section. Briefly, functions are defined, and functions are invoked. I can give you directions , perhaps orally, perhaps by text, to my house, which is analogous to defining a function. At that point, I am not directing you to come to my house. At some later time, I can direct you to go to my house, and this is analogous to invoking the function.

Programs can be considerably shorter as well as easier to modify through the use of functions and variables, so understanding both of these concepts is important. You do not need to accept this or understand this right now. It will be demonstrated later by my sketch for displaying two Daddy logos that takes just one statement more than displaying the Daddy logo just once.

Specifying Positions and Angles

Displaying drawings and images and text on the screen requires a coordinate system. The coordinate system used by most computer languages and many graphical tools is similar to what we learned (but might or might not remember) from high school geometry, with one big difference. Horizontal positions, sometimes called x positions, are specified starting from the left. Vertical positions, sometimes called y, are specified starting from the top of the screen. Figure 1-2 shows the coordinate system with a small circle at the 100, 200 location.

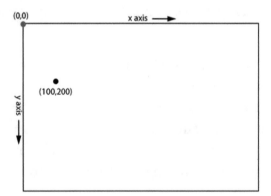

Figure 1-2. *Coordinate system*

If you say to yourself "This is upside down," then I know you understood. Another important point is that the unit is very small, so if your code positions something at 100, 200 and later at 101, 201, you probably will not detect the difference. Your intuition regarding this will improve with experience.

Note

As a teaser, Processing has facilities for 3D as well as 2D. We get to 3D in later chapters.

In this chapter, my Daddy logo has a smile made by specifying an arc of an ellipse. To produce the arc, I need to write code to indicate a starting angle and an ending angle of the arc. The system used in most computer languages is not the standard one in which a right angle is 90 degrees, a U-turn is a 180, and snowboarders do 1800s. (I am writing this during the Olympics, and yes, snowboarders did tricks measuring 1800 and bigger.) It might be upsetting to realize this, but the notion of degrees with a circle consisting of 360 degrees was invented by people. I typically offer my students extra credit to identify where and when this happened. Instead, in most programming languages, we use a measure called *radians*. Think of wrapping a circle with lengths equal to one radius. How many lengths will this take? You know the answer: It is not a whole number, it is 2 times π, where π is an irrational number often approximated by 3.14159. In our programming, we will use the built-in values TWO_PI, PI, HALF_PI, and QUARTER_PI. You will see radians in use, so be patient.

Colors

There are different ways to specify colors in computer languages and computer applications, and Processing supports more than one. In this text, we stick with grayscale and RGB (red/green/blue). Because of how these values are stored, the range of grayscale is from 0 (black) to 255 (white), and the values for redness, greenness, and blueness are specified by a number from 0 to 255. This approach is used in many applications. If you want to use a certain color that you see in a photo, you can open the image file in Adobe Photoshop or the online Pixlr or some other graphics tool and use the eye drop on the pixel (picture element) you want, and an information window will tell you the RGB value. See also the mention of the Color Selector in the "Things to Look Up" section.

Development Environment

Programmers need to prepare programs and test programs. We also need to save our work to come back to it another time. We might need to send the program to someone else. Processing has what is termed an *integrated development environment*, the Processing Development Environment (PDE), which provides a way to prepare and make changes to a program as well as test it and save it. To give you a different example, Hypertext Markup Language (HTML) documents containing JavaScript are prepared and saved using a text editor, such as Sublime. The resulting files are opened (and run) using a browser, such as Chrome. In the Appendix, I will show you how to use an editor for p5.js, which is a version of JavaScript incorporating Processing features.

Role of Planning

I close this first "Programming Concepts" section by noting that preparing programs such as a Processing sketch generally involves planning and design. It might be best to step away from the keyboard. Some of the plans might need to be modified when you get to writing the code, but it is best to have plans!

Under the Covers

As I indicated earlier, Processing is a language built on Java. This means that the Processing code you write is Java code that the development environment puts into a larger Java program prepared for handling Processing sketches. In Java, there are no functions, but, instead, what are termed *methods*. I will introduce methods for our use in Processing in Chapter 4.

The PDE (Processing Development Environment) makes use of *libraries*, collections of methods holding the built-in functions of Processing, such as functions to draw a rectangle.

In the big Java program, there are calls to functions that we write, or, to put it more accurately, we code the body of the function. For example, all Processing sketches contain a function called setup, the purpose of which is to do what the name implies. It nearly always includes a statement that defines the width and height of the window, for example. The big Java program invokes the setup program once at the start of the sketch. Similarly, we can write the body of a function named draw. The Java program invokes this function over and over, the frequency defined by the *frame rate*, which can be reset by assigning a value to the built-in variable frameRate. This enables us to build applications producing animations and responding to events such as a user clicking the mouse button. There are many other functions for which we, the programmers, specify the response to an event, for example, keyPressed or mouseClick.

The Java program also defines *default* settings. Processing and other computer languages and many computer applications provide powerful features. If we needed to specify each aspect of each feature before anything happens, it would be tremendously burdensome. It is important to be aware that certain things can be adjusted, though, as you will see in our very first example later, with the discussion on default values for font, text size, fill color, and stroke color.

The design and capabilities of Processing provide us a way to get started creating and implementing our ideas quickly.

Processing Programming Features

In this section, I explain the concepts focusing on Processing features. There will be small coding examples to prepare for the larger (although not too large) examples covered later in the chapter.

To use Processing, you need to go to the `processing.org` website and follow the directions to download and install Processing on your computer.

Processing Development Environment

To describe the PDE in abstract terms is too difficult, so let's get started. Once you have downloaded and installed Processing, open it. At the top of the PDE window, you will see the Processing File toolbar.

Click File, which will open a drop-down menu. Select New. The toolbar will change to hold more options. A window that looks like Figure 1-3 will appear on your screen. The number after sketch_ will be different than what you see here. I believe in saving early, and often so, at this point, you can think about where you want to save your Processing work in terms of the file system on your computer. I leave that to you. You also should give some thought to what you will name each sketch. I suggest the name `first0` for this one. Click File, then select Save As..., and proceed with a file name and a location in the usual way for your operating system.

Figure 1-3. *Window for new sketch*

Using Save As… in the PDE produces a folder, in this case named first0, which contains a file named first0.pde. The examples explored in future chapters will consist of folders containing additional items. For example, a Processing sketch named myFamily that makes use of an image file aviva.jpg and an image file daniel.jpg will be a folder named myFamily containing a file named myFamily.pde and a folder named data that contains the two files aviva.jpg and daniel.jpg. The relationship of these files is shown in Figure 1-4.

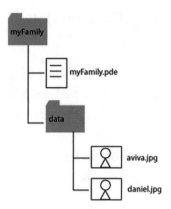

Figure 1-4. *Typical file structure for a sketch*

Functions

Processing uses the term *function* for grouping together one or more statements into something that can be invoked (called). Functions are defined with *header* statements and then the *body*, a sequence of statements, contained within brackets. You will see in this chapter and every chapter definitions for the setup function, a function that Processing expects the programmer to supply. The header is

```
void setup()
```

The term *void* indicates that this function does not produce or return a value. The opening and closing parentheses with nothing between them indicate that this function does not expect any parameters.

The Daddy logo example includes a function called daddy that does the work of drawing the cartoon. Its header is

```
void daddy(int x, int y, int w, int h)
```

The parameters are the things between the parentheses. The parameter list is the place for the programmer to give names and specify the data type. This means that when I wrote the code to invoke daddy, which is necessary because daddy was something I made up, not anything Processing expects, Processing will check that the values cited in the call are the correct type.

I feel obliged to show you an example of a function that does produce a value, a standard one supplied in many textbooks.

```
float calculateTax (float bill, float rate) {
    return (bill*rate);
}
```

The header indicates that this function calculates a floating-point value, sometimes called a decimal number. The code includes what is termed an expression: `bill*rate`. The asterisk indicates multiplication.

Because it generates a value, a call of this function can be used in an expression. With this function defined, I could write an expression (part of a statement) with something like this:

```
Total = 150.53 + calculateTax(150.53, .07);
```

Processing will assign the `150.53` to the parameter `bill` and the `.07` to the parameter rate, perform the multiplication `bill * rate`, which in this case is `150.53 * .07`, and return the result so it is available to be added to `150.53`. The variable `Total` will be set to 161.0671.

I hope the names of these variables are suggestive. My examples are more complex and more interesting and, because context is given, more understandable, in later chapters.

Angles

Processing provides us built-in variables—`PI`, `TWO_PI`, `HALF_PI`, and `QUARTER_PI`—to use when requiring specification of angles. These names are case-sensitive. Figure 1-5 shows the designation of some angles.

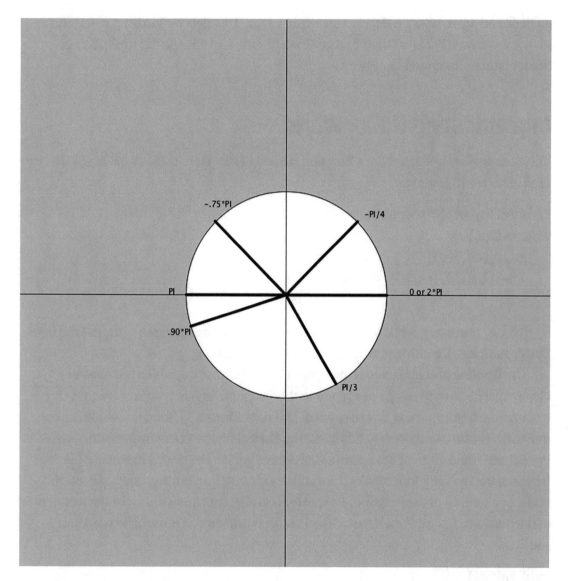

Figure 1-5. *Diagram showing some angles in radians*

In Processing, angles start at 0 and move clockwise around the circle as the number increases. Notice the location of PI/3. However, you can designate a negative angle. The angle labeled –PI/4 could also be specified as PI+.75PI or 1.75*PI.

Processing provides a function named radians for converting from the degree system to radian measure. So radians(90) will produce a floating-point number very close to PI/2, and radians(180) will produce a floating-point number very close to PI. We can go back and forth between degrees and radians, but I suggest building up your intuition in radians. One way to do that is to examine my code and change the smile. You get immediate feedback and can try again.

Implementing Hello, World

In Processing, we need to write a function named setup. Here is the code for my first try at a Hello, World program.

```
// a Hello, world program
void setup() {
    size(900,600);
    text("Hello, world",100,200);
}
```

It is not necessary, but it is good practice to put a comment at the start, as I did here. The // indicates a comment, which is ignored by Processing.

The first line of actual code is the header line of a function, which has several elements. The term *setup* gives a name to the function. As I indicated earlier, we define a setup function to get our sketch started. The parentheses, (), after the name indicate that there are no parameters to this function. Parameters are extra information passed to the function, and you will see examples of parameters in the Daddy logo example. The brackets, the opening { on the first line and the closing } on the last line, mark off the body, or contents, of the function. People follow different conventions for the location of the brackets. They do not have to be where they are but can instead be what you see here:

```
void setup()
    {size(900,600);
    text("Hello, world",100,200);}
```

My general advice is to not be skimpy about line breaks or blank lines. I also need to tell you that indentation is not required and is not interpreted by Processing, *but* I advise you to use indentation for functions and for compound statements such as the if and for loop constructs we see later because it will make your code easier for you to understand. There are Auto Format under edit and a keyboard shortcut (Command+T) for automatic indentation.

The first statement within the body of the function specifies the size of the display window. The width is set at 900 and the height at 600. When you run or execute the program, you will see what these settings produce.

The second and last statement within the body of the function does the work of displaying the string "Hello, world" at the position 100 pixel units from the left side of the display window and 200 pixel units from the top.

You should save the program, which you do by clicking File and then selecting Save. Select Save rather than Save As... to save the file in the same place as you indicated in the first Save As... command. Of course, you could wait to rename the program and then use Save As..., but my motto is to save early and often.

The next step is to try the program by running it. Do this by clicking on the play (triangle/arrow) button in the upper left of the screen shown in Figure 1-6.

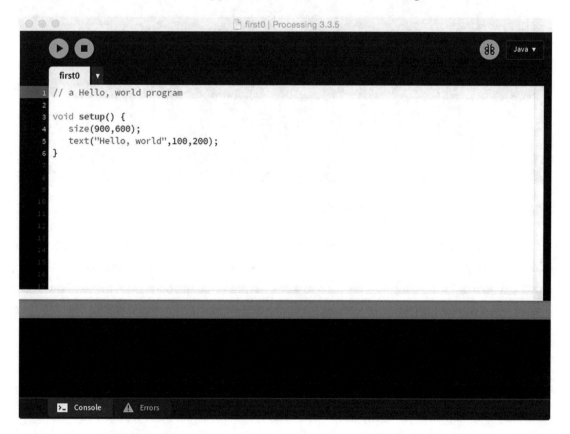

Figure 1-6. *The first sketch*

The result will be disappointing, but it is educational. You should see what is shown in Figure 1-7, namely, the phrase "Hello, world" in tiny, white letters.

Figure 1-7. *Result of running* first0

Now, perhaps you do not see anything. Perhaps the program did not even start. This could happen if you made any *syntactic* mistakes, or mistakes of form. To put it in practical terms, Processing can detect syntactic errors but cannot correct them. Examine Figure 1-8. I made a mistake, omitting a comma between the 100 and the 200. The Processing program shows that there is a problem in the statement indicating the call to the function text. The message, called an *error message*, does not say what I know happened: it does not say anything about a missing comma. It does say that the function text() expects three parameters. Error messages might not tell you everything, but they generally are helpful. One of the most common syntactic mistakes is a problem with brackets or parentheses. Processing can detect when there are too many or too few but does not indicate exactly where the problem is.

Figure 1-8. *Example of a syntactic mistake and error message*

In addition to syntactic mistakes, we could make *semantic mistakes*, mistakes of meaning or faulty logic. If you or I had written "Hellowold," the rules of Processing would accept it, but it might not be what we intended. Similarly, if we intended to draw a red circle and instead drew a blue one or if we produced a drawing with the left eye not on the face, that would be a semantic mistake. Processing does not help us notice or fix these. We are on our own.

You can say that the program shown in Figure 1-6 and producing the result shown in Figure 1-7 represents a semantic error. I will say it was a success—the desired message was displayed—but we can do better. Remember my mention of default values? The call to the text function makes use of the current settings for text size, text font, text color, and text alignment. I will show you an improvement. To encourage good habits, go to the File menu, select Save As..., and save with a new name, `first1`. The improved sketch will change the text size and the color. I leave font and alignment to you.

The Processing function `fill()` sets the color of a shape or the color of text, and the function `stroke()` sets the color of the outline of a shape. If we use just one number, the color is grayscale, or black to white. The value should be a number from 0 to 255, where 0 is black and 255 is white. If we use three numbers, the numbers specify the amounts of redness, greenness, and blueness. As with positions and angles, you will gain intuition on this as you use it.

Here is the complete code for the improved sketch; notice that two statements have been added to the original sketch, and I also changed the comment at the start.

```
// improved Hello, world program, setting size and color
void setup() {
    size(900,600);
    textSize(30); //bigger than default
    fill(250,0,250); //changed color for text
    text("Hello, world",100,200);
}
```

The call to the function textSize sets the new size. The call to the fill function sets the color. Save the sketch and then run this program; it will produce what is shown in Figure 1-9.

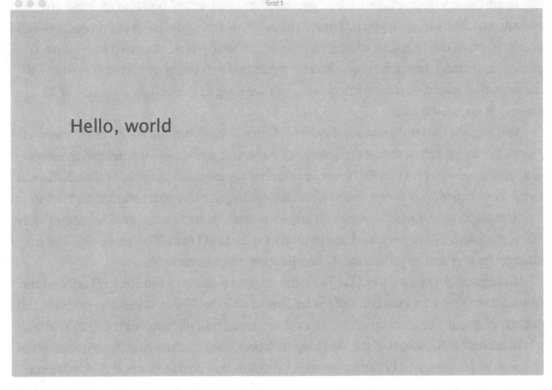

Figure 1-9. *Result of first1, the improved sketch*

Because Processing facilitates much more than displaying text, I describe one more program here. Click File, select Save As..., and save this file with the name first2. Now modify the program with the addition of one more statement. I provide the whole sketch, but it is just the line with the call to the ellipse function that is to be added. The ellipse is centered at 180, 200. Its width is 300, and its height is 200. Ellipses can be specified in different ways depending on the setting of a variable named ellipseMode. You can look this up to see the possibilities.

```
// a Hello, world inside of ellipse
void setup() {
    size(900,600);
    ellipse(180,200,300,200);//I fiddled with these values
    textSize(30); //bigger than the default
    fill(250,0,250); //changed color for text
    text("Hello, world",100,200);
}
```

Do take my comment "I fiddled" seriously; that is, I tried a few things until the result was what I wanted. Save and run the program. You should see what is displayed in Figure 1-10.

Figure 1-10. *Hello, world inside an ellipse*

Why is the ellipse white with a black border? The answer is that the default value for fill is 255, producing white, and the default for stroke is 0, producing black. I strongly urge you to put the book down (or close the window on whatever application you are reading the e-book version) and do some experiments. Put a call to the fill function and a call to the stroke function before the ellipse command. Change "Hello, world" to something else. Draw a circle instead of an ellipse. Try stuff!

This activity with Hello, world examples introduced the basics, but not every feature required for the Daddy logo project. Here is a list of what additional Processing constructs will be used, with short explanations.

- Declaration of variables, including initialization. An example of this is

    ```
    int skinnyFaceWidth = 60;
    ```

    This sets skinnyFaceWidth as a variable of data type int and an initial value of 60. I say initial value, but in fact, this variable and many of the others do not change: they are not assigned different values.

- The `color` data type and the `color` function: This is an unusual but acceptable situation of one name being used for two distinct things. In Processing, `color` is a data type similar to `int` or `float`. The `color` function is used to produce a value of data type `color`. The following code could appear:

```
color skinTone = color(255,224,189);
```

  I advise you to not use the same name for different things even if they are related.

- The `ellipseMode` function: Processing provides different ways to specify an ellipse. For example, a programmer can specify the center or the upper left corner. I use it here to introduce the idea. A call to

```
ellipseMode(CENTER);
```

  means that the parameters specify the center of the ellipse. In different situations, you might find one way more natural than the other.

- Expressions, making use of arithmetic operators: You will read later in the "Planning" section how my code defines certain variables in terms of other variables. For example, the center of the arc that is the mouth is set to be a certain distance, namely, one tenth of the height, further down the screen than the center of the ellipse that is the lower part of the peanut shape. My code converts (the technical term *cast* is used) the results to be rounded to an integer.

```
int mouthYoffset = int(.10*h);
```

- Definition of a programmer-defined function, `daddy`, with parameters: Defining what are called programmer-defined functions is the main lesson of this chapter. The function I define is called `daddy`, and its parameters are used to specify the position and the dimensions of the Daddy figure.

- Definition of the `draw` function and turning off the invocation of `draw`: In the Daddy logo example, the `draw` function calls the `daddy` function two times (wait for the next section). Normally, the `draw` function gets invoked over and over. How often `draw` is invoked is called the *frame rate*, and you can change this. It would not do any harm to repeat this, but I decided to show how to turn it off through the use of `noLoop()`.

These all are best explained in the context of use, so be patient to read what follows.

Implementing the Daddy Logo

With the introduction using the Hello, world examples, and hoping you have done some noodling around in Processing on your own, I move on to the Daddy logo. I describe my thought process when planning the sketch and then explain declaration of variables, the use of expressions, `color` data type and `color` function, the `draw` function, and programmer-defined functions.

Planning

My approach to producing the peanut shape is to draw two ellipses, one slightly on top of the other, with no borders. Borders are turned off by a call to the function `noStroke()`. The drawing of borders is turned back on by a call to `stroke` with the desired color. I won't quite call this a hack, but it is a trick. To make the mouth, I used the `noFill()` function because I just wanted the outline.

My plan is to define a function called `daddy` with parameters indicating the position of the Daddy logo cartoon and the width and height of the peanut-shaped figure. The two ellipses, eyes, mouth, and hair will each be placed using horizontal and vertical values derived from the parameters. I also will make use of global variables. I could have achieved the same effects by putting a lot of code inside the `setup` function because this is just a static drawing. However, I am using a function as well as defining the contents of `draw` and making use of variables to model good practices. This approach does require me to work out the relative position of the two ellipses (the upper and lower parts of the face) and the relative positions of each of the circles representing eyes, the arc that represents the mouth, and the two arcs that represent the one hair on the top of the head.

Doing this work, figuring out these relationships, allows me (through my code) to produce a Daddy or peanut shape at different horizontal and vertical positions and different widths and heights.

I define a programmer-defined function called daddy. The header line is

```
void daddy(int x, int y, int w, int h)
```

This defines daddy as a function expecting four parameters, each integer (whole numbers), with the names x, y, w, and h. You could think of parameters as additional information sent with the invocation of the function. Normally, I would choose longer names but decided that these were clear enough, standing for the horizontal position, the vertical position, the width, and the height. The parameters will each be referenced in the body of the function. Their values will be the values set by a call to the function. The function is called twice, both in the draw function:

```
daddy(ctrx,ctry,faceWidth, faceHeight);
daddy(3*ctrx, 2*ctry,skinnyFaceWidth, skinnyFaceHeight);
```

This is a chicken-and-egg situation. I haven't told you what is inside my daddy function. All I can say now is that the first call of daddy will set the x appearing inside the function to the value of ctrx, the value of y appearing inside the function to the value of ctry, and so on for w and h. The ctrx and ctry are variables that I have named. They will be the horizontal coordinate and the vertical coordinate of the center of one of the two circles used in the Daddy cartoon.

The variables cited in these two lines are global variables, to be explained soon. Just from looking at these two statements, assuming that skinnyFaceWidth and skinnyFaceHeight are appropriately named, we can make a safe guess that the skinny Daddy figure is three times as far from the left and twice as far down the screen, and that is indeed what appears in Figure 1-1.

Execution of code starts with the setup function. The draw function is invoked next. In this particular case, the first statement in the draw function is executed, which means control goes to the daddy function. All the statements in the daddy function are executed with the parameters referenced in the call in the first statement. Then control returns to draw, and the second statement is executed. This means control goes again to the daddy function with all the statements executed with the new set of parameters. Control returns to draw, and the last statement is executed. As you see here, this last statement is noLoop();. The effect of this is to stop looping; that is, stop any further invocation of draw.

Note

I could have left off turning off looping and you would not have noticed. Processing would have drawn the two cartoons over and over in the same place.

Global variables are declared outside of functions, whereas *local variables* are declared inside of functions. Global variables are used inside of functions and persist, or stay around when a function completes. In contrast, local variables go away when the function completes. The benefits of local variables and the more elaborate scoping rules of many computer languages and many other features apply more in big, or at least bigger, programming projects involving more than one person than they do in teaching examples. Still, it is a good practice to think about what values you want to persist and what values are only used within a function.

Some of the expressions defining variables in terms of other variables produce floating-point numbers, which are then cast to integers. (I could have made everything integers but decided to do it this way mainly to show you casting.) The critical thing is that all the settings for the eyes and the mouth and the lower and upper ellipses that produce the peanut shape are defined in terms of x, y, w, and h. For example, inside the daddy function, there is the declaration with initialization of a local variable that will be used for the horizontal positioning of the eyes.

```
int eyeXoffset = int((15.0/80.0)*w);
```

This statement sets up eyeXoffset as a variable of data type int and initializes it to be a fraction of the value of w, which is the width of the upper ellipse. This value is rounded off to be an integer. How did I arrive at the fraction 15.0/80.0? Experimentation. Why don't I write it 15/80? Because division of integers always rounds down to the largest integer not larger than the value. This means 15/80 produces 0, whereas 15.0/80.0 produces 0.1875. So although my code casts to integer when the calculation is over, I do not want the intermediate value to be an integer.

By the way, there are two eyes, but only one variable with the name eyeXoffset. If you examine the code, you will notice that in one place, the expression uses addition for eyeXoffset and in another, the expression indicates subtraction.

One last step in planning is to produce a function table. Table 1-1 shows the functions for the Daddy logo sketch.

Table 1-1. *Daddy Logo Functions*

Function name	Invoked by	Invokes
setup	Underlying Java program	
draw	Underlying Java program	daddy (two places)
daddy	draw	

Daddy Logo Program

My daddyLogo sketch starts with comments.

```
// This produces a peanut-like shape that was a self-portrait by my father
// he sometimes used it as a signature.
// daddy using variables and function
// this version draws two different faces
```

Creating comments such as these at the start is a good practice. You also should put comments throughout the code. This is a case of "Do as I say, not as I do," as I omit comments in the code because I produce Table 1-2 with an explanation of each statement.

The sketch continues, first with the declaration of the global variables, then with the definitions of setup, draw, and daddy. The general procedure for programming in Processing requires me to define a setup and a draw. I chose to name and define a function I call daddy. The advantage of doing that is that I could put in multiple calls to the function and produce cartoons at distinct places in the display window of distinct widths and heights. If I tried to do this with what I call naked numbers, I would eventually produce the same thing but probably have some situations with eyes outside the head.

Note

When programmers need to refer to any built-in Processing function or variable, we need to use the name accurately, including case. However, when we make up our own names, it is totally up to us, as long as we are consistent. I could have decided that the width of the skinny face would be held in a variable named `skinniW`, but if I later referred to it as `skinnyW`, Processing would have called it an error. Therefore, misspelling of names is fine, if you are consistent. Also be willing to use longer names, perhaps with camel casing because that will help you understand your program and be consistent.

Table 1-2 explains the coding using a two-column table, as promised.

Table 1-2. *Code for Daddy Logo Sketch*

`int ctrx = 100;`	Horizontal location for first face
`int ctry = 160;`	Vertical location
`int faceWidth = 80;`	Width of the lower part of first face
`int faceHeight = 100;`	Height of both parts of first face
`int skinnyFaceWidth = 60;`	Width of second face
`int skinnyFaceHeight = 130;`	Height of second face
`int eyeSize = 10;`	Eye size for both faces
`color skinTone = color(255,224,189);`	Color of faces
`void setup()`	Header for required `setup` function
`{`	Opens `setup` function
`size(800,600);`	Specifies size of window
`}`	Closes `setup` function
`void draw()`	Header for `draw`
`{`	Opens `draw` function body
`daddy(ctrx,ctry,faceWidth, faceHeight);`	Calls daddy function to make first face

(continued)

Table 1-2. (*continued*)

`daddy(3*ctrx,`
`2*ctry,skinnyFaceWidth,`
`skinnyFaceHeight );`
	Calls daddy function to make second face

`noLoop();`	Turns off looping: no more draw
`}`	Closes draw function
`void daddy(int x,int y,` `int w, int h)`	Header function for daddy function
`{`	
`noStroke();`	Turns off outline to produce peanut shape by drawing two ellipses
`fill(skinTone);`	
`int eyeXoffset =` `int((15.0/80.0)*w);`	Calculates x offset for eyes
`int eyeYoffset = int(.35*h);`	Calculates y offset for eyes
`int mouthYoffset =` `int(.10*h);`	Calculates y offset for mouth (note that there is no x offset, as the smile is in the middle)
`int mouthWidth = int(.5*w);`	Calculates the width of the ellipse that will be used for the mouth
`int mouthHeight = int(.3*h);`	Calculates the height of the ellipse that will be used for the mouth
`int hairOffsetY =` `eyeYoffset*3;`	Calculates the y offset of the hair
`int hairRadius = 3*eyeSize;`	Calculates the radius of the hairs
`ellipse(x,y,1.2*w,h);`	Draws lower ellipse
`ellipse(x,y-h/2,w,h);`	Draws upper ellipse
`stroke(0);`	Turns outline back on

(*continued*)

Table 1-2. (*continued*)

`fill(0);`	Sets `fill` to black for the eyes

`ellipse(x-eyeXoffset,`
`y-eyeYoffset,`
`eyeSize,eyeSize);`
	Draws left eye (to the viewer's left)

`ellipse(x+eyeXoffset,`
`y-eyeYoffset,`
`eyeSize,eyeSize);`
	Draws right eye

`noFill();`	Turns off `fill` in preparation for the hair and mouth

`arc(x,y-`
`hairOffsetY,hairRadius,`
`hairRadius,-PI/2,PI/2);`
	Draws the first part of the hair

`arc(x,y-hairOffsetY-`
`hairRadius,`
`hairRadius,hairRadius,PI/2,`
`PI*3/2);`
	Draws the second part of the hair

`stroke(240,0,0);`	Sets the color of `stroke` to red for the mouth

`arc(x,y+mouthYoffset,mouthWid`
`th,mouthHeight,`
`QUARTER_PI,3*QUARTER_PI);`
	Draws the mouth

`}`	Closes daddy function

Things to Look Up

The examples in this chapter made use of ellipses and arcs, which are pieces of ellipses. Processing also supports drawing rectangles, triangles, and lines, and you can look these up. The functions are `rect`, `triangle`, and `line`. The Processing document provides an explanation and short examples, which you can try and then modify. There also is a way to define your own shapes using `beginShape`, `vertex`, and `endShape`. Shapes respond to the current `fill` and `stroke` settings. There will be examples of each of these in later chapters, but you can start your exploration now.

Processing provides alternative ways to specify an ellipse or a rectangle. Look up `ellipseMode` and `rectMode`. The default methods are different for ellipse and rectangle.

The Hello, world examples demonstrated some ways to modify how text is displayed. You can change fonts (see `loadFont` or `createFont`), and you can change the alignment of text using `textAlign`. You can set the size of the text, either in the `createFont` statement or using `textSize`.

As I mentioned, Processing does provide a function called `radians` that converts from degrees to radians. You can look it up and use it, but, again, I urge you to practice working directly with radians, using the built-in constants `PI`, `HALF_PI`, and so on.

The PDE, under Tools on the toolbar, has a Color Selector tool. This can provide the RGB values into your program.

How to Make This Your Own

With this and anything else, proceed slowly. You can copy all the code and make sure it runs and produces exactly what is shown in the picture. You then can do some or all of the following:

- Add a third instance of the Daddy logo somewhere else in the window. This requires the addition of just one more statement to the `draw` function.

- Change the values of the global variables, including those indicating widths, heights, and also skin color.

- Change the `daddy` function itself while still thinking of it as some sort of face or head.

  - Add a nose, perhaps by using two lines. Look up `line`.

- Make the smile bigger. You can make the arc cover more of the same ellipse, change the size of the ellipse, or do both.

- Substitute a frown for the smile.

- Make the hair longer. Add another hair or two.

- Look up how to draw rectangles and add a hat.

- Change the daddy function totally; that is, create a function that produces a small drawing with parameters setting the horizontal and vertical positions and other attributes such as width and height. How about pumpkins? How about houses? How about flowers? (For flowers, or anything with curved lines that are not arcs, you might want to wait for later chapters.) Remember the technique of defining variables in terms of other variables. This is critical.

What You Learned

You learned how to create a Processing sketch. This included the roles of setup and draw, although you will learn more about draw in later chapters. You also saw how to draw an ellipse and an arc, which is a piece of an ellipse. You learned the roles of fill, stroke, noFill, noStroke, and noLoop.

The most important concept in this chapter was how to expand the language by creating a function. Functions have a specific format, with a header giving the name, the return value (more on this in later chapters), and specification of the parameters. Another concept, perhaps equally important, is the notion of a variable, a way of associating a value with a name. This example did not show all the power of functions or variables but provided an introduction. One benefit of defining the function with parameters is that the relationships among the different values are specified, so there will be no eyes outside the head, for example. Another benefit was the ease in drawing two cartoons, not just one, and at different places in the window.

What's Next

Chapter 2 introduces event handling: how to set up a response to mouse actions. It also introduces stochastic processing, a fancy way of modeling events that have a random or probabilistic aspect. The chapter provides examples of the `for loop`, a type of compound statement, and the use of expressions to produce polygons. There will be two examples. In one, you let your user, viewer, player, or audience click the mouse on the display window and a polygon will appear at that spot. The polygons start off as triangles and increase the number of sides until a set limit is reached and go then back again to triangles. The other example is what I categorize as a *coin toss*. However, I use two photos of family members. You can find and use photos of the head and the tail of an actual coin or any two photos you wish.

CHAPTER 2

Interactions

Abstract

In this chapter, you will learn how to prepare a Processing sketch that reacts to events such as clicking your mouse on the screen.

In this chapter, you will learn how to prepare a Processing sketch that reacts to events such as clicking your mouse on the screen.

Note

I use the term *player* for the person running the program. No matter what term is used, you, the program designer and builder, should have the future user in mind when you are doing the work. You are the user, player, or client when you are testing the program. There is a snide comment that only two industries refer to their customers and clients as users: illegal drugs and computing. Do think about an appropriate name for your example.

The examples for this chapter are a sketch in which polygons are drawn where the player clicks the mouse (see Figure 2-1) and a coin-toss type of application, which, in my example, alternates between different images of my granddaughter (see Figure 2-2 for one of them and Figure 2-9 for the other). You should choose two of your own pictures.

© Jeanine Meyer 2022
J. Meyer, *Programming 101*, https://doi.org/10.1007/978-1-4842-8194-9_2

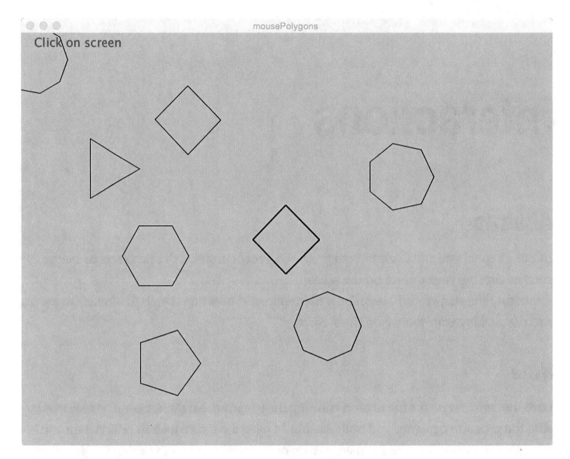

Figure 2-1. *Polygon drawing sketch, after many clicks*

The program also keeps track of totals, which my code classifies as heads or tails even though there are no images of coins.

coinflipImages

Heads   Tails

4   3

Figure 2-2. *Window of my "coin-toss" sketch after several clicks*

These examples provide an opportunity to explain important programming concepts such as events. There will be some mathematics here, and this is a good thing, even a great thing, because of the power it gives us to build beautiful, fun, and useful programs.

Programming Concepts

In this section, I provide background on programming event handling and producing (simulating) random phenomena along with other features common to programming languages. These facilities are present not just in Processing or Java, but in many programming languages, although the details differ.

Events

The term *event* is not that easy to define in programming, although it is easy enough to give examples: a mouse click on the screen or a key press or the passage of a specified amount of time or the player responding to a prompt for a file name. The capability of event-based or event-driven programming is that programmers can specify the event and what we want to have happen when the event is detected (the event handling) and the underlying system does the work of detecting if and when the event happens and follows through on our directions. This is a tremendous boon to programming as you will see when I explain how some, although not all, events are handled in Processing and describe the examples. It means that we can focus on one thing at a time.

Randomness

Building a computer program means specifying everything. What if you want to build a game in which certain actions do not occur all the time, but according to a set specific probability? In addition to games—and I am not implying that games are not serious business, because they are, but–what if you want to simulate for serious study a phenomenon such as traffic in which certain conditions arise based on probabilities? The programming would seem to be impossible. However, most programming languages have functions that produce values within a set range that are random or, more accurately, appear random according to the probabilistic pattern specified. This is called *pseudorandom processing*. It is still the object of ongoing research, but I will assume the pseudorandom features in the implementation of Processing are completely reliable.

Displaying Images from Files

Most programming languages have facilities for incorporating the use of image files, but this is an area in which Processing excels. It is important to keep in mind that image files are large and complex objects. Moreover, there are different types of encodings for images, indicated by the file name's extension, such as `.gif`, `.jpg`, `.tiff`, and `.png`.

Calculations, Including Built-in Functions

You might say that programming languages specialize in performing calculations. Mathematical *operators*, such as + and *, are used to form *expressions*. Programming languages typically have a large set of built-in functions, such as the trigonometric functions and functions to produce random values.

Programming courses once typically started with attention to precedence rules. Consider an expression

```
a + b * c
```

Is it evaluated by first multiplying the values of b and c and then adding in the value of a or are the value of a and the value of b added together and then that sum added to the value of c? All programming languages have set rules for this, and they tend to be the same: Multiply b and c first and then add in a. The precedence rules follow the silly mnemonic Please Excuse My Dear Aunt Sally (PEMDAS) for performing operations in the correct order: parentheses, exponent, multiplication, division, addition, and subtraction. However, my strong advice to you is to use parentheses and break up long expressions into parts, possibly over several statements.

Looping

Looping, or doing the same thing over and over again, is a feature of all programming languages. One construct for looping that appears essentially the same in different languages is the for-loop. A variable, called the loop or index variable, is declared and given an initial value. An operation that changes the variable as the looping proceeds is defined, and a condition to govern if the looping is to be continued also is defined. You will see for-loops in use in drawing polygons.

Processing Programming Features

Processing has multiple facilities for mouse events and key events. In this chapter, I explain the implementation of a program responding to a mouse click on the screen. More elaborate examples are covered in later chapters.

In the previous chapter, I explained how programmers provide the body of the setup function and the draw function. The Processing system invokes these functions at the appropriate times. Similarly, Processing has functions such as mouseReleased and others that provide a way to specify the response—the event handling—for given events. When the mouse button is pressed and then released, the mouseReleased function, if provided by the programmer, is invoked. Therefore, setting up the response for the mouse button being released requires us to have a draw function, even if there is nothing in the body of the function, and write something in the body of the mouseReleased function.

Obtaining information on which key is being pressed is done using the keyPressed function. This will be demonstrated in Chapters 5 and 7. See also the remarks in the "Under the Covers" section later in this chapter.

To access the mouse position, I use the built-in variables mouseX and mouseY inside the mouseReleased function. This allows me to write code that positions something at the point at which the player has released the mouse.

The polygon-drawing sketch draws regular polygons of varying number of sides centered at the mouse position. The coin-toss sketch displays one or a choice of two images positioned with the upper left corner at the mouse position. Further details follow in the "Implementing the Polygon Sketch" section.

Responding to the passage of time to produce animation is discussed in Chapter 3. In Chapter 10, I describe how to implement the absence of an event, making a cube rotate when the mouse is dragged on the screen or making it move "by itself" after no action. In this chapter, I also discuss prompting a player for a file name and responding when a file name is given.

Processing has a built-in function named random that can take one parameter and produce a floating-point number from zero up to but not quite including the parameter. The call random(1) will produce a fraction from 0 up to but not including 1.

Note

We do not write the random function, but if we did, the header line would be

```
float random(float upper)
```

which indicates that the function returns a floating-point number. In fact, there is an alternative form of random, with the header

```
float random(float lower, float upper)
```

This indicates that the function can be invoked with two parameters: one the lower and one the upper limit. The result is something greater than or equal to the lower limit and less than the upper limit.

There is one more detail that I want to clear up just in case it worries you. Can we use integer values or integer variables in places calling for floats? The answer is yes, and that is what I do for this example. We cannot do the reverse and use a float when an integer is the designated value.

My code compares the output of random(1) with the number .5. If it is greater or equal to that number, one choice is made (which I call Heads, although it is displayed as one picture of Annika). Otherwise, if it is not greater than or equal, the program takes the other path.

Images are incorporated into a Processing sketch by first using the Processing toolbar: select Sketch/Add a file... to bring each image file into the sketch folder. The sketch folder will now contain a subfolder named data, which will hold all the image files, and the PDE file. (If and when tabs are used, the code in each tab produces a new PDE file. This will be demonstrated in a later chapter.) In the code, the image files are referenced using a global variable of type PImage. The setup function would have a statement that uses the function loadImage to assign a value to the global variable. Finally, somewhere in the code, the programmer would use the image function to make the image appear in the display window. The image function displays the image with the original dimensions or with specified dimensions. Here are fragments of code, based on the assumption that an image file named smirk.JPG has been added to the sketch. Please be aware that case matters in file names and in extensions. So smirk.jpg would not work if the image in the data folder was smirk.JPG.

```
PImage myGD;
void setup() {
    size(1000,1000);
    myGD = loadImage("smirk.JPG");
}
void draw() {
    image(myGD,10,10);
    image(myGD,20,20,300,300);
}
```

The result, as shown in Figure 2-3, suggests that the picture at its full size is very big, in fact, bigger than the $1,000 \times 1,000$ window set up for the sketch. The first call to image is not a syntactic error, even though it could be viewed as unsuccessful. The result is to fit in as much of the image possible. Notice also that the picture is drawn twice, with the second version up near the top, with the dimensions changed to 300×300. Supplying the width and height parameters can result in a distorted image, so it is good practice to determine the actual dimensions of an image and make the dimensions you specify proportional. This is a case of "Do as I say, not as I do," because I ignored the actual dimensions and made the images 100×100. I am more careful in examples later in the text.

Figure 2-3. *Drawing two versions of a large image*

The for-loop in Processing provides a way to do repeated operations involving variables. The following example adds up the numbers from 1 to 10.

```
sum = 0;
   for (int i=1; i<=10; i++) {
       sum = sum + i;
   }
```

This works because, first of all, the variable sum is initialized to zero. Then the for-loop starts with the variable i set to the value 1. This value is less than or equal to 10, so the body of the loop is executed. The body contains the one assignment statement: taking the current value of the variable sum and adding the current value of the variable i to it. The for-loop now increments the value of i by executing the expression i++. This is shorthand for i = i + 1. So now, the variable i holds the value 2. This value is less than or equal to 10, so the body of the for-loop is executed. The assignment statement sets the variable sum to be its current value + 2. So now sum holds the value 3. Jumping ahead, the variable sum has been set to 1 + 2 + 3 + 4 + 5 + 6 + 7 + 8 + 9 + 10. The value of i is 10 and then incremented to 11. This is not less than or equal to 10 so the for-loop terminates.

For the polygon example, I use a for-loop to draw the sides of the polygon by calculations using trigonometric functions that, in turn, use angles calculated based on the number of sides of the polygon.

The coin-toss example makes use of a font other than the default font. Two options are available: loadFont and createFont. I leave it to you to research the difference in the Processing reference.

Under the Covers

It is a requirement in Processing that the draw function must be present for mouseReleased and similar mouse and keyboard events to be handled. What is taking place here is that the presence of the draw function, even with an empty body (see the code later), signals to the Java program constructed with our Processing code to include a call to the draw function and perform checking on the mouse, the keys, or both. It also means that variables such as mouseX and mouseY have valid values. All these tasks require actions, but they are "under the covers," and we do not have to be concerned with them. The frequency of invoking draw and checking for events and updating mouseX and other variables is set by the function frameRate. My code sets the frame rate to 6, which is relatively slow. You can evaluate if it makes the sketch not responsive enough.

The PDE and then the execution of a Processing sketch could be one of several programs running on the computer. The issue for the operating system is what program is the one to get the information about events. The technical term for this is *focus*. In some cases, it will be necessary to click the display window of the sketch to give it the focus. That generally happens naturally for mouse events but might not happen for keystrokes. I will repeat this for the examples involving the keyboard.

Polygon Sketch Operation Overview

My design objective for this sketch was to demonstrate interactivity and showcase the use of a for-loop. A deeper goal was to show that something complex could be handled by a small amount of mathematics. Finally, I wanted the examples in this chapter to be only a little more complex than the ones in the first chapter, making use of global variables and a function with parameters indicating the position and the attributes of a drawing of a certain type. You can evaluate how well I did after reading the "Implementing the Polygon Sketch" section.

My sketch will include a function named polygon that draws a polygon of a specified number of sides. The program starts with a four-sided polygon (you will see why I would call it a diamond, rather than a square) in the center of the window (see Figure 2-4). You also will notice that there are directions: Click on screen.

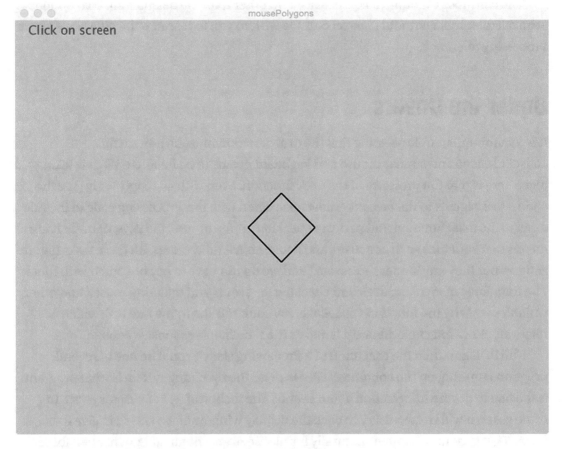

Figure 2-4. *Starting window for polygon sketch*

When the player clicks the window, a triangle appears as shown in Figure 2-5. The position of the triangle is based on where on the screen the player clicks. Subsequent clicks produce more polygons with the number of sides of the polygon going from three to ten and then back to three. The first figure I included in this chapter for the polygon sketch, Figure 2-1, shows the sketch after seven clicks. Notice that one polygon is partially outside the display window at the upper left corner. My instructions should have said "window" and not "screen," but my sloppiness gives me a chance to point out two things: (1) Processing will not consider it an error if our code specifies drawing something outside or partially outside the window boundaries, and (2) the Processing/Java system needs to manage the whole computer screen, including other programs running at the same time.

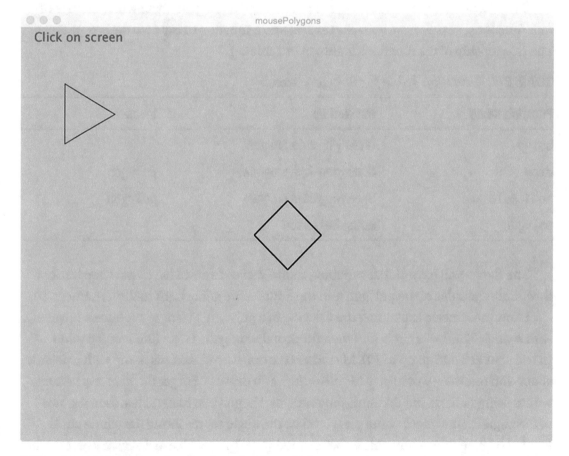

Figure 2-5. *Polygon sketch after the first click*

Implementing the Polygon Sketch

Next, I describe the implementation. As we move ahead, think about the similarities to the examples you have already seen.

Planning

To do the program, I will create a function called `polygon` and have statements that invoke the function. There is no correct answer as to which is to be done first, and sometimes, I go back and forth. The trick is to not be paralyzed and do nothing. Trust in yourself that you will complete the job.

Before writing any code, I know, as I have hinted in the text, that I will make use of four functions: `setup`, `draw`, `mouseReleased`, and a function of my own design, `polygon`. The relationship of the functions is shown in Table 2-1.

Table 2-1. *Function Table for Polygon Sketch*

Function name	Invoked by	Invokes
`setup`	Underlying Java program	
`draw`	Underlying Java program	`polygon`
`mouseReleased`	Underlying Java program	`polygon`
`polygon`	`mouseReleased`	

The sketch will have global variables, namely, `choice` and `limit`, that keep track of the number of sides of the polygon and the limit before going back to three, namely, `10`.

I now must tackle explaining the drawing of a polygon! I want to produce a polygon with *n* sides. Think of a circle and then think of dividing the circle into *n* equal parts (*n* will start at 3 and go up to 10). My father (the one who signed his name with a peanut shape and one hair) would give his pie order as 30 degrees. Forget the degrees, because we are using radians, but do think about angles. If a polygon has *n* sides, then the size of the angle for one piece of the pie would be the angle representing the whole circle divided by *n*. In Processing, this is the expression TWO_PI/n. Please do not try or feel bad because you do not want to try to calculate what this is in degrees for different values of *n*. It is the correct amount, and after all, you want to cultivate your intuition in terms of calculations. Let the computer do the arithmetic.

Figure 2-6 shows a circle with an angle A and a triangle. The *n* for this example is 6. The heavy horizontal line represents the horizontal distance from the center to the point on the circle, and the heavy vertical line represents the vertical distance from the horizontal axis to the point on the circle. The size of these lines is provided for us by the trig functions. Recall, if you can, the definitions of sine and cosine. I use radius to indicate the length of the line from the center to the circle. This means that the size of the horizontal line is radius * cos(A) and the size of the vertical line is radius * sin(A). I use these calculations to determine the position of the point on the circle. If the center of the circle is at x, y, then the horizontal dimension of the point on the circle is x+radius*cos(A). The calculation for the vertical value for the circle diagram is somewhat subtle in terms of the circle diagram. Recall the fact that the coordinate system is upside down! The vertical dimension of the point on the circle is y-radius*sin(A).

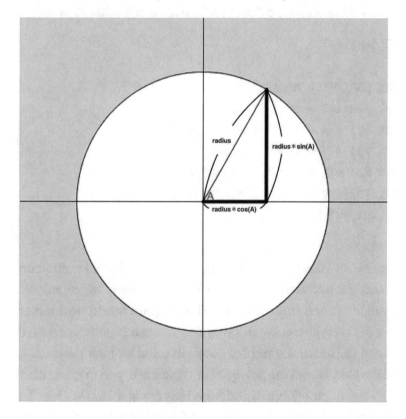

Figure 2-6. *Circle showing angle and lines for cos and sin*

We are not done, but we are close. It appears that I have explained the calculation for one end of one edge of a polygon. A better term for end is *vertex*. What is the code for drawing the whole edge? What is the code for drawing all the edges? This is where the for-loop comes into play. My code will set a variable named angle set to TWO_PI/n where n is the number of sides in the polygon. Then, my code draws a line from the point at an angle equal to zero to a point at an angle equal to angle (too many uses of the name "angle"). The code is clearer than my attempts at prose. Let's define two new variables: pangle1 and pangle2. At the first iteration, pangle1 is equal to zero and pangle2 is equal to angle. At the next iteration, pangle1 is set to angle and pangle2 is set to 2 * angle. I hope you can see where I am going. I use a for-loop to draw the edges. In the body of the for-loop, the variable i assumes the value 0, then 1, and keeps going until it is one less than n. For a three-sided polygon (also known as a triangle), the variable i will be 0, 1, and 2. This means three edges are drawn, which is exactly what we want.

```
for (int i=0;i<n;i++)
    {
        float pangle1 = angle * i;
        float pangle2 = angle * (i+1);
        float xp1 = x + rad * cos(pangle1);
        float yp1 = y + rad * sin(pangle1);
        float xp2 = x + rad * cos(pangle2);
        float yp2 = y + rad * sin(pangle2);
        line(xp1,yp1,xp2,yp2);
    }
```

Notice that I did not use y-rad*sin(pangle1) and so forth. I wanted my circle diagram to be familiar to you from your previous exposure to trig functions and so wanted the triangle to not be upside down. The program would work either way.

You will see the code in context in Table 2-2. You can experiment with this or just accept it, but keep trig functions and for-loops in mind for later projects.

Now that I have explained the polygon function itself, you might ask how it is used in the sketch. Functions are defined, and functions are *invoked* (or *called*). I now show the calling of the polygon function. It will be in the mouseReleased function as indicated already in the function relationship table. I had to decide on the parameters, which are analogous to the parameters for the daddy function in Chapter 1. The parameters specify the position, the size, and the number of sides (i.e., which polygon). The header of my polygon function is

```
void polygon(float x, float y, float w, int n)
```

The first two parameters specify the position of the center of the polygon. The third parameter indicates the size, which is interpreted as twice the radius of the bounding circle, that is, the radius used in the expressions to determine the vertices. The first three parameters are all specified as floats. The fourth and last parameter indicates the number of sides.

The position of the polygon will be based on the mouse location. Processing provides the mouseX and mouseY variables holding the coordinates of the mouse. My code produces a polygon centered at the x, y location held in the parameters. The size of the polygon is a fixed amount, but my code allows flexibility if I want to change it.

Implementation for producing the sequence of polygons, starting with triangles and continuing to ten-sided polygons, then reverting back to triangles, is done in a standard way that you can apply in different programs. One int variable, which I named choices, is initialized at 3 (you cannot have a polygon with fewer than three sides). This variable is incremented using the ++ operator. There is a subtle point here: The value passed from choices++ is the original value of choices before incrementation happens. After this value is used, the variable is incremented by 1. My next piece of code uses an if statement to compare choices with a variable I defined named limit. If the value of choices is bigger than limit, the true clause of the if statement is invoked, and choices is set to 3. I can be self-critical here and suggest that I could and, probably, should have declared a variable with a name such as original and initialized it to 3, to be used in the code in place of the "naked number" 3. The variable original would not be changed. This would make it easier to modify the sketch to produce polygons starting at a different number of sides.

Polygon Sketch Program

The polygon sketch is organized much like the example in the last chapter. First, there are global variables and then definitions for setup, draw, and, for this example, mouseReleased. The sketch also includes my function, polygon (see Table 2-2).

Table 2-2. *Code for Polygon Sketch*

`int choices = 3;`	Starting number for polygons; we start with triangles
`int limit = 10;`	Last number; the biggest polygon has ten sides
`void setup()`	Header for setup
`{`	
`size(800,600);`	Set the size of window
`fill(255,0,0);`	Set the color for instructions
`textSize(18);`	Set text size
`text("Click on screen",20,20);`	Display instructions. Note: the default font is used
`}`	
`void draw()`	Header for draw
`{`	
`polygon(.5*width, .5*height, 100.0, 4);`	Invoke polygon function to draw one four-sided polygon at the center of window
`}`	
`void mouseReleased()`	Header for mouseReleased
`{`	
`polygon(mouseX,mouseY,10 0.0,choices++);`	Draw a polygon with sides equal to the value of choices at the location of mouse and then increment choices
`if (choices > limit) { choices = 3;}`	If choices is over the limit, set (back) to 3
`}`	
`void polygon(float x, float y, float w, int n)`	Header for polygon function
`{`	
`float angle = TWO_PI / n;`	Calculate the angle for a wedge of the polygon
`float rad = w/2;`	Set rad to be half of w parameter

(continued)

Table 2-2. (*continued*)

`for (int i=0;i<n;i++)`	For-loop head going from 0 to 1 less than n parameter
`{`	
`float pangle1 = angle * i;`	Angle for start of edge
`float pangle2 = angle * (i+1);`	Angle for end of edge
`float xp1 = x + rad * cos(pangle1);`	Calculate the x coordinate
`float yp1 = y + rad * sin(pangle1);`	Calculate the y coordinate
`float xp2 = x + rad* cos(pangle2);`	Calculate the x coordinate
`float yp2 = y + rad * sin(pangle2);`	Calculate the y coordinate
`line(xp1,yp1,xp2,yp2);`	Draw the edge
`}`	
`}`	

Coin-Toss Sketch Operation Overview

The second example for this chapter is what I call a coin toss, although, again, I use my choice of images. My program keeps track of the results, calling them Heads and Tails. The opening window is shown in Figure 2-7.

Figure 2-7. *Opening window for coin-toss sketch*

The first click produced what is shown in Figure 2-8, and a couple more clicks results in what is shown in Figure 2-9.

● ● ●   coinflipImages

Heads Tails

1   0

Figure 2-8. *After a first click in the coin-toss sketch*

coinflipImages

Heads   Tails
1   2

Figure 2-9. *After three clicks in the coin-toss sketch*

Implementing the Coin-Toss Sketch

I will describe the planning and then the details of the coin-toss program. Here and in the rest of the book, you will benefit by thinking about what you already know how to do and what is new.

Planning

You know that the setup function does set up the window. For this application, it will be used for other operations that need to be done just once at the start, including creating and setting the font for text, loading in two images, and displaying the direction "Click on the screen." The draw function serves to allow Processing to respond to events, such as the mouse button being released. There is nothing in the body of the draw function, but it needs to be present. The mouseReleased function will be where the main action occurs: performing the choice based on a pseudorandom calculation between two images.

My first step for what I call the coin toss is identifying the pair of image files I will use. I have a large and growing collection of photos of family members, so that is not a problem. After starting a new sketch by clicking File and then New and giving it a name (my choice of name was cointossImages), I then follow the procedure in Processing to use the Sketch drop-down menu and Add a file... two times. This produces a folder named cointossImages that contains two items: a PDE file named cointossImages and a data subfolder. The subfolder contains two files: braid.jpg and smirk.JPG.

Table 2-3 is the function relationship table. Note that I could have defined one of my own functions to do the work done in mouseReleased but chose not to for this sketch.

Table 2-3. *Coin-Toss Functions*

Function name	Invoked by	Invokes
setup	Underlying Java program	
draw	Underlying Java program	
mouseReleased	Underlying Java program	

I did want to keep a tally of the random choices made. I label these Heads and Tails. It could have been Smirk and Braid. I named the variables used for the tally headc and tailc. These are global variables, which means they are declared outside of any function. I could have initialized them in the declaration statements, but instead they are initialized in setup. The mouseReleased function erases the whole window each time. It makes the choice (simulates a coin toss), displays one or the other image, and increases the corresponding variable holding the count. Finally, mouseReleased displays text showing the counts. You can examine the code and, hopefully, appreciate the brevity in Table 2-4.

Table 2-4. *Code for Coin-Toss Sketch*

`PImage coinh,coint;`	Declares `image` variables
`PFont font;`	Declares `font` variable
`int headc,tailc;`	Holds counts
`void setup() {`	Header for `setup`
`size(600,400);`	Sets the size of window
`frameRate(6);`	Sets (slow) frame rate
`headc = 0;`	Initializes count of heads
`tailc = 0;`	And count of tails
`font = createFont("Arial-Black",20);`	Creates font, sets size
`textFont(font);`	Sets font to be used
`coinh = loadImage("smirk.JPG");`	Sets image used for head
`coint = loadImage("braid.jpg");`	Sets image used for tail
`fill(0,0,240);`	Sets color for instructions
`text("Click on the screen.",100,100);`	Displays instructions
`}`	
`void draw() {`	Header for `draw`
`}`	No body
`void mouseReleased() {`	Header for `mouseReleased`
`background(255);`	Erases whole window
`if (.5<=random(1)){`	Makes random choice
`image(coinh,mouseX,mouseY,100,100);`	Displays head

(*continued*)

Table 2-4. (*continued*)

`headc = headc+1;`	Increments head count
`}`	Closes the `if-true` clause
`else {`	Else: `not-true` clause
`image(coint,mouseX,mouseY,100,100);`	Displays head
`tailc = tailc+1;`	Increments tail count
`}`	Closes the `else` clause
`text("Heads",10,20);`	Displays label "Heads"
`text(headc,10,50);`	Displays head tally
`text("Tails",80,20);`	Displays label "Tails"
`text(tailc,80,50);`	Displays tail tally
`}`	Closes `mouseReleased`

Note about fonts   The polygon example made use of the default font. For the "coin-toss" sketch, I originally inserted a call to the Arial font. This worked perfectly when I wrote it. However, this font does not exist on my current Mac. The Processing system inserts a substitute. The Arial Black font is on my computer. If you get the message about making a substitution, you can try the following code:

```
String[] fontList = PFont.list();

printArray(fontList);
```

to get a list of the fonts on your computer.

Things to Look Up

You could look up the following functions: `mouseClicked`, `mousePressed`, `mouseDragged`, and `mouseMoved`. Processing also keeps track of the current mouse coordinates in the variables `mouseX` and `mouseY` and the coordinates of the mouse at the last iteration of `draw` in the variables `pMouseX` and `pMouseY`. These built-in variables can be accessed in any function, not just the mouse functions. I have other examples making use of these functions and variables, and you also can try your own experiments.

The procedure I have described uploads the image files in the `data` folder located within the sketch folder. (You can look up an alternative way of dragging them into the sketch.) Image files also can be accessed from anywhere on the local computer using a complete address or from a website using a URL. This approach assumes the computer is connected. I will describe these alternative places to get image files in Chapter 6 and Chapter 7. Look up `loadImage`. You can experiment with this. Do keep in mind that loading from the `data` folder or elsewhere on the local computer is not instantaneous. This means that code may fail later in the program because the images are not available. Putting the loadImage command in setup generally does the job, but you can investigate preloading and checking for loading.

How to Make This Your Own

You can take my `daddy` function from Chapter 1 or, even better, take the function you (hopefully) designed and coded for your own figure and substitute it for the `polygon` function to draw your figure at the mouse location. You must code the call with the appropriate set of parameters.

For the coin toss, you should choose your own pair of images.

A good exercise is to think about how to simulate a crooked coin in a more or less exact way. That is, what if I wanted the head image to show up twice as often as the tail image? The answer is to replace the `.5` in the `if` statement with something else. One way to calculate the amount is to think of the interval from 0 to 1 as being made up of two parts: let's call them A and B. If the value returned by `random()` is in the A part, my code will display the head image and increment the head count; otherwise, it will display the tail image and increment the tail count. The following is mathematics, not programming. I start with two simultaneous equations.

```
A + B = 1
A = 2 * B
```

Continuing with the standard algebraic manipulations, I replace A in the first equation with 2 * B.

```
2 * B + B = 1
```

Combining the Bs, I get

```
3 * B = 1
```

This yields a value for B:

```
B = 1/3
```

I can then calculate the value of A. This indicates the value to use in my code. The value of A will be from 0 to 2.0/3.0, and B will be the rest. I could do the division and write .6666666, but instead I let the computer do the work. Using what is called pseudocode, a mixture of code and English, the following suggests what my code will be:

```
if ((2.0/3.0 ) >= random(1))
    { do the head things}
else
    { do the tail things}
```

You can pose different exercises for yourself. The concept that something can be random but not "even money" is important in building games and models for real-life situations such as studying traffic or predicting weather or elections.

What You Learned

This chapter reinforced the lessons started in Chapter 1 on the roles of the setup and draw functions. You saw that mouseReleased was similar to setup and to draw in that it also is invoked by action of Processing. The first example made use of a programmer-defined function, polygon, that was analogous to my definition and use of daddy in Chapter 1.

The chapter featured the use of the image function and explained the procedure for how image files are added into the data subfolder in the sketch folder.

The examples made use of the `random`, `sin`, and `cos` functions. Familiarity with these functions lets us include a wide variety of effects into our programs.

The polygon example featured the use of a `for`-loop. This is a highly useful construct for doing a sequence of similar things. Similarly, Processing provides us the `if` and `if/else` constructs for controlling what statements are executed depending on conditions.

What's Next

Chapter 3 involves the production of animation. It also will introduce arrays, a value that is a set (sequence) of values of the same data type.

Animation Using Arrays and Parallel Structures

Abstract

Animation is the technique of producing a sequence of still pictures fast enough that our eye–mind connection interprets the sequence as motion. This chapter introduces the topic of animation by presenting four sketches. You'll first implement a bouncing ball, namely, a circle that moves in a window, changing direction (bouncing) off the sides. You'll then implement a set of three bouncing balls, a bouncing pentagon, and a bouncing polygon in which the user can change the number of sides by pressing the mouse button. Animation is the exciting concept introduced here. However, how these four distinct sketches relate to each other is just as important.

Before actually implementing the sketches, I present a high-level overview of them and review some of their programming concepts and processing features.

More on the Sketches

Processing has facilities, notably the draw function, that make it relatively easy to produce animations, as draw is invoked over and over.

The static figures in this chapter cannot fully convey the animation. Figure 3-1 shows the bouncing ball sketch. We'll build on the bouncing ball sketch to produce the bouncing balls sketch and the bouncing pentagon sketch and then the bouncing polygon sketch. In the next chapter, which introduces classes, I'll approach going from

© Jeanine Meyer 2022
J. Meyer, *Programming 101*, https://doi.org/10.1007/978-1-4842-8194-9_3

bouncing ball to bouncing balls in a different way and then show bouncing things. Building on one application or taking from one application to build another one is a common and extremely useful technique that I am demonstrating in several ways in this chapter.

Figure 3-1. *Screenshot of a bouncing ball*

Figure 3-2 shows the sketch with a change in the background color and the statement that erases the window before redrawing the circle (ball) in the new position commented out. This causes the whole trajectory to be displayed. You can see the ball "bouncing" off the sides. You might want to produce a nonlifelike but, perhaps, artistic effect by not erasing the window.

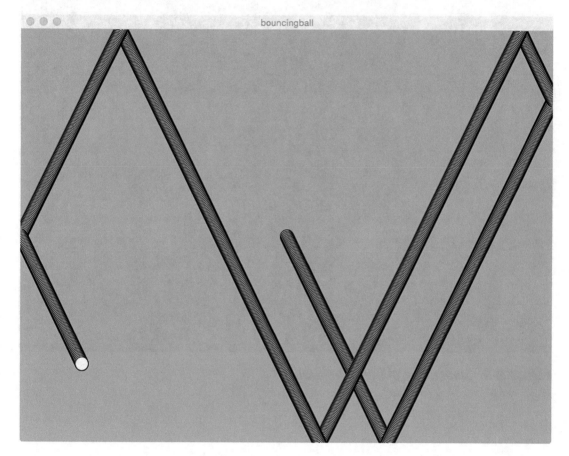

Figure 3-2. *Screenshot of a bouncing ball, with no erasure of window*

Figure 3-3 shows three bouncing balls, each of a different size and each moving at a different rate. I use this example to introduce *arrays* and a technique called *parallel structures*.

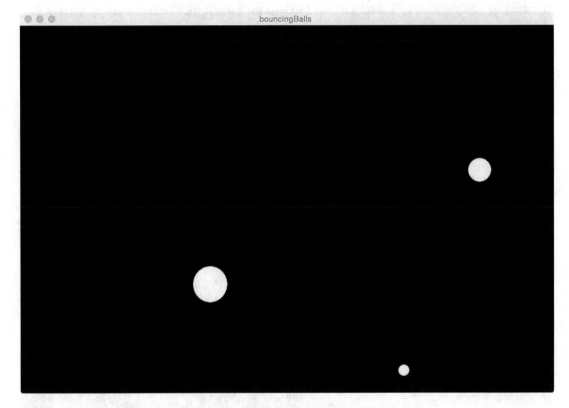

Figure 3-3. *Screenshot of bouncing balls*

Figure 3-4 shows a bouncing pentagon.

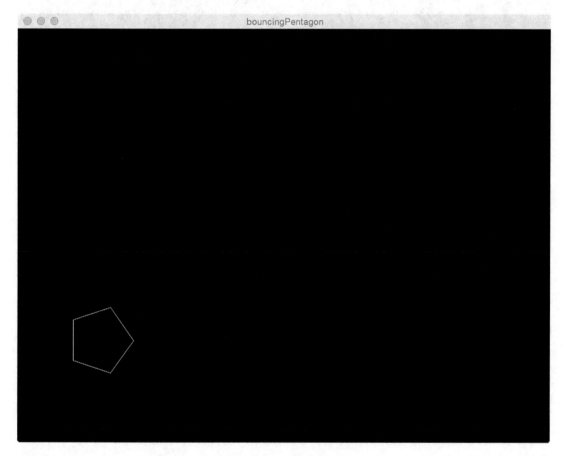

Figure 3-4. *Screenshot of a bouncing pentagon*

The last example starts off as a bouncing pentagon but changes to a random polygon after a mouse click. You know how to draw polygons and you have had an introduction to the use of pseudorandom calculations, so understanding this application will build on what you know. Figure 3-5 shows the sketch after several mouse clicks.

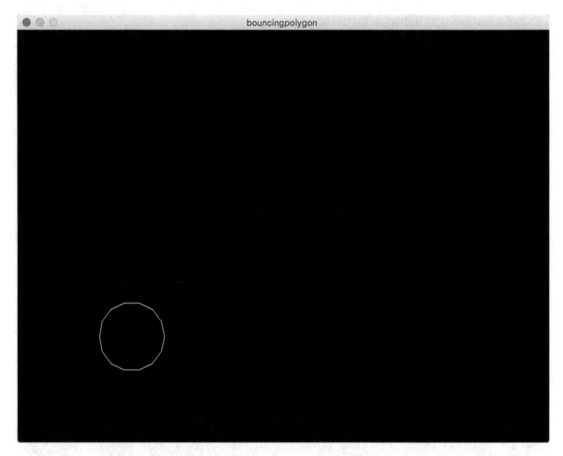

Figure 3-5. *Bouncing polygon*

At this point, you should have a basic understanding of the bouncing concept. The remaining sections show you exactly how to make it happen for several distinct sketches.

Programming Concepts

This section contains general background on many features useful for programming. As I have said before, although there is support for these in most programming languages, the details do vary.

Animation

If you have ever examined a reel of film, you will recall that the reel contained *frames* of still images. Movies are shown at sufficient speed that we see motion. Computer programs can display one scene and then another scene and then another. If the changes are fast and small, the scene appears lifelike. Commercial movies use a rate of 24 frames per second, called the refresh cycle.

Computer animation for production of movies is not done in real time and is still the subject of research and development. Computer games, in contrast, do have to accomplish tasks such as calculating the effects of many objects on many other objects and displaying the results fast enough to appear for the players. Both are worthy subjects of exploration.

Logical Operations

For the simple bouncing ball, you need to understand that there is no ball and there are no walls. What you will see in the code is a set of variables that define the ball's coordinates, its trajectory, and the location of the walls. The choice of variables is dependent on Processing and your imagination, but what is common across programming languages is the use of logical expressions to make decisions such as checking for collisions (simulated collisions) and, if a collision can be deemed to have occurred, what are the changes in variables needed to define the new trajectory. My approach, which works in many languages, is to define the trajectory by specifying a change variable for each dimension. I write code that checks if the ball is at or outside the walls and, if it is, reverse the sign of one or the other of the change variables. The code is presented and explained later. A general concept is that just as we include expressions that add and subtract and multiply and divide, we also can have expressions that make comparisons that return the value `true` or the value `false`. These values, called *Boolean values* after George Boole, can themselves be used in expressions.

Arrays

The bouncing balls example demonstrates the use of sets of values. This can be implemented in most computer languages by a construct called an *array*. An array is a list or sequence of items. The items are constrained to have the same data type in Processing, though not in some other languages. Referencing and changing a specific item requires the use of an *index* value. Typically, the index value goes from 0 to one less than the number of items in the array.

Parallel Structures

Parallel structures refer to the technique of setting up arrays with corresponding values. In the next chapter, I introduce the notion of classes. Parallel structures can be considered a way to address part of the problem that classes address, namely, linking together related values.

Compound Statements

This concept will be illustrated later by multiple `if` statements appearing in a `for`-loop, but because it is a general concept and frequently used, I mention it here. A function (or whatever the appropriate term is for a given programming language) contains one or more statements. Format varies but all programming languages have a construct that includes a check on a condition and then either has one true clause or a true clause and a not-true (`else`) clause. These clauses can contain one or more statements. Similarly, programming languages have one or more looping constructs, containing one or more statements. Any compound statement can go where a simple statement can go. Cautions are provided later in the discussion for Processing.

Pseudorandom Processing

Once a programming language provides some sort of random result, we can use calculations to get a wide variety of results. For example, I wanted to calculate a random choice from a range of integers to designate a polygon to have from 3 to 14 sides. The `random` function called with a parameter n returns a floating-point number from 0 to just under n. I use the function `int` to turn this into an integer. The value calculated by the `int` function is the largest integer not larger than the parameter. (Some programming languages have a function like this and name it `floor`, and that is a good name.) If `nsides` is a variable of data type `int`, then

```
nsides = 3+int(random(12));
```

sets nsides to be a random choice from 3 to 14. The point here is that the random function can be used to make a random choice from a range of integers.

Processing Programming Features

Processing is ideally suited for animation programs because the draw function is invoked at fixed intervals of time.

Caution

Let me insert a warning here, from the Processing documentation. The program attempts to invoke draw at the current frameRate, but it might fail if there is too much to do. This has never been an issue for me, but it is a worthy challenge to see if you can put too much computing invoked for each iteration.

For these examples, I put the work of displaying the ball, balls, or pentagon by code in the draw function. This includes putting the work in a function invoked by draw.

The relevant variables are bx and by for the ball coordinates and dx and dy to define how each coordinate changes at each frame. I use the names dx and dy because in common usage, a change is called a *delta*. Moving the ball means adding the current value to the change value. I write code using logical expressions that checks each updated coordinate against the boundaries of the Processing window. These expressions determine if a comparison expression is true or false.

Logical expressions also might include combinations of comparison operations. The operator that I use to combine two comparisons is the || operator. This performs a logical OR test. The logical expressions I use for checking about the walls check for either of two things being true. The built-in variable width holds the width of the window, and height holds the height. Note that bx and by define the center of the ball; it is this value that is used to determine if a collision has taken place. I could do the slightly more complex checking for the edge of the circles but decided that I liked the way this looks. The code follows.

```
bx = bx + dx;
if ((bx>=width)||(bx<=0))
    {dx = -dx;}
by = by + dy;
```

```
if ((by>=height)||(by<=0))
    {dy = -dy;}
```

Here is what the first three lines do.

- Adjust bx, the horizontal coordinate, by dx, the change value for the horizontal coordinate.

- Check if *either* the new value of bx is equal to or greater than the width, the built-in variable holding the width of the window, meaning it is off the screen to the right, *or* if bx is equal to or less than 0, meaning it is off the screen to the left.

- If either of these is true, change the sign of dx. If it was positive, it becomes negative; if it was negative, it becomes positive. The modified dx will be used at the next iteration.

See if you can interpret the next three lines, that is, what happens for the vertical coordinate.

I repeat that the assignment statement dx = -dx; does the right thing if dx is originally positive or originally negative. This fact lets me combine the bx>=width condition with the bx<=0 condition. Notice the operator || is a logical OR. If either of the two comparisons is true, the ball is considered to have hit a wall, and the delta for that dimension, dx or dy, must be changed for the next iteration. The calculations are again done separately for each dimension. You might need to consider the different cases to accept that this works.

For the bouncing balls example, I make use of sets of values (i.e., multiple arrays) for holding the information about the balls.

Array variables, like any variables, need to be declared. The statements

```
int[] counts;
float[] distances;
```

declare two arrays. They do not create the array, specifically, set up space for it in memory, and they do not populate the array: assign items to the array. The counts array will hold integers, and the distances array will hold floating-point numbers. As is always the case, you can name variables whatever you want. Processing does not care, so the names should be meaningful to us, the programmers. I am using plurals here in this made-up example to be suggestive.

To reference an item in an array, you use an *indexing expression*, such as counts[2] or counts[myCount]. This assumes, of course, that the array has been created and populated.

Here is the standard example demonstrating the use of arrays and a for-loop.

```
void setup() {
    float[] scores = {90, 85, 70, 95};
    float sum = 0;
    float average;
    for(int i=0;i<scores.length;i++) {
    sum = sum + scores[i];
    }
    average = sum/scores.length;
    println("The average is "+average);
}
```

The code makes use of a couple of new features. The code declares and defines an array with four items, all in one statement. You can look at the name of the array and guess that the values are intended to be scores on tests. The expression scores.length holds the number of items in the array, namely, four. The code computes the average (mean) by initializing a variable named sum to be zero. A for-loop goes through the items in the array and adds each, one at a time, to sum. Notice the expression scores[i]. After the for-loop, the variable average is assigned the result of sum divided by scores.length. Of course, I could have used four because I knew it, but knowing the construction scores.length prepares us for situations when this is not the case. The function println causes a message to appear on what is called the console, shown in Figure 3-6. The println function is highly useful for debugging.

```
chapter3_Average_example | Processing 3.3.5

                                                          Java ▼

chapter3_Average_example  ▼
1  void setup() {
2    float[] scores = {90, 85, 70, 95};
3    float sum = 0;
4    float average;
5    for(int i=0;i<scores.length;i++) {
6        sum = sum + scores[i];
7    }
8    average = sum/scores.length;
9    println("The average is "+average);
10 }
11



The average is 85.0

  Console      Errors
```

Figure 3-6. *Example showing the results of* `println`

You might have noticed that this `setup` function does not have a `size` statement. A small window does appear using default values.

In the bouncing balls example, my code declares and initializes each array in one statement. I have decided that there will be three balls, so the declaration of the set of *x*-coordinate values is

```
float[] bxs = {900/2,900/4, 900 * .75};
```

I know I will set the width of the window to 900. This initialization places one ball in the center in terms of *x* coordinate, one over to the left and one over to the right. These values are arbitrary.

If I wanted to declare the array variable and specify its size, but not supply the values of the items, I could use the following code:

```
float[] bxs = new float[3];
```

Alternatively, if I need to wait until some later time when the number of items is determined, say, by the setting of a variable named count, I would use the following declaration:

```
float[] bxs;
```

and later

```
bxs = new float[count];
```

The new operator creates the array. The values of the items still need to be set.

Yes, you do need to be careful about brackets, sometimes called braces, { and }, vs. square brackets [and] vs. parentheses (and). Index values are specified within square brackets. Sets of things, including items in arrays and sets of statements in functions, make use of braces. Parentheses are used in header statements for functions, for calls of functions, and for specifying precedence of operations, among other things.

Implementing a Bouncing Ball

My discussion of general programming concepts and Processing features probably provides enough background for you to move on to the "Program" section, but at the risk of being redundant, I will describe my planning process.

Planning

My plan for the bouncing ball was to make something simple to demonstrate animation. I first need to define the variables necessary to specify the ball, namely, a circle. A circle is an ellipse with equal width and height, and that value is stored in the variable I named balldiam. The ball's position is held in the variables bx and by, and the changes in position are held in the variables dx and dy. All these are global variables; that is, they are defined outside of any function.

Note

The variables' names for this sketch are pretty short. Perhaps they could be longer. Do not avoid typing long[er] names. We tend to spend more time staring at our code rather than typing it, so making names meaningful is more important than making them short.

The sketch just uses two functions: `setup` and `draw`. In this case, there is code in both. The action is all in the `draw` function, which is invoked over and over. I do not change the default frame rate, which is 60 frames per second. You might want to experiment with decreasing that number to see when you notice the ball move in jerky steps. Now is the time to appreciate the design of Processing.

The `draw` function includes the statement

```
background(0);
```

This has the effect of erasing everything by making the whole window black. You can use a different number for the parameter. The circle is then drawn again at a new position. As I explained earlier, an `if` statement is used to make the determination if a change in the delta values is warranted. Erasing and then redrawing the circle representing the ball is what makes the sketch produce animation. The functions are described in Table 3-1.

Table 3-1. *Bouncing Ball Function Table*

Function name	Invoked by	Invokes
setup	Underlying Java program	
draw	Underlying Java program	

Program

Table 3-2 describes the coding. Notice that the code starts with the declaration of global variables.

Table 3-2. *Bouncing Ball Code*

`float bx,by,dx,dy;`	Declare four variables for x and y positions and x and y changes
`int balldiam = 20;`	Declare and initialize the size of the ball
`void setup() {`	Header of `setup`
`size(800,600);`	Set the dimensions of window
`bx = width/2;`	Set bx to be horizontal center. The built-in width variable is set by the call to size
`by = height/2;`	Set by to be vertical center
`dx = 1;`	Set horizontal change
`dy = 2;`	Set vertical change
`}`	Close `setup`
`void draw(){`	Header of `draw`
`background(0);`	Erase the window
`ellipse(bx,by,balldiam, balldiam);`	Draw the ball (namely, a circle at the current bx, by position
`bx = bx+dx;`	Increment bx
`if ((bx>=width)|| (bx<=0))`	Check if at or beyond the vertical bounds
`{dx = -dx;}`	If so, change horizontal change variable
`by = by + dy;`	Increment by
`if ((by>=height)|| (by<=0))`	Check if at or beyond top or bottom bounds
`{dy = -dy;}`	If so, change vertical change variable
`}`	Close `draw`

You will see most of this code again or statements highly similar to those in this sketch in the next examples.

Implementing a Set of Three Bouncing Balls

The bouncing balls sketch is built by modifying the bouncing ball sketch, making use of the technique of parallel structures.

Planning

One array holds the x-coordinate values for each ball. Another holds the y coordinates. A third array holds the values for changing the x coordinate, and a fourth holds the values for changing the y coordinate. One more array holds the diameters for the different balls. The values at index J in each of the arrays together represent the information necessary to display the Jth ball. This technique, parallel structures, provides a systematic way to handle information on sets of things.

My code does not change the number of items in each array, just the value of individual items in the bxs, bys, dxs, and dxy arrays. It is possible to change the number of items in an array, and this will be demonstrated in later examples. Processing also has its ArrayList construct that you can look up (see the "Things to Look Up" section). What I want you to appreciate now is that the compilation process for Processing (and Java) seeks to produce efficient code; for that to happen, we need to specify that a variable is an array holding items of a specific data type and that there will be a set number of items.

Program

The modification of the bouncing ball sketch to produce the bouncing balls sketch is pretty much statement by statement. Each of the global variable declarations is replaced by a declaration of an array. As I indicated before, the values are arbitrary. The setup function consists of just the one statement specifying the dimensions of the window. I chose to put the initializations in the declaration statements.

The new draw function will start with a background statement as in the original bouncing ball and then have one for-loop. The header of the for-loop is

```
for (int i=0;i<bxs.length;i++)
```

There is an assumption here that the arrays are all the same size. If this is not true, there will be errors caught at runtime.

The body of the for-loop contains statements that correspond to the ones in the original bouncing ball sketch but refer to items in an array. The function relationship table is the same as the one for the simple bouncing ball shown in Table 3-1. The code is shown in Table 3-3.

Table 3-3. *Bouncing Balls Code*

`float[] bxs = {450, 225, 675};`	Declaration and initialization of the x coordinate array
`float[] bys = {450, 300, 150};`	Declaration and initialization of the y coordinate array
`float[] dxs = { 3,2,1};`	Declaration and initialization of the horizontal change (delta) array
`float[] dys = {3,1,2};`	Declaration and initialization of the vertical change (delta) array
`int[] balldiams = {20,40,60};`	Declaration and initialization of the diameters array
`void setup() {`	Header of setup
`size(900,600);`	Set window dimensions
`}`	Close setup
`void draw(){`	Header of draw
`background(0);`	Erase window
`for (int i=0;i<bxs.length;i++)`	Go through all items
`{`	Start the for-loop
`ellipse(bxs[i],bys[i],balldiams[i], balldiams[i]);`	Draw the ith circle using the current information
`bxs[i] = bxs[i]+dxs[i];`	Add current horizontal change (delta) value for the ith ball
`if ((bxs[i]>=width)||(bxs[i]<=0)) {dxs[i] = -dxs[i];}`	The whole if statement, including the if-true clause
`bys[i] = bys[i] + dys[i];`	Add current vertical change (delta) value for the ith ball
`if ((bys[i]>=height)||(bys[i]<=0)) {dys[i] = -dys[i];}`	The whole if statement, including the if-true clause
`}`	End the for-loop
`}`	End the draw function

Implementing Pentagon Bouncing

For this sketch, I go back to the original single bouncing ball and modify it to produce a pentagon in place of a circle. It makes sense to use the bouncing ball sketch as a base. Let's say you want to bounce a pentagon. Copy and paste the polygon function definition from the sketch described in Chapter 2. Because that sketch displayed polygons with black edges against a gray (default) background, if you want to keep the black background, you will need to change the color of lines. The function call stroke(255) changes the color of lines to white. I also changed the balldiam variable to be bigger. The last step is to replace the call to ellipse with a call to polygon. For a pentagon, this is

```
polygon(bx,by,balldiam,5);
```

A screenshot is shown in Figure 3-4.

Planning

To produce this sketch, I use what I already have (see Chapter 2), namely, a function that produces a polygon with the position, size, and number of sides specified in the function parameters. The call to the polygon function is substituted for the statement invoking the ellipse function. It does not matter that ellipse is part of the basic Processing language and polygon is something I made up.

The function relationship table, Table 3-4, has one additional row from the table for the bouncing ball and bouncing balls.

Table 3-4. *Bouncing Pentagon Functions*

Function name	Invoked by	Invokes
setup	Underlying Java program	
draw	Underlying Java program	polygon
polygon	draw function	

This is essentially the same program. Examine the code in Table 3-5 and notice the changes.

Table 3-5. *Bouncing Pentagon Code*

`float bx,by,dx,dy;`	Declare position and change variables
`int balldiam = 100;`	Declare and initialize the size of bounding circle for pentagon
`void setup() {`	Header for `setup`
`size(800,600);`	Set the dimensions of window
`bx = width/2;`	Set horizontal coordinate
`by = height/2;`	Set vertical coordinate
`dx = 1;`	Set horizontal change variable
`dy = 2;`	Set vertical change variable
`stroke(255);`	Set line color to white
`}`	
`void draw(){`	Header for `draw`
`background(0);`	Erase window
`polygon(bx,by,balldiam,5);`	Invoke function to draw pentagon
`bx = bx+dx;`	Increment horizontal variable
`if ((bx>=width)||(bx<=0))`	Check if at or beyond vertical bounds
`{dx = -dx;}`	If so, reverse x change variable
`by = by + dy;`	Increment vertical variable
`if ((by>=height)||(by<=0))`	Check if at top or bottom bounds
`{dy = -dy;}`	If so, reverse y change variable
`}`	Close `draw` function
`void polygon(float x,` `float y, float w, int n)`	Header for `polygon` function; parameters are `x`, `y` position, `w` for size, and `n` for number of sides
`{`	
`float angle = TWO_PI / n;`	Set angle by dividing circle into n parts
`float rad = w/2;`	Set radius to half of size parameters
`for (int i=0;i<n;i++)`	for-loop header

(*continued*)

Table 3-5. *(continued)*

`{`	
`float pangle1 = angle * i;`	Starting angle for this wedge
`float pangle2 = angle *` `(i+1);`	Ending angle
`float xp1 = x + rad *` `cos(pangle1);`	Compute x location for start
`float yp1 = y + rad *` `sin(pangle1);`	Compute y location for start
`float xp2 = x + rad*` `cos(pangle2);`	Compute x location for end
`float yp2 = y + rad *` `sin(pangle2);`	Compute y location for end
`line(xp1,yp1,xp2,yp2);`	Draw line connecting points
`}`	Close the `for`-loop
`}`	Close the `polygon` function

Implementing Bouncing Polygons

I decided to squeeze in one more example. It is not because I think there is anything wrong with bringing in the `polygon` function and not fully using it in Bouncing Pentagon, but I thought you would appreciate the addition. My last example is my attempt to add mystery. The sketch will make full use of the `polygon` function, with the number of sides of the polygon changing. The change is done by placing a call to the `random` function in the `mousePressed` function. It makes use of a global variable, `nsides`, that is set in `mousePressed` and used in the call to `polygon` present in the `draw` function. A screenshot for this is shown in Figure 3-5.

Planning

My goal now is to provide the viewer a way to change the type of polygon that is bouncing. What I do is define a new global variable and initialize it to 5.

```
int nsides = 5;
```

Then I modify the bouncingPentagon sketch by adding a definition for mousePressed that changes nsides using a calculation with random. I modify the call to the polygon function to use nsides for the last parameter and not the number 5. The variable nsides needed to be global, meaning that the value persists and that it is accessible by all functions. Declaring it outside of any function makes it global. The variable is assigned a value in one function, mousePressed, and used in another, draw.

The function relationship table, Table 3-6, has one more row than bouncingPentagon.

Table 3-6. *Bouncing Polygons Functions*

Function name	Invoked by	Invokes
setup	Underlying Java program	
draw	Underlying Java program	polygon
polygon	draw function	
mousePressed	Underlying Java program	

Program

The bouncing polygons sketch is essentially the same as the bouncing pentagon, with the addition of the definition of the mousePressed function. Examine the code in Table 3-7. The places where there are additions or changes are marked by bold text in the comments.

Table 3-7. *Bouncing Polygons Code*

`float bx,by,dx,dy;`	Declare position and change variables
`int balldiam = 100;`	Declare and initialize the size of bounding circle for pentagon
`int nsides = 5;`	Declare and initialize `nsides`
`void setup() {`	Header for `setup`
`size(800,600);`	Set the dimensions of window
`bx = width/2;`	Set horizontal coordinate
`by = height/2;`	Set vertical coordinate
`dx = 1;`	Set horizontal change variable
`dy = 2;`	Set vertical change variable
`stroke(255);`	Set line to white
`}`	Close `setup`
`void draw(){`	Header for `draw`
`background(0);`	Erase window
`polygon(bx,by,balldiam, nsides);`	Invoke polygon at position bx, by, with size `balldiam`, and (current) value of `nsides`
`bx = bx+dx;`	Increment horizontal variable
`if ((bx>=width)||(bx<=0))`	Check if at or beyond vertical bounds
`{dx = -dx;}`	If so, reverse x change variable
`by = by + dy;`	Increment vertical variable
`if ((by>=height)||(by<=0))`	Check if at top or bottom bounds
`{dy = -dy;}`	If so, reverse y change variable
`}`	Close `draw` function
`void polygon(float x, float y, float w, int n)`	Header for polygon function; parameters are x, y position, w for size, and n for number of sides

(continued)

Table 3-7. (*continued*)

`{`	
`float angle = TWO_PI/n;`	Set angle by dividing circle into n parts
`float rad = w/2;`	Set radius to half of size parameters
`for (int i=0;i<n;i++)`	for-loop header
`{`	
`float pangle1 = angle * i;`	Starting angle for this wedge
`float pangle2 = angle * (i+1);`	Ending angle
`float xp1 = x + rad * cos(pangle1);`	Compute x location for start
`float yp1 = y + rad * sin(pangle1);`	Compute y location for start
`float xp2 = x + rad* cos(pangle2);`	Compute x location for end
`float yp2 = y + rad * sin(pangle2);`	Compute y location for end
`line(xp1,yp1,xp2,yp2);`	Draw line connecting points
`}`	Close the `for`-loop
`}`	Close the `polygon` function
`void mousePressed() {`	Header for `mousePressed`
`nsides = 3+int(random(12));`	Set `nsides` to be 3 + integer from 0 through 11
`}`	Close `mousePressed`

Under the Covers

Processing is doing a considerable amount of work here. Most specifically, the implementation is invoking the `draw` function over and over. The power of Processing also is demonstrated by the action of `mousePressed`. First of all, it is the underlying Java program that invokes `mousePressed` when the mouse button is pressed. Second, the code in `mousePressed` changes the global variable `nsides` that is referenced in `draw`.

Perhaps you have wondered why arrays in Processing and, indeed, most computer languages are indexed starting from 0 and not 1. Consider the following: If an array of values is stored starting at an address in memory, say, at *A*, then the location of the first item would be at *A*. The location of the second item would be at *A + 1 * size_of_one_item*. The location of the item pointed to be the index *J* would be at *A+J*size_of_one_item*. You can see that this works if the index values go from 0 to one less than the number of items. You also can go back to Chapter 2 and notice that the `for`-loop for specifying the angles works with the index value for the loop starting at 0 and not 1. Of course, doing it another way just requires some different coding, but this does work nicely.

One of the design points behind the creation of Java many years ago was runtime checking on array bounds. In many of the existing languages, this was not done, so strange and hard-to-catch errors occurred.

Things to Look Up

There are several operators for comparing numbers in addition to the `>=` and `<=` used in these examples, for example, `>` and `<`. The single equal sign (`=`) is not a comparison operator, but the operator for assignment. The double equal sign (`==`) is the comparison operator. Look these up.

There are operators that work on logical values: `||` and `&&`. Take note of `|` and `&` and also note the operator `!` for logical not.

Shapes are a construct that could be used to make a shape with `fill` and `stroke` colors. Look up `beginShape` and `vertex`. You will see examples of shapes later in the text. It is an alternative way to do polygons.

You can read about arrays in the Processing documentation. A later example shows the use of `append` to add an item to an existing array.

There are other types of arrays; look up `ArrayList` and `HashMap`.

You can investigate mousePressed vs. mouseClicked vs. mouseReleased.

How to Make This Your Own

Bounce other things, again going back to what you did in Chapter 1, or try something new.

Think about having an array that specifies the color of each ball (circle). Look up the `color` function and the `color` data type. Hint: In the for-loop, use `fill`.

Think about the physics: Make the bouncing thing slow down when it hits a wall or invent your own physics. You can change colors, for example. A frequent idea of my students is to look up how to incorporate sound and play a sound file when it hits a wall. You will need to use a library for this. Examples making use of libraries come later.

Change the walls. I did the simplest thing, letting the virtual container be the window itself.

Move on completely from these examples and think about how responding to mouse events and making use of random can be used in a new project.

What You Learned

This chapter showed you how to produce animation by using the full power of the `draw` function. The examples included expressions with comparison operators and logical operators. The `if` construct was used to check on the position of things.

The chapter introduced arrays and their use in parallel structures. The `for`-loop, introduced in Chapter 2, was used to manipulate sets of things.

The chapter demonstrated the power of event-driven programming. Along with the power of functions and variables, programmers can focus on one thing at a time: What needs to be done in (by) `setup`, what in `draw`, what in `mousePressed`, and what in functions we invent?

What I can call a metalevel lesson in this chapter was building new sketches based on old ones. This is the way programmers work, so it is not just for instruction. I modified (enhanced) the sketch for a single bouncing ball to build a sketch that has three balls. Then, returning to the original single bouncing ball sketch, I took the code that draws a polygon from the polygon example in Chapter 2 and added it to the bouncing ball sketch, making certain small changes. I modified it once more to make the bouncing polygon. This is a powerful approach and something for you to focus on, along with the delight of making programs in which things move. Be sure to follow the suggestions in the "How to Make This Your Own" section and go off on your own to build new sketches.

What's Next

The next chapter introduces classes and objects of classes. The examples include another bouncing sketch, this one involving a set of different things: circles, rectangles, and images. Other examples are making a path and then seeing an image travel on the path and a jigsaw puzzle. Classes are an important, practical organizing tool in programming.

CHAPTER 4

Classes

Abstract

This chapter introduces the concept of a class, a way to associate data and code. A class defines a set of objects that are defined by a set of variables and a set of procedures, which are termed methods, that make use of those variables. In the previous chapter, I showed the use of arrays to hold similar items of information. The technique of using a set of such arrays is termed parallel structures. Classes are a more structured way to model things, with the models consisting of information and behavior. I want to inspire you to view defining classes as a way to make programming easy and practical and not the application of some abstract technique.

This chapter introduces the concept of a *class*, a way to associate data and code. A class defines a set of *objects* that are defined by a set of variables and a set of procedures, which are termed *methods,* that make use of those variables. In the previous chapter, I showed the use of arrays to hold similar items of information. The technique of using a set of such arrays is termed *parallel structures*. Classes are a more structured way to model things, with the models consisting of information and behavior. I want to inspire you to view defining classes as a way to make programming easy and practical and not the application of some abstract technique. The chapter includes the concept of inheritance for classes along with dynamic arrays, phases of operation, and providing a way to allow for a margin or tolerance in checking.

© Jeanine Meyer 2022
J. Meyer, *Programming 101*, https://doi.org/10.1007/978-1-4842-8194-9_4

The examples of this chapter include bouncing objects (a circle, two rectangles, and an image), a program in which the user creates a path and then an image travels on the path just made, and a jigsaw puzzle in which parts of a puzzle are jumbled up, the player attempts to position the pieces in the proper positions, and the player gives up and chooses to set the pieces to move slowly into place. The sketches are different in terms of the amount and the type of player interactions, but they all make use of the programming techniques of classes. The operation of each of the three sketches is described in the Overview sections.

Programming Concepts

This section contains general background on classes, phases of operations, and the idea of providing for tolerance or margin in making certain determinations. Each concept applies to one or more of the three examples. Remember: I explain the concepts first and then show the concepts in context in the sections on each example.

Classes

Classes were developed as a strategy to make programming structured. Classes help groups of people work together and over time on large projects. Some of the benefits are less obvious when working on the small projects we undertake when learning programming. Still, I hope you will appreciate the potential of classes.

The use of classes is called *object-oriented programming* (OOP). The basic idea is to specify a set of variables and a set of methods. Objects of the class are created by executing one of the methods, which is called the *constructor*. The variables are accessed and changed only through the methods (this is not always true, but close enough for now); that is, after creating the class, if a programmer tried to change the variables directly and not through one of the methods, it would be a syntax error. Moreover, many, although not all, of the programming languages supporting classes also supported a way to create a hierarchy of classes, based on a concept called *inheritance*. A *subclass*, also called a *child class*, shares some, but not all, variables and methods of the *superclass*, also called the *parent class*. One feature, which you will see in use, is that the parent constructor is invoked in the child constructor using the function super. The term *encapsulation* also is used for putting together data and code (methods) that act on the data. *Information hiding* refers to the fact that the exact workings of the methods may be hidden from view. My approach is to move quickly to see classes in use.

The bouncing things demonstrate the use of classes and inheritance. Some of the code for handling the circle, rectangle, and image is the same, and some is different. You might argue that if the code is the same, it could simply be cut and pasted where it is appropriate, but the OOP approach is more disciplined. It also means that the code that is the same appears just once and can be debugged just once. Wait and see.

Phases of Operations

Many programs have distinct phases or states. For example, making a path and then watching an image travel on the path has those two states:

1.   The player moves the mouse and positions (x and y coordinates) are stored, and a short line segment is added to the path displayed.

2.   After the player releases the mouse button, the image is made to move along the path.

Because there are just two phases (creating the path and moving the image along the path), a Boolean variable can be used to distinguish between them. In contrast, the jigsaw puzzle has three states:

1.   The pieces are placed randomly in the window. The player attempts to put the puzzle together by moving (dragging) individual pieces.

2.   The puzzle has been put together by the player; that is, the program determines that the puzzle is complete. At this point, nothing can happen until the player clicks on one of the two buttons.

3.   The player has clicked the Restore button, and the pieces slowly move into their proper positions in the complete jigsaw puzzle.

For the situation with more than two phases and others like it, it is necessary to use an integer variable.

More complex situations might require more elaborate definitions. My motivation in bringing it up is to prepare you for the descriptions of these examples and to provide assurances that what appear to be complex situations might be addressed by thinking about different program states.

Tolerance or Margin

Earlier in this chapter, I used the phrase "close enough" in describing the jigsaw puzzle game. For many applications, and not just games, it would be much too strict to require our players, users, or customers to locate a position on the screen or exactly position items being dragged on the screen by the mouse, the trackpad, or a finger (especially a finger). The pixel unit is simply too small. Similarly, if there is an application asking for numbers or even the spelling of a name, you need to decide if you want to require exact answers or be more flexible. For positioning pieces in the jigsaw puzzle, I declare and set a variable I call tolerance. You will see it in use.

Processing Programming Features

As a gentle introduction before plunging into the examples, I will describe an implementation of bouncing balls using a class named Ball and a single array that holds Ball objects. This is an alternative to the implementation in Chapter 3 using parallel structures for the information.

Classes

Using classes in Processing requires planning as well as coding. I need to determine what information defines a ball object and then how the program is to create a ball object and what is to be done with the ball object. These actions are often called the *behaviors*. The information is represented by the variables, and the behaviors, including creating each ball object, are represented by the methods. From Chapter 3, you and I know what is involved with a bouncing balls program. Here is a sketch containing a definition of the class named Ball using the format of Processing. The sketch starts with a declaration of a variable named b. The data type is Ball. Do not be concerned. The whole sketch is read in by the PDE, and so the definition of the class Ball can be used. The setup function creates a Ball object by invoking the Ball method. This also is termed the constructor method: it creates a Ball.

```
Ball b;
void setup() {
   size(100,100);
    b = new Ball(10,20,3,6,20);  //create a Ball object
}

void draw () {
  background(200);  //erase the window
  b.moveAndShow();  //move and show the Ball b
}
class Ball {
    float bx;
    float by;
    float dx;
    float dy;
    int balldiam;
Ball (float x, float y, float vx, float vy, int diam) {
    bx = x;
    by = y;
    dx = vx;
    dy = vy;
    balldiam = diam;
  }
  void moveAndShow() {
    ellipse(bx,by,balldiam,balldiam);
    bx = bx + dx;
    by = by + dy;
    if ((bx>=width) || (bx<=0)) {dx = -dx;}
    if ((by>=height) || (by<=0)) {dy = -dy;}
  }
}
```

I follow the convention that classes have names starting with a capital letter. I
have included the declaration of five variables with the class. Each Ball object (now I
am using capital B) has those five variables. The next piece of code is the *constructor*
method, indicated by having the same name as the class name and, also, not having

a return value declaration. Otherwise, it appears as a regular function. The code in the constructor stores the parameters in the variables. This is more or less standard, although there are situations in which parameters are used in the creation of an object, but not retained in variables. The next piece of code is a typical function, with a header including the designation of the return type or void, a name, moveAndShow, and parameters. In this case, the return is void, and there are no parameters. The code in moveAndShow should be familiar to you. Yes, there are several brackets, but use your mind and your finger to match them up: one set { } for the whole class and one set for each method.

Before showing how the class is used, that is, how the methods are invoked to create and move each Ball object, I need to explain how the information on a set of balls is created and referenced.

Definition of Images, Rectangles, and Ellipses

As you already have seen, Processing provides a way to position images, rectangles, and ellipses in terms of locations and dimensions. In fact, there are multiple ways or, to use the technical term, modes. The default way to specify a rectangle is to define the location of the horizontal and vertical values and then specify the width and the height. This is termed CORNER. The default way to specify an ellipse is to provide the horizontal and vertical values of the CENTER and then the width and height values. The default way to specify an image is the same as the rectangle. To specify the center for the image, we would use

```
imageMode(CENTER).
```

Note   The uppercase is important. You can look these up, and you will find that it can be worth changing.

Dynamic Arrays

In the previous chapter, arrays were used to hold information on the bouncing balls. The number of balls and, therefore, the size of each array and the initial values were all known when I wrote the program and expressed in the declaration statements. In the bouncing balls, and the other examples in this chapter, I do know everything, but my implementation requires that I create the objects during program execution. This means I need to create and populate the arrays *dynamically*.

For each of the implementations for the alternate bouncing balls, bouncing things, make a path and travel, and jigsaw, I make use of a single array holding objects. These arrays are constructed dynamically because code has to be executed to create each thing.

For the bouncing balls, an array is declared as a global variable. This declaration, with an initialization, is

```
Ball[] balls = {};
```

This statement declares balls to be an array of things of data type Ball. To put it another way, the data type for balls is Ball[]. The balls array can only contain items of data type Ball. Processing determines that Ball has indeed been defined as a class so the data type exists. It is okay that the class definition is later in the sketch. Processing scans the whole sketch. My definition of the Ball class has extended the language. The statement also initializes the array to be an empty array, {}, which is a legitimate value.

I need to show you two things: how to create a single Ball object and how to store them, or more precisely, references to the objects, in the balls array.

The way to create a single Ball object is first to declare a variable of type Ball:

```
Ball oneBall;
```

and, later, include code such as this:

```
oneBall = new Ball(width/2, height/2, 1, 2, 20);
```

The term new is an operator used just for this purpose, creating new objects.

The way my code stores them in the balls array combines the creation of the new object with adding them, called append, to the array. My code needs to explicitly refer to the data type of the array, which it does:

```
balls = (Ball[]) append(balls,
    new Ball(width/2,width/2,3,3,20));
balls = (Ball[]) append(balls,
    new Ball(width/4,width/3,2,1,40));
balls = (Ball[]) append(balls,
    new Ball(width*.75,width/6,1,2,60));
```

The (Ball[]) term applies what is called a *cast*. It takes the output of the append function and makes it an array of type Ball[]. The append works for any array, so we need to do this cast operation to establish the correct data type. This is not something I expect you to have figured out for yourself, so that is why I am telling you.

I need to show you one more thing: the draw function. It is much simpler than the one using the parallel arrays because the action is in the moveAndShow method.

```
void draw(){
    background(0);
    for (int i=0;i<balls.length;i++) {
        balls[i].moveAndShow();
    }
}
```

I will get to the explanation of bouncing things soon. The draw for that sketch has just one more statement.

Tolerance and OK-So-Far Coding

This determination of the jigsaw puzzle being complete is done using what I call *ok-so-far coding*. I program a for-loop that compares where a piece is with where it should be. Before the loop, the variable oksofar is set to true. This should be defined in terms of a horizontal distance and a vertical distance from the first piece. This allows the player to position the jigsaw anywhere in the window. As soon as my code determines that either the horizontal distance or the vertical distance is greater than the value in the variable I named tolerance, the oksofar variable is set to false, and the for-loop is exited using the break; statement. The ok-so-far coding and the use of break to exit for-loops (and other types of loops) have applications much wider than jigsaw puzzles and other games.

Bouncing Objects Overview

My bouncing objects sketch is more complex than just one bouncing ball, namely, it includes four objects, three different types. Figure 4-1 shows a screenshot of two circles, a rectangle, and an image. The objects appear to move and to bounce against the edges of the window. These are three different types of objects with classes defining the types of objects. The feature called *inheritance* provides a systematic way to use the same code for all the types when possible and different code when required by the differences among the types.

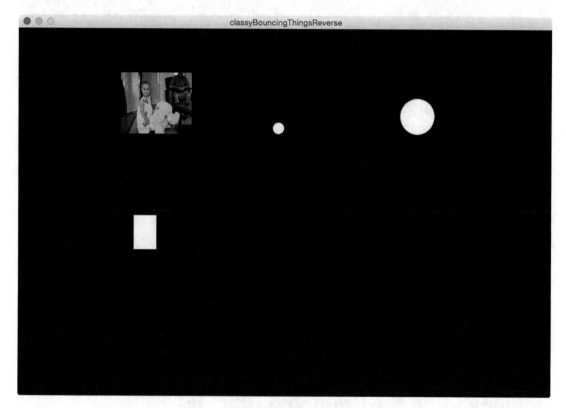

Figure 4-1. *Bouncing circles, rectangle, and image*

One extra feature, requested by one of my students, is to reverse the direction of the image of Annika riding the elephant after hitting a wall. This is shown in Figure 4-2.

Figure 4-2. *Screenshot of bouncing things, with image facing the other direction*

Implementing the Bouncing Objects

The bouncing things sketch features three types of objects bouncing within the window: a circle, a rectangle, and an image. It turns out that this is a perfect candidate for demonstrating inheritance, a way of building one class on another.

Planning

When planning this sketch, I knew I wanted three types of things bouncing around. I decided to call them Ball, Box, and Picture. For bouncing balls, the variables defining the things would include variables for position, size, and the change variables. For Ball and Box, I use these, and no other variables would be needed. To define a Picture object, I also use the variables for position, size, and change, but there would be two more variables, each a PImage created by a call to loadImage. At this point, because of my experience, I also knew how to define a base class that I named Thing.

I started off by planning to write a constructor and one other method, moveAndShow. It then occurred to me that moving any of the objects and checking for hitting the boundaries would be the same coding for all three types of bouncing things. However, displaying the thing needs to be different. This insight led me to plan to specify two methods: show and move.

Just like the classy bouncing balls, I will make use of one array to hold references to all the things. The declaration of this array is

```
Thing[] things = {};
```

and I use coding in the setup function, making use of append, to populate the array.

Now, here comes the explanation of the inheritance mechanism. It does exactly what I need. The subclasses will inherit the methods of the superclass unless the subclass has a different method of the same name. I define a class named Thing and then three more classes: Ball, Box, and Picture. The header line for the Box class will be

```
class Box extends Thing
```

Box is called the *subclass*, and Thing is the *superclass*. The header lines for the Ball and Picture classes follow the same format.

Within the definition of each subclass, I have the option of adding variables and defining methods, including methods with the same names as methods in the parent class. Such a method in the subclass is said to *override* the method in the superclass. For the bouncing things example, the Thing class will have a move method that the three subclasses inherit. There will be a show class that is empty in the Thing class that will be overridden by methods in each of the three subclasses. (It is possible to have a method in a superclass that is overridden by methods in some subclasses but not others, although this is not the case for this example.)

The inheritance and subclass–superclass structure is what enables me to write a for-loop in the draw function that has the statements

```
things[i].show();
things[i].move();
```

Make note of the dot (.) notation for invoking a method of an object. Processing will invoke the appropriate show and the appropriate move without any more work on my part. If a particular Thing object has its own show function defined in a subclass, that is the method that will be invoked.

By the way, when, to be somewhat redundant, one of my students did request the extra feature for the picture reversing when hitting a wall, it was relatively easy to do because the show coding for the Picture was isolated. By the way, I decided that I liked the picture disappearing behind the wall, which occurs because I used the CORNER mode, the default.

Note

There is an alternative way to produce a reverse image using the scale transformation. I decided to create the reverse image outside of Processing, which provides the opportunity to use a different image entirely.

The function table for bouncing things is shown in Table 4-1.

Table 4-1. *Bouncing Things Functions*

Function name	Invoked by	Invokes
setup	Underlying Java program	
draw	Underlying Java program	The show and move methods
Thing	super	
Ball	Setup	Calls Thing by calling super
Box	Setup	Calls Thing by calling super
Picture	Setup	Calls Thing by calling super
Thing method move	Draw	
Ball method show	Draw	
Box method show	Draw	
Picture method show	Draw	

Program

You now can examine the whole sketch in Table 4-2. The coding is shorter than it would be if I repeated the coding that was the same for the different types of things. It also means that code is debugged once, not multiple times, and changes can be made in one place. Another benefit is that there is no coding by me along these lines: *If this thing is a box, do this with it.* The underlying Processing implementation handles all that.

Table 4-2. *Bouncing Things Code*

`Thing[] things = {};`	Declared and initialized; will hold all the Things
`void setup() {`	Header for `setup`
`things = (Thing[]) append(things,new Ball(width/2,width/2,3,3,20));`	Creates new Thing and appends to things; this one is a `Ball`
`things = (Thing[]) append(things,new Box(width/4,width/3,2,1,40,57));`	Creates new Thing and appends to things; this one is a `Box`
`things = (Thing[]) append(things,newPi cture(width/5,width*.6,2,3,120,100, "annikalookright.jpg","annikalook. jpg"));`	Creates new Thing and appends to things; this one is a `Picture`
`things = (Thing[]) append(things,new Ball(width*.75,width/6,1,2,60));`	Creates new Thing and appends to things; this one is a `Ball`
`size (900,600);`	Sets the size of window
`}`	Closes `setup`
`void draw(){`	Header for `draw`
`background(0);`	Sets black background
`for (int i=0;i<things.length;i++) {`	For-loop, going through things
`things[i].show();`	Shows the ith thing
`things[i].move();`	Moves the ith thing
`}`	Closes for-loop
`}`	Closes `draw`
`class Thing {`	Class definition of Thing
`float bx;`	The (current) x coordinate
`float by;`	The (current) y coordinate
`float dx;`	Amount to increment bx
`float dy;`	Amount to increment by
`int wdiam;`	Width

(continued)

Table 4-2. (*continued*)

`int hdiam;`	Height
`Thing (float x, float y, float vx, float vy, int w, int h)`	Constructor for Thing; will be called using super function
`{`	
`bx = x;`	Sets object variable from parameter
`by = y;`	Sets object variable from parameter
`dx = vx;`	Sets object variable from parameter
`dy = vy;`	Sets object variable from parameter
`wdiam = w;`	Sets object variable from parameter
`hdiam = h;`	Sets object variable from parameter
`}`	Closes Thing
`void move() {`	Header for move
`bx = bx + dx;`	Increments x coordinate
`by = by + dy;`	Increments y coordinate
`if ((bx>=width) || (bx<=0)) {dx = -dx;}`	Checks if at or beyond left and right window "walls"; if so, changes sign of dx
`if ((by>=height) || (by<=0)) {dy = -dy;}`	Checks if at or beyond top or bottom window "walls"; if so, changes sign of dy
`}`	Closes move
`void show() {`	Header for show method
	No code; it is overridden by show in subclasses
`}`	Closes show method
`}`	Closes Thing class
`class Ball extends Thing {`	Header for Ball class
	No additional variables

(*continued*)

Table 4-2. (*continued*)

`Ball (float x, float y, float vx,` `float vy, int diam) {`	Header for constructor for Ball class
`super(x,y,vx,vy,diam,diam);`	Invokes Thing constructor
`}`	Closes Ball constructor
`void show(){`	Header for show method
`ellipse(bx,by,wdiam,hdiam);`	Displays an ellipse
`}`	Closes show method
`}`	Closes Ball class
`class Box extends Thing {`	Header for Box class
	No additional variables
`Box (float x, float y, float vx, float` `vy, int w, int h) {`	Header for constructor for Box class
`super(x,y,vx,vy,w,h);`	Invokes Thing constructor
`}`	Closes Box constructor
`void show(){`	Header for show method
`rect(bx,by,wdiam,hdiam);`	Displays a rectangle
`}`	Closes show method
`}`	Closes Box class
`class Picture extends Thing {`	Header for Picture class
`PImage pic;`	Additional variable
`PImage picR;`	Additional variable
`Picture (float x, float y, float vx,` `float vy, int w, int h, String` `imagefilename, String imagefilenameR)` `{`	Header for constructor for Picture class
`super(x,y,vx,vy,w,h);`	Invokes Thing constructor

(*continued*)

Table 4-2. (*continued*)

`pic = loadImage(imagefilename);`	Loads in the image and sets variable
`picR = loadImage(imagefilenameR);`	Loads in the image and sets variable
`}`	Closes `Picture` constructor
`void show() {`	Header for `show` method
`if (dx>0) {`	Determines which picture to show by checking sign of `dx`
`image(pic,bx,by,wdiam,hdiam);}`	Shows one picture, closes `if-true` clause
`else {`	`else`
`image(picR,bx,by,wdiam,hdiam);`	Shows the alternate picture
`}`	Closes `else` clause
`}`	Closes `show` method
`}`	Closes `Picture` class

Make Path and Travel Path Overview

The path making and image travel sketch is an example of a program with multiple phases, namely, drawing a path and then moving an image on the path. Figure 4-3 shows a path drawn by dragging the mouse. This is the first phase. Note that I need to modify this and other sketches to obtain the desired screenshots. In normal operation, after the player releases the mouse key, the next phase starts immediately.

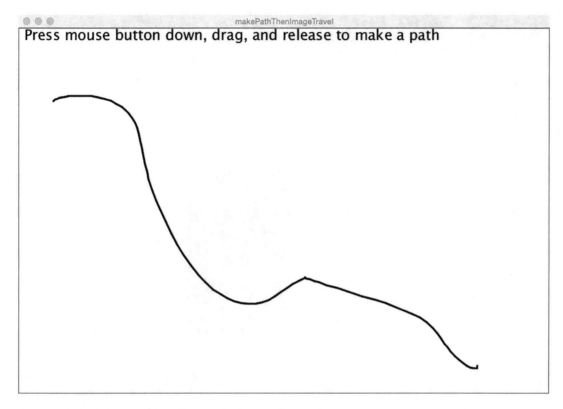

Figure 4-3. *Screenshot of a path drawn by a player*

As soon as the mouse button is released, the first phase stops. The path is erased, and the image is moved along the path. Figure 4-4 shows a screen capture of the sketch with the image somewhere along the path.

makePathThenImageTravel

Press mouse button down, drag, and release to make a path

Figure 4-4. *Image travels on the path*

Figure 4-5 shows a screenshot of the sketch modified to remove the erasing of the screen for a time-lapse photography effect. Notice that it is the center of the image that rides along the path.

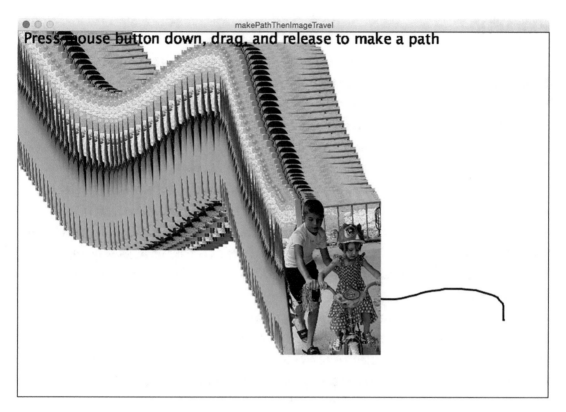

Figure 4-5. *Screenshot of the sketch modified to show images and path*

A player, viewer, or user makes a path by pressing down on the main mouse button and dragging. The path is marked by a black line that grows. Releasing the button will start a new phase: The window is cleared, including the path line, and an image appears to move along where the path was. The image moves at the same speed as the path was drawn.

Implementing the Make Path and Travel Path

One thing to keep in mind is that this example could be viewed as two stubs, or partial programs to build on. One stub is the making of a path, including drawing it on the screen and recording the locations. The other stub is following a path: moving an object, in this case, an image, along a set of locations. Consequently, the sketch has two phases—creating the path and making the image travel on the path—although the first phase has two parts: starting the path creation process and adding to it.

Planning

My plan for the make path and travel path sketch is to construct the path using the mouse event functions. I needed to review the mouse event functions to see how they worked: when they were invoked and how they worked together. It turned out that `mousePressed` is invoked when the mouse button is pressed and `mouseDragged` is invoked when the mouse has been moved if and only if the mouse button is pressed. This last fact saves me from declaring, initializing, setting, and resetting my own Boolean variable. The `mouseReleased` function is invoked when the button is released. All the coding involved with making the path could be done in these mouse event functions. I would define a class, `Location`, that would store a pair of floats representing the horizontal and vertical coordinates. The sequence of `Location` objects would be stored in an array. The `mouseX` and `mouseY` variables hold the values to define the `Location` object.

Making the path has two aspects: forming and storing the information in a new `Location` object and drawing the next small piece of the path in the window. For the second part, Processing supplies `pmouseX` and `pmouseY`, which, as the names suggest, are the previous *x* and *y* coordinates. If these two variables did not exist, I could define and use my own, but Processing does the work for me.

I declare and make use of a variable I name `pathmade` to signal the change from making a path to moving the image along a path. The work of moving the image is done in the `draw` function, and that is all that is done in this function. The variable p, a local variable in the `draw` function, is declared and set:

```
Location p = path[pathI];
```

where `pathI` points to an item, the next item, in the path array.

I made the decision to position the image so that its center is moving along the path as opposed to the upper left corner. I do some work in `setup` to modify the dimensions of the image to make it small enough to look okay in the window. This is accomplished by modifying the original width and height by dividing each by 3. I then compute the values of half the modified width and half the modified height and store these values in global variables so this does not need to be done for each iteration. With these values, the statement to display the image is

```
image(biker,p.xp-half_imageW,p.yp-half_imageH,imageW,imageH);
```

See the "Things to Look Up" section for an alternative approach.

The dot notation is the way to access the variables. Some purists would say that I should use methods for accessing and setting variables of objects, often called getters and setters. The argument is that restricting access serves to prevent errors and provides a way to insert code around every access and setting of variables.

You might be asking, "What is the timing for the mouseDragged event? What is the timing for displaying the image on the path?" The correct answer is that it is based on the frame rate. However, another and perhaps better answer is that it is the same for making the path and using it for the image to travel.

Table 4-3 shows the functions and the relationships for the make path and move image along path sketch.

Table 4-3. *Make Path and Move Functions*

Function name	Invoked by	Invokes
setup	Underlying Java program	
draw	Underlying Java program	Does access the xp and yp variables of a Location object
Location	mousePressed, mouseDragged	
mousePressed	Underlying Java program	Location
mouseDragged	Underlying Java program	Location
mouseReleased	Underlying Java program	

Program

The major programming techniques for making the make a path and image travel sketch are the use of a class to define Location objects and the use of a Boolean variable, pathmade, to determine the phase or state of the sketch. The Location class is pretty simple as there is just one method, the constructor method.

Three mouse event functions are used to define the path, with mousePressed starting things off by resetting the path array to be an empty array and then immediately adding (appending) the current mouse location. This function also sets the index variable, pathI, to 0 and the Boolean variable pathmade to false. The mouseDragged function is called over and over as long as the mouse button is pressed. It is used to append more

105

locations to the path array. The mouseReleased function finishes up the path creation phase by setting pathmade to true. It is typical in these cases to need to think about the very first entry of a list such as the path array and then subsequent entries. The code follows in Table 4-4.

Table 4-4. *Make Path and Move Image Code*

`Location[] path = {};`	Will hold positions on the path; starts off as empty array, which is different than having no initial value
`Boolean pathmade = false;`	Indicates which phase
`int pathI = 0;`	Index into path array
`String instructions = "Press mouse button down, drag, and release to make a path";`	Instructions displayed in the window
`float imageW;`	Width of image; this is calculated
`float imageH;`	Height of image; this is calculated
`float half_imageW;imageMode(CENTER);`	Changes from default of CORNER. Used to have center of image ride along the path; it is calculated
`float half_imageH;`	Used to have center of image ride along the path; it is calculated
`PImage biker;`	Will hold the image
`void setup() {`	Header of setup function
`size(900, 600);`	Dimensions of window
`background(255);`	Window will be white
`biker = loadImage("bikerchickWGrant. jpg");`	Loads in the image
`imageW = biker.width/3;`	Displays at smaller width
`imageH = biker.height/3;`	Displays at smaller height
`half_imageW = imageW/2;`	Calculated amount of half the width

(continued)

Table 4-4. (*continued*)

`half_imageH = imageH/2;`	Calculated amount of half the height
`strokeWeight(3);`	Thickness of line for path
`fill(0);`	Black for instructions text
`textSize(24);`	Sets size for all text
`text(instructions,10,20);`	Displays instructions
`frameRate(30);`	Slows down frame rate
`}`	Closes `setup` function
`void draw() {`	Header for `draw` function
`if (pathmade) {`	If `pathmade`, will display image
`background(255);`	Erases window
`text(instructions,10,20);`	Redisplays instructions
`Location p = path[pathI];`	Sets current position on path
`pathI++;`	Increments the index variable for next time
`image(biker,p.xp-half_imageW,` `p.yp-half_imageH,imageW,imageH);`	Displays image, with adjustment so center of image is on the path
`if (pathI>=path.length)` `{pathI = 0;}`	After end of path is reached, resets to start travel again at start of path
`}`	Closes clause if (`pathmade`)
`}`	Closes `draw` function; the `draw` function does nothing if path making is in process
`void mousePressed(){`	Header for `mousePressed` function
`path = new Location[0];`	Sets path array to be empty by creating a new, empty array
`pathI = 0;`	Sets `pathI` for indexing to 0
`pathmade = false;`	No drawing of image
`path = (Location[]) append(path,new` `Location(mouseX,mouseY));`	This will be the first item in `path`

(*continued*)

Table 4-4. (*continued*)

`}`	Closes `mousePressed` function
`void mouseDragged(){`	Header for `mouseDragged`; only invoked if button is pressed
`path = (Location[]) append(path,new Location(mouseX,mouseY));`	Creates new location object at current mouse location and adds to the `path` array
`line(pmouseX,pmouseY,mouseX,mouseY);`	Draws a line from last mouse position to current one
`}`	Closes `mouseDragged` function
`void mouseReleased() {`	Header for `mouseReleased` function
`pathmade = true;`	Set up to now draw image
`}`	Closes `mouseReleased` function
`class Location {`	Class definition for `Location` objects
`float xp;`	Object variable
`float yp;`	Object variable
`Location (float x, float y) {`	Constructor function
`xp = x;`	Stores x parameter
`yp = y;`	Stores y parameter
`}`	Closes the `Location` (constructor) function
`}`	Closes the class definition

Jigsaw Overview

The last example is a simple jigsaw puzzle. The pieces are all equal-sized rectangles created dynamically with horizontal and vertical cuts. They are positioned randomly in the window. There are two buttons: Mix up and Restore. Figure 4-6 shows an opening window. The player moves pieces around by dragging, and as soon as the pieces are close enough to the correct relative positions, the puzzle is deemed done.

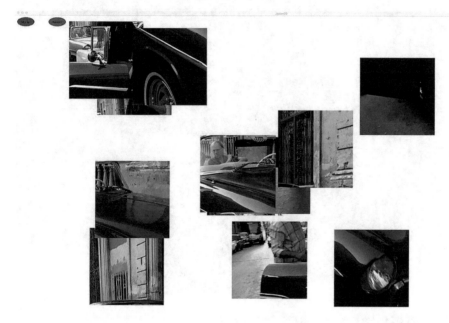

Figure 4-6. *Opening window for jigsaw*

If the player is impatient or just enjoys watching what I think of as a slow dance, pressing the Restore button will cause the pieces to move slowly to their proper positions. Figure 4-7 shows the pieces on their way to the correct relative positions.

Figure 4-7. *Pieces on the way to restored positions*

The restored picture is shown in Figure 4-8. This is my daughter in Cuba, getting out of one of the famous, painstakingly maintained cars from the 1950s.

Figure 4-8. *Restored picture*

Implementing the Jigsaw

The jigsaw puzzle is the longest sketch so far, but if you think about what you already know and read the "Planning" section and then scan the program before plunging into the details, you will find that it is not too difficult to understand.

Planning

I have made programs for jigsaw puzzles before in which I used another program to create the pieces. I also have experimented with having pieces snap together. I decided for this sketch to use the original image and cut it up in the program. This means the pieces are all the same rectangular shape.

I decided to set the Processing window to be the full display. Then I wrote code to make a new image to fit the window. You can examine the code in the setup function that does this work. It is more complex than you might have expected because I need to retain what is called the *aspect ratio* of the original image. I used the createImage function to create a new PImage variable and used the copy function to set the contents of the new PImage variable. The individual pieces are created using these same two functions.

I created a Button class and a Piece class, and as was the case in previous examples, there are an array, buttons, that holds the two Button objects, and an array, pieces, that holds the Piece objects. The work of making the pieces is split between a function, makePieces, and the constructor Piece.

The movement of the pieces by the player makes use of the mouse event functions in similar ways to the make a path and image travel example. For the jigsaw, the mouseReleased function checks if the puzzle should be considered done. The Processing function abs, which performs the mathematical absolute function, is used so the positive or negative discrepancies from the correct value are treated the same.

The Restore button causes what I call a dance of the pieces back into position. My code calculates how much each piece is to move horizontally and vertically in each frame of the restore dance in arrays called deltaxs and deltays.

Table 4-5 is the function table for jigsaw.

Table 4-5. *Jigsaw Functions*

Function name	Invoked by	Invokes
setup	Underlying Java program	makeButtons, makePiIeces
draw	Underlying Java program	drawButtons, drawPieces, and variables of Piece object
makeButtons	Setup	Button (twice)
makePieces	Setup	Piece (multiple times); note: mixes up pieces
drawButtons	Draw	Button.display
Button	makeButtons	Button
Piece	makePieces	Piece
mouseClicked	Underlying Java program	Button.isOver, mixUpPieces; uses Piece variables
mousePressed	Underlying Java program	Piece.isOver
mouseDragged	Underlying Java program	Adjusts Piece px and py
mouseReleased	Underlying Java program	Computations involving Piece variables
drawPieces	Draw	Piece.display; computations involving Piece variables
mixUpPieces	mouseClicked	Sets Piece px and py variables
Button.isOver	mouseClicked	
Button.display	drawButtons	
Piece.isOver	mousePressed	
Piece.display	drawPieces	

Program

The jigsaw sketch is the longest one so far (see the code in Table 4-6). Do not be concerned: the sketches will not all be getting longer and longer in the next chapters. Give each of the functions a quick scan and then look at the global variables' declarations and the comments. After that, you can skip around, examining a function in detail. Table 4-5 will be helpful. (Making a functions table for your own projects before you start the detailed programming is recommended.)

The intent when the player drags a piece around is for the piece to move smoothly with the mouse virtually stuck to the initial point of contact. To accomplish this, it is necessary for the code to calculate what I term the offsets in x and y from the location of the piece as defined for the upper left corner and the location of the mouse. You will see this in the program.

You might notice that because I know that I am slicing up the image into three rows with four pieces in each row and using the variables NHor set to 4 and NVer set to 3, I know NoP is 12. I am building flexibility into the coding just in case I want to change things in the future, such as slicing the puzzle up into more pieces.

Note   Please accept that my version of jigsaw is not as sophisticated as what you may have played. For example, pieces do not snap together. Also, pressing Restore and Mix up in combination or in too quick succession can produce a flash.

Table 4-6. *Jigsaw Code*

`Piece[] pieces;`	Holds references to the jigsaw pieces
`PImage original;`	Original image
`PImage originalA;`	Image modified to fit in window
`int phase = 0;`	Keeps track of phases
`Button[] buttons;`	Holds references to the two `Buttons`
`int NHor = 4;`	Number of pieces in a row
`int NVer = 3;`	Number of pieces in a column
`int NoP = NHor * NVer;`	Number of pieces
`float oriWidth;`	Width of original image
`float oriHeight;`	Height of original image
`float oriRatio;`	Ratio
`int adjustedWidth;`	Target width
`int adjustedHeight;`	Target height
`int wedgeW;`	Width of a piece
`int wedgeH;`	Height of a piece
`int pieceMoving = -1;`	Keeps track of which piece is being dragged. The -1 serves as a null value
`int offsetx;`	Horizontal offset of mouse from the upper corner of image
`int offsety;`	Vertical offset of mouse from the upper corner of image
`int tolerance = 20;`	Margin for pieces being off from correct position relative to first piece
`int travelBackFrames;`	Number of frames to dance back to proper position
`int[] deltaxs = new int[NoP];`	Holds horizontal deltas for the dance back
`int[] deltays = new int[NoP];`	Holds vertical deltas for the dance back

(*continued*)

Table 4-6. (*continued*)

`void setup(){`	Header for `setup`
`frameRate(30);`	Sets `frameRate`
`travelBackFrames = 30*2;`	Number of frames for the restore dance
`original = loadImage("cubaOldCarR.jpg");`	Loads in original image
`size(displayWidth,displayHeight);`	Sets window to full screen
`oriWidth = original.width;`	Stores width of image
`oriHeight = original.height;`	Stores height of image
`oriRatio = oriHeight/oriWidth;`	Computes ratio
`adjustedWidth = round` `(min(.75 * displayWidth,oriWidth));`	Calculates first try at target width
`adjustedHeight = round(min(oriRatio * adj` `ustedWidth,.75*displayHeight));`	Calculates (using ratio) target width
`adjustedWidth = round(` `adjustedHeight/oriRatio);`	Recalculates target width
`wedgeH = round(adjustedHeight/NVer);`	Calculates width of pieces
`wedgeW = round(adjustedWidth/NHor);`	Calculates height of pieces
`originalA = createImage(adjustedWidth,` `adjustedHeight,RGB);`	Creates new `PImage` object to hold adjusted image

`originalA.copy(original,0,0,`
`round(oriWidth),`
`round(oriHeight),0,0,`
`adjustedWidth,adjustedHeight);`
	Now puts data into `originalA` using calculated values

`makeButtons();`	Invokes `makeButtons`
`makePieces();`	Invokes `makePieces`
`}`	
`void makeButtons() {`	Header for `makeButtons`
`buttons = new Button[2];`	Creates array for the two `Button` objects

(*continued*)

Table 4-6. (*continued*)

`buttons[0] = new Button(50,30,80,40,` `color(200,0,0),"Mix up");`	Creates the `Mix up` button
`buttons[1] = new Button(200,30,80,40,` `color(0,100,0),"Restore");`	Creates the `Restore` button
`}`	Closes `makeButtons`
`void drawButtons() {`	Header for `drawButtons`
`for (int i=0;i<buttons.length;i++)`	Loop through the buttons
`{`	Loop clause
`buttons[i].display();`	Invokes display method
`}`	Closes loop clause
`}`	Closes `drawButtons`
`void mouseClicked() {`	Header for `mouseClicked`
`int mx, my;`	Declares variables to hold mouse positions
`mx = mouseX;`	Holds `mouseX`
`my = mouseY;`	Holds `mouseY`
`if (buttons[0].isOver(mx,my))`	Checks if over the `Mix up` button
`{`	`If true` clause
`mixUpPieces();`	Invokes `mixUpPieces`
`phase = 0;`	Sets to phase for working on puzzle
`}`	Closes `if true` clause
`if (buttons[1].isOver(mx,my))`	Checks if over the `Restore` button; note that both will not be `true`
`{`	Opens `if true` clause
`phase = 2;`	Sets for restore dance
`for (int i=0;i<NoP;i++)`	Loop through all pieces
`{`	Opens loop clause

(*continued*)

Table 4-6. (*continued*)

`deltaxs[i] = floor(((100.0 +`
`pieces[i].locx)`
`- pieces[i].px)/travelBackFrames);`
	Calculates how much this piece will move each frame horizontally

`deltays[i] = floor(((100.0 +`
`pieces[i].locy)`
`- pieces[i].py)/travelBackFrames);`
	Calculates how much this piece will move each frame vertically

`}`	Closes for loop clause
`}`	Closes if over `Restore`
`}`	Closes `mouseClicked`
`void mousePressed() {`	Header for `mousePressed`
`int mx =mouseX;`	Stores `mouseX`
`int my = mouseY;`	Stores `mouseY`
`for (int i=0; i<NoP;i++)`	Loop through pieces
`{`	Opens loop clause
`if (pieces[i].isOver(mx,my))`	Checks if over this piece
`{`	Opens `if true` clause
`pieceMoving = i;`	Stores which piece is being moved
`break;`	Leaves `for`-loop
`}`	Closes if over this piece
`}`	Closes for loop clause; no action if not over any piece
`}`	Closes `mousePressed`
`void mouseDragged() {`	Header for `mouseDragged`
`if (pieceMoving>= 0)`	Checks if an actual piece is moving
`{`	Opens `if true` clause
`pieces[pieceMoving].px= mouseX- offsetx;`	Adjusts x coordinate of this piece

(*continued*)

Table 4-6. (*continued*)

`pieces[pieceMoving].py= mouseY -offsety;`	Adjusts y coordinate of this piece
`}`	Closes `if` clause
`}`	Closes `mouseDragged`
`void mouseReleased(){`	Header `mouseReleased`
`pieceMoving = -1;`	Sets for no piece being moved
`int firstx = pieces[0].px;`	Calculation is in terms of piece 0, so stores x position
`int firsty = pieces[0].py;`	Stores y position
`boolean oksofar = true;`	Starts with `oksofar` true
`for (int i=1;i<NoP;i++)`	Looks through the remainder of the pieces
`{`	Opens `for`-loop clause
`int pxi = pieces[i].px;`	Stores the x value
`int pyi = pieces[i].py;`	Stores the y value
`int perfectpx = firstx + pieces[i].locx;`	This is what the x value should be
`int perfectpy =firsty + pieces[i].locy;`	This is what the y value should be
`int errorx = abs(perfectpx-pxi);`	This is x discrepancy
`int errory = abs(perfectpy-pyi);`	This is y discrepancy
`if ((errorx>tolerance) || (errory>tolerance))`	Checks if either one is greater than tolerance
`{ oksofar = false;`	No longer okay
`break;`	Leaves `for`-loop
`}`	Closes `if` true clause
`}`	Closes `for`-loop
`if (oksofar) {`	Are pieces all close enough

(*continued*)

Table 4-6. (*continued*)

`text("Close enough.`
`You can click Restore or Mix up to try`
`again.",500,20);`
	Displays message

`phase = 1;`	Sets phase to 1
`}`	Closes `if oksofar` true clause
`}`	Closes `mouseReleased`
`void makePieces(){`	Header for `makePieces`
`pieces = new Piece[NoP];`	Creates `pieces` array to hold pieces; values will be put in later
`int alli = 0;`	Index variable into `pieces` array
`for (int i=0;i<NHor;i++)`	Loop for the columns
`for (int j=0;j<NVer;j++)`	Loop for the rows
`{`	Opens clause
`int rx =` `round(random(.75*displayWidth));`	Generates random x value for positioning piece
`int ry =` `round(random(.75*displayHeight));`	Generates random y value for positioning piece
`pieces[alli] = new Piece(wedgeW*i,wedgeH*` `j,rx,ry,wedgeW,wedgeH);`	Creates `Piece` object; the first two parameters indicate distance from the 0th piece, the next two where to place the piece now (calculated using random), the width and the height
`pieces[alli].display();`	Displays `Piece` just created
`alli++;`	Increments `alli`
`}`	Closes `for`-loops
`}`	Closes `makePieces`
`void mixUpPieces() {`	Header for `mixUpPieces`

(*continued*)

Table 4-6. (*continued*)

`for (int i=0;i<NoP;i++)`	For-loop through pieces
`{`	Opens loop clause
`int rx = round(random(.75*displayWidth));`	Generates random horizontal position up to .75 of width
`int ry = round(random(.75*displayHeight));`	Generates random vertical position up to .75 of height
`pieces[i].px=rx;`	Sets the `Piece` object variable
`pieces[i].py=ry;`	Sets the `Piece` object variable
`}`	Closes `for`-loop
`}`	Closes `mixUpPieces`
`void draw() {`	Header for `draw`
`if (phase == 0)`	For `phase == 0`
`{`	Opens `if true` clause
`background(255);`	Erases window
`drawPieces();`	Draws the pieces
`drawButtons();`	Draws the buttons
`}`	Closes `if phase==0` clause
`if (phase == 2)`	For `phase == 2` (dance)
`{`	Opens `if true` clause
`for (int i=0;i<NoP;i++) {`	Loop over pieces
`pieces[i].px=pieces[i].px+deltaxs[i];`	Sets the x value by the calculated amount
`pieces[i].py=pieces[i].py+deltays[i];`	Sets the y value by the calculated amount
`}`	Closes `for`-loop
`background(255);`	Erases window
`drawPieces();`	Draws the pieces

(*continued*)

Table 4-6. (*continued*)

`drawButtons();`	Draws the buttons
`if (abs(pieces[0].px-100)` `<5*tolerance)` `{`	Checks if the first (index 0) piece is close to the specified x position and, if so, snaps pieces into place
`for (int i=0;i<NoP;i++) {`	Loop over the pieces
`pieces[i].px=100+pieces[i].locx;`	Sets the x value
`pieces[i].py=100+pieces[i].locy;`	Sets the y value
`}`	Closes for-loop
`phase = 0;`	Sets phase to 0
`}`	Closes if 0th piece is close enough
`}`	Close of phase was 2
`}`	Closes draw
`void drawPieces() {`	Header for drawPieces
`for(int i=0;i<NoP;i++)`	For-loop over pieces
`{`	Opens loop clause
`pieces[i].display();`	Displays the ith piece
`}`	Closes for-loop
`}`	Closes drawPieces
`class Button {`	Header for class Button
`int cx,cy;`	For center of button
`int bw, bh, bwsq, bhsq;`	Dimensions, calculated values for determining isOver
`color col;`	color
`String label;`	label
`Button (int x,int y,int bwid,` `int bht,color c, String lab) {`	Header for Button constructor

(*continued*)

Table 4-6. (*continued*)

cx = x;	Set variable
cy = y;	Set variable
bw = bwid;	Set variable
bh = bht;	Set variable
bwsq = bw*bw;	Calculate and set
bhsq = bh*bh;	Calculate and set
col = c;	Set variable
label = lab;	Set variable
}	Closes Button
boolean isOver(int x,int y) {	Header for isOver method
float disX = cx- x;	Calculate and set
float disXsq = disX * disX;	Calculate and set
float disY = cy - y;	Calculate and set
float disYsq = disY * disY;	Calculate and set
float v = (disXsq / bwsq) + (disYsq/bhsq);	Calculation for over an ellipse
return (v<1);	Returns true or false
}	Closes isOver
void display() {	Header for display
fill(col);	Sets fill with the color
ellipse(cx,cy,bw,bh);	Draws an ellipse
fill(0);	Sets fill to black
textAlign(CENTER,CENTER);	Sets alignment
text (label,cx,cy);	Displays label
}	Closes display

(*continued*)

Table 4-6. (*continued*)

`}`	Closes the Button class
`class Piece {`	Header for Piece class
`int locx;`	Holds relative x distance from 0th piece
`int locy;`	Holds relative y distance from 0th piece
`int px;`	x coordinate
`int py;`	y coordinate
`int pw;`	Width
`int ph;`	Height
`PImage content;`	Image
`Piece (int locxC, int locyC,` `int x, int y, int w, int h)`	Header for constructor
`{`	Open method
`locx = locxC;`	Store variable
`locy = locyC;`	Store variable
`px = x;`	Store variable
`py = y;`	Store variable
`pw = w;`	Store variable
`ph = h;`	Store variable
`content = createImage(pw,ph,RGB);`	Creates a new PImage object
`content.copy(originalA,locxC,` `locyC,pw,ph,0,0,pw,ph);`	Copies over the portion of the image for this piece
`}`	
	Closes constructor
`boolean isOver(int mx,int my) {`	Header for isOver for a Piece object
`if ((mx>=px) && (mx<=(px+pw))` `&& (my>=py) && (my<(py+ph)))`	Is the mx, my position on the rectangle of the piece

(*continued*)

Table 4-6. (*continued*)

`{`	Opens `if true` clause
`offsetx = mx- px;`	Calculates the x offset from upper left corner so piece moves smoothly
`offsety = my- py;`	Calculates the y offset
`returntrue;`	Returns `true`; yes, it is over this piece
`}`	Closes `if true` clause
`else {`	Not over
`return false;`	Returns `false`
`}`	Ends `else` clause
`}`	Closes `isOver`
`void display() {`	Header for `display`
`image(content,px,py,pw,ph);`	Displays this piece
`}`	Closes `display`
`}`	Closes `Piece` class

Under the Covers

Now I can provide a further explanation of functions vs. methods and, briefly, how Processing is implemented. Java does not have stand-alone functions; it only has classes and methods of the classes. Inventors Ben Fry and Casey Reas, joined soon by Dan Shiffman and over time by a large community of developers, defined a class called PApplet. The code for our Processing sketch will be housed within a class that extends the PApplet class definition. All our functions are methods of this class.

Java has a system of access modifiers that can define limits on what code can access what methods. This is not to keep things secret in a security sense, but to impose limits that Java can check to keep programmers from making mistakes and, more generally, make it possible for teams of people to work together. However, for Processing sketches to work, code in what we have called the underlying Java program must be able to invoke the setup, draw, mouseReleased, and other Processing functions. This means that setup and so on need to have the access modifier `public` in the header. You only need to know this if you decide to port your Processing code into Java yourself. The PDE does this for us.

I am being repetitive, but I do want to emphasize that making use of subclasses and superclasses means that Processing does a considerable amount of work for us. Consider the `for`-loop in the bouncing things sketch in which the appropriate method is invoked to display a circle or a rectangle or an image.

Things to Look Up

You can read about classes in the Processing documentation for a complementary exposition on the topic.

An alternative way to address the orientation of the image is to just have one image file and use the transformation expression `scale (-1,0)` to produce the reversed image. There will be examples making use of transformations in 2D and 3D, but you can explore these features now.

One of the technical reviewers, Joe McKay, suggested the use of the `ImageMode` function—it can be used to change how the location of an image is interpreted. Look up `ImageMode(CENTER)` to see how to ease the calculation of the image traveling on the path. There are several different modes to explore. More generally, be aware of default settings!

Processing has a facility to use tabs to break up a sketch into parts, such as putting each class definition in its own tab. Do read about this and consider it for your projects.

How to Make This Your Own

My vague term "things" is intended to inspire you to build sketches with bouncing things other than circles, rectangles, and images. You can build on what you did in the previous chapter when I urged you to build on bouncing ball to bounce something else.

Taking lessons from the make path and travel program and the jigsaw program, think about creating a path in different ways. Perhaps your user can click on a few points and store the locations and then have something move incrementally from point to point.

You can study the bouncing things sketch and the make a path sketch and try to move objects along more complex paths. Consider using random movement, although too much randomness tends to just be a mess.

What You Learned

This chapter introduced the idea of classes defining objects, with specification of data, the variables, and behaviors, the methods. You will see more uses of classes in the rest of the book. The three examples certainly were different, but they each made use of the techniques associated with OOP.

The examples made extensive use of calculations to determine values for repositioning objects and if it is time to change the phase of the application. The ok-so-far testing provided an opportunity to present the `break` statement for for-loops. The variable I named `tolerance` provided a way to express a check on values that is constrained but not exact. This all provides you with insight into the use of logic and data in programming.

What's Next

I call the next chapter "More Interactions." The interactions featured in the examples involve the use of the mouse, the use of arrow keys, and the use of the keyboard to input text. One of the applications adds data to a file stored in the sketch folder.

CHAPTER 5

More Interactions

Abstract

This chapter continues with classes and with more interactions by providing three new sketches. The first example is a game in which the player uses a slingshot to hit a chicken. You'll then create a snake sketch, which is my version of a snake game. The final sketch tests the interpretation of what a player sees. It was inspired by a psychology student who wanted to record reactions from test participants.

More on the Sketches

The slingshot sketch makes use of the same mouse event functions that you learned about in the previous chapter to perform a dragging operation, moving the circle representing the rock and lengthening the two lines representing cords in the slingshot. Releasing the mouse button releases the rock, which then travels in an arc. If the chicken is hit, the image is replaced with feathers.

The snake sketch responds to pressing the arrow keys and grows when it passes over food, represented by circles. The game ends when the snake goes off the window or passes over itself, or a set period of time has elapsed.

In the image test sketch, a photo is shown for a short period of time, and then the user is asked to write a response. An important feature of this sketch is the use of a comma-separated value (CSV) table. The player's responses are added to and stored in the table for later examination. This example increases your battery of interactions to include text and files.

© Jeanine Meyer 2022
J. Meyer, *Programming 101*, https://doi.org/10.1007/978-1-4842-8194-9_5

Programming Concepts

The general programming techniques and concepts relevant to the examples in this chapter include ballistic motion, the single character data type vs. String data type, taking in and outputting tabular data, the *Case* statement, measuring the passage of time, and *Regular expressions*.

Ballistic Motion

One of the earliest uses of computers was in the calculation of trajectories for missiles. The topic is called ballistic motion, namely, simulation of motion under forces such as gravity. It might be too fancy a description for my slingshot program. Figure 5-1 shows a screenshot from the sketch modified to show the rock's motion as a parabolic arc. You also can see the feathers picture on top of the chicken because the window has not been erased.

Figure 5-1. *Screenshot from slingshot showing arc*

The approach used for the slingshot is related to a mathematical technique called *finite differences*. My code starts off the flight of the rock by computing the angle of the cord going from the rock to the top of the slingshot. The cord represents a vector. My code *resolves* the vector into horizontal and vertical components. The horizontal component is used as the horizontal delta factor to change the position of the rock each frame. The vertical component is used as the vertical delta factor. Leaving the slingshot, the rock's position for each frame is calculated based on the two factors. The vertical factor changes each frame as gravity acts on the rock; the horizontal one does not. (Ballistic calculations for underwater torpedoes need to modify the horizontal factor as well to allow for resistance by the water.) This approach does work. Some readers might wonder why there is not a square somewhere in the code because parabolas arise from squaring! Rest assured that this is a parabola.

Character (char) Data Type vs. String Data Type

Most programming languages support two distinct data types: the character, often abbreviated as char, a data type for single characters, and the complex data type String for zero, one, or more characters. I will go into more detail when I explain how Processing handles characters and strings of characters.

Use of Files

Although the focus in most Processing sketches is on interactions with the user, Processing along with other programming languages provides ways to access, modify, and save files, and also to create and then save files. The files have an existence independent of the program.

Case Statement

In the examples shown so far, you have seen the if statement in use. Most programming languages provide an additional way to check on certain types of conditions that might fit the problem better even though the use, often multiple use, of if or if-else could handle the situation. The underlying program checks if the condition satisfies one of several *cases*. In the "Processing Programming Features" section, I indicate how the implementation in other languages might be different.

Elapsed Time

Programming applications often require a check on time elapsed since something happened. Computers come with internal clocks, and we can put them to work.

Regular Expressions

Regular expressions are a way to define a pattern and detect if a character string contains instances of the pattern. A pattern also can be defined that indicates the absence of a string or class of strings. Capabilities include extracting portions of the string that match parts of the pattern so that they can be rearranged. The invention and use of Regular expressions predate Java. Processing, Java, and many other programming languages have facilities for defining a Regular expression and using it to check on a string. If a programming language or other tool contains functions for Regular expressions, these functions will perform much better—and faster—than anything we can program in the language ourselves, so it makes sense to be aware of the capability. It is possible to look up Regular expression patterns for things such as an email address, a web address (URL), credit card numbers, and Social Security numbers, and this is a way to explore the topic.

Processing Programming Features

The programming concepts that I choose to discuss in this chapter are quite varied, although they each are present in the examples. Now, I discuss the Processing features for these techniques individually.

The char Data Type

The char data type in Processing holds a single character or symbol. A variable of data type char is initialized or assigned a value using single quotation marks:

```
char mykey = 'J';
```

The String data type, in contrast, is a complex data type. It is a class with its own set of methods. Processing will automatically cast (convert) char values into String values in situations such as concatenation with a String object or printing on the console or using text to display in the window, but it still can be critical to realize the difference between the two data types. The key and keyCode variables, typically used in the keyPressed function, refer to char values. The code I found in the Processing documentation to handle keyboard input makes use of the function str to convert a char into a String, so this is what you will see in the image test code, although the str could be omitted.

The keyPressed Function, key, and keyCode

Just as there is a mousePressed function that is invoked by the underlying Java program when the mouse button is pressed, there is a keyPressed function invoked when a key on the keyboard is pressed. The built-in variable keyCode is set if the key is one of the special keys such as Enter, Backspace, or Delete. The built-in variable key is set for the letters, numbers, and other symbols.

For accepting text from the keyboard, I use an approach found in the Processing documentation. The task is to do two things: display the text as it is typed in the window—this is not done automatically—and store the result after the player is done as indicated by pressing the key labeled either Return or Enter. It makes use of two global variables: myText and answer. The myText variable is used for the immediate display. The answer variable is set only when the player has clicked the Return or Enter key.

Table Files

The type and purpose of the file determine what Processing functions are available. You already have read about (and hopefully used) loadImage to make use of an image file to be stored in a variable of data type PImage. Processing supports a data type named Table. For the image test sketch, you will see the use of loadTable and saveTable as well as some other functions. For this example, I prepared a spreadsheet file using Microsoft Excel, saved it as a CSV file, and uploaded that file to the data subfolder for the sketch.

The Switch Statement

Processing provides the switch statement for handling cases. The value on which the case determination is made must be a primitive data type such as char or int. A String will not work. Another thing that will not work is a variable. This means I cannot use my favorite example: calculating the days in a month, using the name or three-letter abbreviation for the month. Here is an implementation of the dice game known as craps. Notice that there are two phases to the game, corresponding to a first throw and corresponding to a follow-up throw. A throw of 7 or 11 wins on a first throw; 2, 3, or 12 loses. If the first throw is anything else, the value is stored as the *point*, and there must be a follow-up throw. For the follow-up throw, throwing the point means a win; throwing a 7 means a loss, and anything else means that there must, again, be a follow-up throw.

```
boolean first = true;
int point;
void setup() {
    size (600,500);
    textSize(20);
}
void draw() {
}
void mouseClicked() {
    background(100);
    int choice = 1+ int(random(12));
    text("you threw "+str(choice),100,60);
    if (first) {
        switch(choice) {
            case 7: case 11:
                text("you win",100,100);
                break;
            case 2: case 3: case 12:
                text("you lose",100,100);
                break;
            default:
                text("follow up throw. Your point is "+str(choice),
                100,100);
                first = false;
                point = choice;
        }
    }
    else {
        switch(choice) {
            case 7:
                text("you lose",100,400);
                first = true;
                break;
            default:
                if (choice==point) {
```

```
            text("you win", 100, 400);
            first = true;
          }
      }
    }
}
```

The break statement means that control jumps out of the switch statement. The requirement for a break; statement makes it possible to combine cases as I have done for 7 and 11 and for 2, 3, and 12. A specification of all other cases is done using the label default. It is tempting to write else, but that is not what works in Processing.

As I hinted earlier, some other languages—JavaScript, for example—have different case statements. For example, JavaScript does allow strings and variables as case designations. The Visual Basic and VB.net languages allow specification of cases using expressions and lists and, as a result, do not require something like a break; statement.

There are situations, such as detecting the arrow keys, that are better suited to switch statements as opposed to if statements, so I encourage you to add them to the features you know how to use.

The millis and Other Time Functions

The function used to indicate elapsed time is the millis function, which returns the number of milliseconds (thousandths of a second) since the program started. With this function, we can write code to determine the difference between two points of time in the running of a program. If you want to convert from milliseconds to seconds, simply divide by 1,000.

Processing provides access to the internal clock with additional functions, including second, minute, hour, day, month, and year. You need to check on the ranges of the values returned. The month function returns a number from 1 to 12; the hour function returns an integer from 0 to 23.

The match Function for Regular Expressions

Processing provides the match function for checking if a String in the first parameter matches the pattern specified in a Regular expression in the second parameter. My use of Regular expressions in the image test program might be considered overkill, but I felt it important to introduce the topic. You can set up complex tests and perform complex manipulation of strings using Regular expressions.

ArrayList

An ArrayList is a construct for holding a sequence of values and is an alternative to arrays. It is easier to remove an element from an ArrayList and, consequently, was a good fit for holding the set of the Food elements. The declaration you will see in context in the "Program" section is

```
ArrayList<Food> foods = new ArrayList<Food>();
```

You will see uses of the add method when the Food items are positioned randomly in the window. The following code fragment uses the get method for an ArrayList to get a reference to the Food item at a particular slot in the foods ArrayList and, if it is closeEnough to the head segment of the snake, remove the item from the foods ArrayList. You can examine the closeEnough code in the whole program given later.

```
    if (closeEnough(newHeadx,newHeady,
        foods.get(i).fx,foods.get(i).fy)) {
    foods.remove(i);
```

Under the Covers

Data are represented in the electronic circuitry of the computer using sets of on–off switches. An on–off switch holds one *bit* of information, where bit stands for binary digit. It is easy to see how this can represent true or false, that is, a value of Boolean data type. A set of eight bits is called a *byte*. There also is a byte data type.

You can think about a set of bits as representing patterns. One bit can hold two different patterns. Two bits can hold 00, 01, 10, and 11, for four different patterns. Three bits can hold 000, 001, 010, 011, 100, 101, 110, and 111, for eight different patterns. The formula that is a string of N bits can hold 2^N distinct patterns. Check it out for N = 4.

A char value is represented using two bytes (16 bits) according to a system called UNICODE. Older computer languages used a system called ASCII that held seven or eight bits. A string of length 8 can hold 2^8 or 256 different patterns. This certainly is enough for our letters, numerals, and standard symbols, but not enough for all the languages of the world, which is the goal of the UNICODE effort.

Numbers are represented using the binary number system. What does this mean? In life, we use the decimal number system. This is a place-value system with base 10. You learned this in elementary school when you learned how to do addition with two-digit numbers. The decimal number 36 stands for 3 times 10 plus 6 times 1. More formally, 36 stands for 3 times 10^1 plus 6 times 10^0. The number 2,017 stands for 2 times 10^3 plus 0 times 10^2 plus 1 times 10^1 plus 7 times 10^0. Anything raised to the zeroth power is 1. Now, apply this methodology to base 2. The number 111 in the binary system stands for 1 times 2^2 plus 1 times 2^1 plus 1 times 1. This is equal to 7 in the decimal system.

A byte, or a set of eight bits, can hold a number from 0 to 255. This fact should explain why the range 0 to 255 shows up frequently in computer work. In Processing, the fill function expects either one integer or float value, from 0 to 255, to indicate a level of grayscale, or three integers or float values, each from 0 to 255, to represent a degree of redness, greenness, or blueness. By the way, fill also can accept a fourth parameter, the alpha, which specifies opacity, by which you can set levels of transparency. See references to more on fill in the "Things to Look Up" section.

You might ask why the designers of computers chose to use binary. A plausible answer is that designing and building switches with two states is considerably easier than designing and building switches with ten states. Yes, the computer hardware designers needed to accept that there would be more switches to hold the same value, but it would be easier to build. Another way to express this is to consider the circuitry required for arithmetic operations. The addition table for binary contains four items:

0 + 0 is 0

1 + 0 is 1

0 + 1 is 1

1 + 1 is 1 carry a 1

Now recall the addition "number facts" you needed to learn in elementary school. There were ten times ten facts! Even reducing it based on the fact that addition is commutative, the fancy way to say that A + B is the same as B + A still leaves 50. The circuitry required to support binary arithmetic is much, much simpler.

When our code places something in an array, you might wonder what happens. If it is an array of integers, then a copy of the integer is constructed and placed in the area of storage set up for the array. If the array is to hold character strings or objects created by constructors in classes we define, the array will hold a reference to the object. Similarly, when our code invokes a function (or a method associated with a class), the `int` parameters will be copies of the integers within the function for `int` parameters. This is known as *pass by value*. For parameters that are objects or strings, what is passed to the function are references to the strings and other objects. You might need to be aware of this if the function changes the value of the parameter. If the parameter is an integer, any integer variable used in the function call will not be changed. However, if the function expected an array and the function changed the array, the array used in the function call will be changed.

Slingshot Operation Overview

In this example, the programming makes use of the same mouse event functions that you learned about in the previous chapter to perform a dragging operation, moving the circle representing the rock and lengthening the two lines representing cords in the slingshot. The player presses the main mouse button down over the rock in the slingshot and drags it back from the rest of the slingshot. When the player releases the mouse button, the rock will start its flight, which travels in an arc. The initial horizontal and vertical change factors (deltas) are computed based on the length and the angle of one of the straps. The rock stops when it hits the chicken or reaches ground level. If the chicken is hit, the image is replaced with feathers.

Players should aim for the chicken, but the program does not depend on this. If the player aims the rock away from the chicken, the program will send the rock off in the direction calculated. The rock will eventually return to the ground level and stop.

The opening screen is shown in Figure 5-2.

Figure 5-2. *Opening screen of slingshot*

Implementing the Slingshot Sketch

Although you might think that the slingshot program is very different from bouncing things or a jigsaw puzzle, the implementation resembles the first in its use of classes and inheritance and the second in the dragging operation.

Planning

The slingshot sketch features a slingshot, a rock, a chicken, and some feathers. These four items are each implemented as objects in three different classes, each of which is a subclass of a class named Thing. At the start of the sketch, objects named mySlingshot, chickenPicture, and myRock are appended into an array named scene. The feathersPicture is swapped in later, replacing the chickenPicture. The draw function displays the appropriate items using the method show, which has been overridden for each subclass. The general technique of using an array such as my scene array will be useful.

The implementation using classes of the rock and the chicken picture and the feathers picture is straightforward. The slingshot is a different story. My approach is to define a slingshot by five positions, or, to be more accurate, one absolute position and four other positions defined as offsets, that is, relative terms to one location given in absolute terms. Figure 5-3 shows the different parts of the slingshot in terms of the names given in the code. The tx_ty label marks the position given in absolute terms and corresponds to the tx and ty variables defined in the Thing class definition.

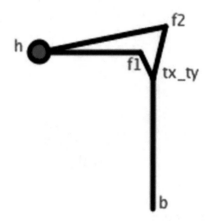

Figure 5-3. *Names of points defining slingshot*

Note that the code in setup that creates the Rock object positions it at the actual h location. I think this is a case in which writing and reading the code are easier than formulating and reading the English prose.

The sketch has four phases. The opening phase lasts until the player presses the mouse button when the mouse is on top of the Rock as determined by the myRock. isOver method. The second phase is when part of the slingshot and the rock are in motion. In this phase, variables determining the appearance of the slingshot are changed in the method called movePocket, and the myRock is moved by the move method. The next phase is initiated by mouseReleased. The delta factors are calculated, and the myRock is set into flight in the mouseReleased function. This phase ends when myRock hits the chicken or hits the ground. The noLoop() function is invoked, stopping all interaction. The function table is shown in Table 5-1. Give it a quick review and then go on to examine the program itself.

Table 5-1. *Slingshot Function Table*

Function name	Invoked by	Invokes
setup	Underlying Java program	`Slingshot, Rock, Picture`
draw	Underlying Java program	show methods, `chickenPicture.hits, simulateRockInAir, myRock.getTx, myRock.getTy` (in two places)
Thing	Invoked by super	
SlingShot	setup	Calls Thing by calling super
Rock	setup	Calls Thing by calling super
Picture	setup	Calls Thing by calling super
Thing method move	draw called as inherited method for `myRock.move`, `simulateRockInAir`	
Slingshot method show	draw called as item in scene array	
Slingshot method movePocket	draw	
Slingshot methods: getActualF1x, getActualF1y, getActualHx, getActualHy	initspeeds	
Slingshot method initspeeds	calculateSpeeds	Slingshot methods: getActualF1x, getActualF1y, getActualHx, getActualHy
Rock method show	draw called as item in scene array	
Picture method show	draw called as item in scene array	

(continued)

Table 5-1. *(continued)*

Function name	Invoked by	Invokes
simulateRockInAir	draw	myRock.move
calculateSpeeds	mouseReleased	
Rock method getTy	draw in two places to check for hitting chicken and hitting ground	
Rock method getTx	draw (just for hitting chicken)	
Rock method isOver	mousePressed	
Picture method hits	Draw	
mousePressed	Underlying Java program	myRock.isOver
mouseReleased	Underlying Java program	calculateSpeeds

Programming the Slingshot Sketch

The slingshot program is shown with comments in Table 5-2. The global variables and the class definitions are first. Although I could have said this for prior examples, I feel the need to say it at this point: this is my implementation of slingshot. Others might have done it differently. You might notice and be concerned about certain things: the move method is not used for mySlingshot or chickenPicture, or feathersPicture, but just for myRock. There is no cost in this, and defining these distinct items as subclasses of the Thing class made sense to me and it worked. The division of labor in calculateSpeeds, initSpeeds, and the getActual methods could be different. I define "getter" methods to demonstrate their use. The getTx and getTy were not necessary because I did not make the object variables *private*. However, I wanted to contrast with the methods that perform a computation to return the actual values for certain mySlingshot variables.

Table 5-2. *Slingshot Sketch*

`Slingshot mySlingshot;`	The single slingshot object
`Rock myRock;`	The single rock object
`float rockD = 15;`	Diameter used for `myRock`
`float horSpeed, verSpeed1,` `verSpeed2;`	To simulate ballistic motion
`float gravity = .05;`	Arbitrary value designed to produce a nice arc
`float adjust = 20;`	Arbitrary scale factor on initial speeds
`PImage chicken;`	Variable for the image file of the chicken
`Picture chickenPicture;`	Variable for the `Picture` object for the chicken
`PImage feathers;`	Variable for the image file for the feathers
`Picture feathersPicture;`	Variable for the `Picture` object for the feathers
`int targetIndex;`	Holds the `index` into the `scene` array indicating the position held originally by `chickenPicture` and, if and when the chicken is hit, where `feathersPicture` will go
`Boolean rockInMotion = false;`	Rock is in motion in the sling and once released
`Boolean slingInMotion = false;`	After mouse is pressed on the rock and until mouse is released
`Thing[] scene = {};`	Will hold all `Thing` objects to be displayed
`class Thing {`	Header for the `Thing` parent class
`float tx;`	Horizontal position
`float ty;`	Vertical position
`Thing (float x, float y) {`	Constructor
`tx = x;`	Set variable
`ty = y;`	Set variable
`}`	Closes constructor method
`void show() {`	To be overridden

(continued)

Table 5-2. (*continued*)

`}`	Closes show method
`void move(float dx, float dy) {`	Moves are done incrementally; that is, arguments indicate changes
`tx = tx + dx;`	Makes the horizontal adjustment
`ty = ty + dy;`	Makes the vertical adjustment
`}`	Closes move method
`}`	Closes Thing class
`class Rock extends Thing {`	Header for Rock subclass
`float rDiam;`	Variable for size of rock
`Rock (float x, float y, float diam) {`	Header for Rock constructor
`super(x,y);`	Invokes parent constructor
`rDiam = diam;`	Sets size
`}`	Closes constructor
`void show() {`	Header for show method
`fill(200,0,200);`	Sets color (always the same)
`ellipse(tx,ty,rDiam, rDiam);`	Displays circle
`}`	Closes show method
`Boolean isOver(float mx, float my) {`	Header for isOver method
`return (dist(mx,my,tx,ty)<rDiam/2);`	Returns `true` or `false` depending on if mouse on rock
`}`	Closes isOver method
`float getTx() {`	Header for getTx method
`return tx;`	Returns the value of variable
`}`	Closes getTx method
`float getTy() {`	Header for getTy method
`return ty;`	Returns the value of variable

(*continued*)

Table 5-2. (*continued*)

`}`	Closes getTy method
`}`	Closes Rock class
`class Slingshot extends Thing {`	
`float hx,hy;`	Moving part of slingshot; note that all variables are offsets from tx and ty, defined in Thing
`float f1x,f1y,f2x,f2y,bx,by;`	Stationary part of slingshot, along with tx and ty

`Slingshot (float f1xa,float f1ya,`
`float f2xa, float f2ya, float x,`
`float y, float bxa, float bya, float`
`hxa, float hya) {`
	Header for constructor

`super(x,y);`	Invokes parent constructor
`f1x = f1xa;`	Set variable
`f1y = f1ya;`	Set variable
`f2x = f2xa;`	Set variable
`f2y = f2ya;`	Set variable
`bx = bxa;`	Set variable
`by = bya;`	Set variable
`hx = hxa;`	Set variable
`hy = hya;`	Set variable
`}`	Closes constructor method
`void show() {`	Header for show method
`strokeWeight(4);`	Sets the thickness of line
`line (tx, ty, tx+bx, ty+by);`	Draws line from center to base
`line (tx, ty, tx+f1x, ty+f1y);`	Draws line from center to first prong
`line (tx, ty, tx+f2x, ty+f2y);`	Draws line from center to second prong
`line (tx+f1x, ty+f1y, tx + hx,` `ty+hy);`	Draws line from first prong to pocket

(*continued*)

Table 5-2. (*continued*)

`line (tx+f2x, ty+f2y, tx +hx, ty+hy);`	Draws line from second prong to pocket
`}`	Closes show method
`float getActualHx() {`	Header for method
`return (tx+hx);`	Returns actual x coordinate, calculated by adding in base `tx`
`}`	Closes method
`float getActualHy() {`	Header for method
`return (ty+hy);`	Returns actual y coordinate, calculated by adding in base `ty`
`}`	Closes method
`void movePocket(float dx, float dy) {`	Header for method
`hx += dx;`	Makes incremental x adjustment
`hy += dy;`	Makes incremental y adjustment
`}`	Closes method
`float getActualF1x() {`	Header for method
`return (tx+f1x);`	Returns actual x coordinate, calculated by adding in base `tx`
`}`	Closes method
`float getActualF1y() {`	Header for method
`return (ty+f1y);`	Returns actual y coordinate, calculated by adding in base `ty`
`}`	Closes method
`float[] initSpeeds() {`	Header, returns an array with two values
`float actF1x, actF1y,actHx,actHy;`	Variables used in calculations
`float angle;`	Angle variable

(*continued*)

Table 5-2. (*continued*)

`float[] answer = {0,0};`	Declares and initializes variable to be an array
`float lenOfSling;`	Variable used in calculations
`actF1x = getActualF1x();`	Extracts value
`actF1y = getActualF1y();`	Extracts value
`actHx = getActualHx();`	Extracts value
`actHy = getActualHy();`	Extracts value
`lenOfSling = dist(actF1x,actF1y,actHx,actHy)/ adjust;`	Calculates extension of `sling`, adjusted
`angle = -atan2(actF1y-actHy,actF1x-actHx);`	Computes angle using vertical and horizontal differences
`answer[0] = lenOfSling*cos(angle);`	Sets the x value to be returned
`answer[1] = -lenOfSling*sin(angle);`	Sets the y value to be returned; need to adjust for upside down coordinates
`return answer;`	Returns answer
`}`	Closes method
`}`	Closes class
`class Picture extends Thing {`	Header for `Picture` class
`PImage pic;`	Will hold the picture
`float picW;`	Will hold the width of picture
`float picH;`	Will hold the height of picture
`float padLeft;`	Calculated amount used for a hit
`float padRight;`	Calculated amount used for a hit
`float padTop;`	Calculated amount used for a hit
`float padBot;`	Calculated amount used for a hit
`Picture (float x, float y, PImage pica) {`	Header for constructor for `Picture`

(*continued*)

Table 5-2. (*continued*)

`super(x,y);`	Invokes parent constructor
`pic = pica;`	Sets pic
`picW = pic.width;`	Extracts the picture width
`picH = pic.height;`	Extracts the picture height
`padLeft = x+picW/4;`	Calculates for hit calculation
`padRight = x+picW*.75;`	Calculates for hit calculation
`padTop = y+picH/4;`	Calculates for hit calculation
`padBot = y+picH*.75;`	Calculates for hit calculation
`}`	Closes constructor
`void show() {`	Header for `show` method
`image(pic,tx,ty);`	Draws pic at its location
`}`	Closes `show`
`Boolean hits(float x, float y) {`	Header for `hits` method
`return ((x>padLeft)&&(x<padRight)&&(` `y>padTop)&&(y<padBot));`	Returns `true` if x,y is near the center of picture
`}`	Closes `hits` method
`}`	Closes `Picture` class
`void setup() {`	Header for `setup`
`size(1300,600);`	Specifies window dimensions
`frameRate(25);`	Slows down frames
`mySlingshot = new Slingshot(-10,-20,` `10, -40, 170,400, 0,100, -90,-20);`	Creates `mySlingshot` object
`scene = (Thing[])` `append(scene,mySlingshot);`	Starts the definition of `scene`: an array of `Thing` objects
`targetIndex = scene.length;`	Used to swap feathers for chicken
`chicken = loadImage("chicken.gif");`	Loads chicken image

(*continued*)

Table 5-2. (*continued*)

`feathers = loadImage("feathers.` `gif");`	Loads feathers image
`feathersPicture = new` `Picture(600,400,feathers);`	Creates `feathersPicture` object
`chickenPicture = new` `Picture(600,400,chicken);`	Creates `chickenPicture` object
`scene = (Thing[])` `append(scene,chickenPicture);`	Appends to `scene`; it will be at `targetIndex`

`myRock = new Rock(mySlingshot.`
`getActualHx(),mySlingshot.`
`getActualHy(),rockD);`
	Creates `myRock` object

`scene = (Thing[])` `append(scene,myRock);`	Appends to `scene`
`background(255);`	Sets background to white
`}`	Closes `setup`
`void draw () {`	Header for `draw`
`background(255);`	Erases the window
`for (int i=0;i<scene.length;i++){`	Goes through all items in `scene`
`scene[i].show();`	And shows each one
`}`	Closes `for`-loop
`if (rockInMotion) {`	If rock is in motion
`if (chickenPicture.hits(myRock.` `getTx(),myRock.getTy()))`	Checks if rock hits the chicken
`{`	If it does
`rockInMotion = false;`	Resets Boolean
`scene[targetIndex] =` `feathersPicture;`	Swaps in the feathers image
`}`	Closes `if hits` clause

(*continued*)

Table 5-2. (*continued*)

`simulateRockInAir();`	Continues the motion of rock in the air (rock will move one more frame if it hits the chicken)
`if (myRock.getTy()> height) {`	Checks if `myRock` is at the bottom of the window
`rockInMotion = false;`	Sets Boolean to stop the motion of `myRock`
`noLoop();`	Freezes the display and stops all mouse interactions
`}`	Closes if rock at bottom of window clause
`}`	Closes the initial check of rock in motion
`if (slingInMotion) {`	Checks if sling is in motion
`float dx = mouseX - pmouseX;`	Determines change in x
`float dy = mouseY - pmouseY;`	Determines change in y
`mySlingshot.movePocket(dx,dy);`	Adjusts the slingshot variables
`myRock.move(dx,dy);`	Moves the rock
`}`	Closes the sling-in-motion clause
`}`	Closes the `draw` method
`void mousePressed() {`	Header for `mousePressed`
`if (!rockInMotion) {`	If not rock in motion phase
`if (!slingInMotion) {`	Or slingshot in motion phase
`if (myRock.isOver(mouseX,mouseY)) {`	If mouse over rock
`slingInMotion = true;`	Then starts slingshot in motion phase
`}`	Closes `isOver` if
`}`	Closes not `slingInMotion` if
`}`	Closes not `rockInMotion` if
`}`	Closes `mousePressed` function
`void mouseReleased() {`	Header for `mouseReleased`
`if (slingInMotion) {`	Only acts if slingshot is in motion phase

(*continued*)

Table 5-2. (*continued*)

slingInMotion = false;	Stops the phase
calculateSpeeds();	Sets the horizontal and vertical delta values
rockInMotion = true;	Sets the Boolean to specify the next phase
}	Closes if true clause
}	Closes mouseReleased
void calculateSpeeds() {	Header for calculateSpeeds
float[] speeds = mySlingshot. initSpeeds();	Gets values calculated from position in slingshot
horSpeed = speeds[0];	This is the horizontal delta; does not change
verSpeed1 = speeds[1];	This is the initial vertical delta
}	Closes calculateSpeeds function
void simulateRockInAir() {	Header for simulateRockInAir
float dy;	Calculated value for vertical change
verSpeed2 = verSpeed1 + gravity;	Simulates the effect of gravity by calculating next vertical delta (change amount)
dy = (verSpeed1 + verSpeed2)/2;	Calculates average
myRock.move(horSpeed,dy);	Moves the rock
verSpeed1 = verSpeed2;	Prepares for calculation in next frame
}	Closes simulateRockInAir function

Snake Operation Overview

In this project, a snake is made up of a head segment and four other segments. Circles representing food are positioned at random locations in the window. The opening screen is shown in Figure 5-4.

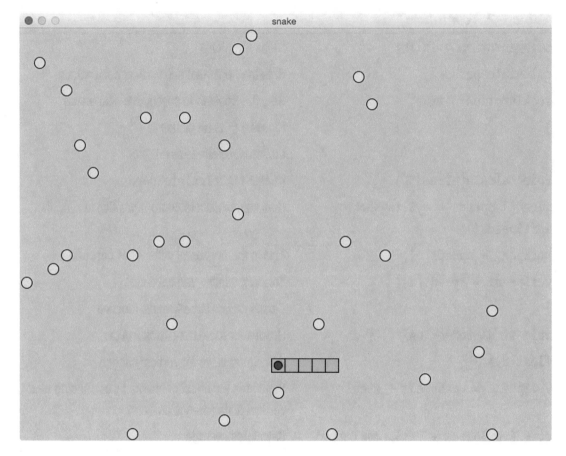

Figure 5-4. *Opening screen of snake*

The snake moves when you press the arrow keys. The snake grows when it passes over food. The game ends if the snake goes off the window or passes over itself, or a set period of time has elapsed. Figure 5-5 shows a screenshot when the time has elapsed. The snake has grown to be 15 segments long.

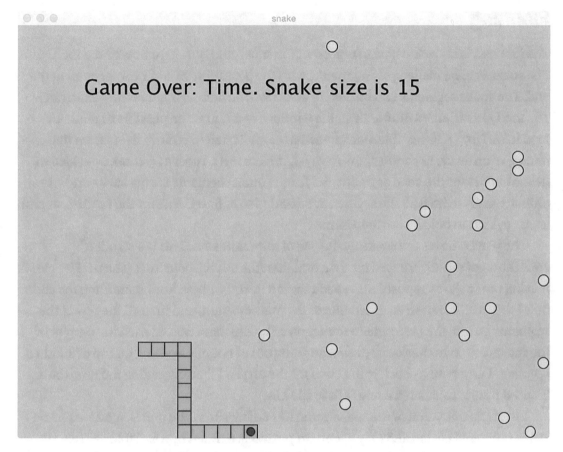

Figure 5-5. *Example of final window for snake game*

Implementing the Snake Sketch

The snake game was one of the first computer games widely distributed, and I am
going by memory on its design. Of course, my motivation is to demonstrate techniques
in programming and features of Processing, and the snake game represents ample
opportunities for both.

Planning

The first task is to decide how to represent the snake and how to represent the food. The snake is to be made up of segments, with the possibility of adding a segment at the end. The snake segments can be held in an array. The first segment has the extra circle. The food is distributed randomly in the window, and it must be possible to remove a food item. Now, it is possible, but somewhat complicated to remove items from the middle of an array. In contrast, the ArrayList class has a remove method. I decided to define classes for the head segment and for the other segments for the snake and use an ordinary array to hold all the segments. I decided to define a class for the food items and an ArrayList to hold all the food items.

The player moves the snake by the use of the arrow keys. This is a standard application of the keyPressed method and then the switch construct. The trickier part is moving the snake by repositioning each segment. You will see from examining the code how I did this: The head segment moves to a new position, and then all the rest of the segments go into the place where the segment before them was. At each movement of the snake, my code checks for the snake going out of bounds or going on top of another segment. I also have a check in the code for the elapsed time exceeding the time limit. Elapsed time is calculated using calls to millis.

My implementation of the snake game has an invisible grid; that is, food items and snake segments are located only at certain positions defined by a variable called unit. I programmed a function call closeEnough that checks if positions are within a margin amount. Note also that I changed the definition of the parameters used for drawing ellipses to be the upper left CORNER as opposed to the center because that is how it is done for rectangles. The functions, methods, and their relationships are shown in Table 5-3.

Table 5-3. *Snake Function Table*

Function name	Invoked by	Invokes
setup	Underlying Java program	placefood, buildfirstsegments
draw	Underlying Java program	foods.get, Food.display, seg.display, endgame
endgame		
placefood	setup	foods.add, Food
buildfirstsegments	setup	HeadSeg, Seg
keyPressed	Underlying Java program	movesnake
movesnake	keyPressed	closeEnough, growSnake, endgame
growsnake	movesnake	Seg
closeEnough	movesnake	
Seg	buildfirstsegments, growsnake	
Seg.display	draw	
Seg.moveTo	movesnake	
HeadSeg	buildfirstsegments	
HeadSeg.display	draw	
Food	placefood	
Food.display	draw	

Programming the Snake Sketch

The code for the snake sketch is shown in Table 5-4. It is long, but much of it is what I would call standard boilerplate code for programs with classes.

Table 5-4. *Snake Sketch*

`float margin = 10;`	Value used to detect the snake head being over food or over another segment
`float cw;`	The specified width of the window
`float ch;`	The specified height of the window
`int unit;`	The unit that defines the implicit grid
`int timeLimit = 30*1000;`	30 seconds for game
`int timeStart;`	Set in `setup`
`ArrayList<Food> foods = new ArrayList<Food>();`	Will hold the randomly positioned food items
`int amountOfFood = 30;`	Number of food items
`Seg[] segs;`	Will hold the snake
`HeadSeg hseg;`	The head of the snake
`void setup() {`	Header for `setup`
`size(800,600);`	Sets the dimensions of the window
`cw = width;`	Stores for later calculation (yes, I know this is 800)
`ch = height;`	Stores for later calculation
`unit = int(min(cw,ch)/30);`	This will define the implicit grid
`ellipseMode(CORNER);`	Easier to check for snake over circle representing food
`placefood();`	Invokes function to distribute food
`buildfirstsegments(5);`	Invokes function to build original snake
`timeStart = millis();`	Stores starting time
`}`	Closes `setup`
`void endgame(String m) {`	Header for endgame
`fill(0);`	Sets for text for final message
`textSize(30);`	Sets for text for final message

(continued)

Table 5-4. (*continued*)

`int snakeL = segs.length;`	Extracts length
`text("Game Over: "+m+" Snake size is "+str(snakeL),100,100);`	Displays final message
`noLoop();`	Stops action; keys no longer work
`}`	Closes endgame
`void draw() {`	Header for draw
`background(200);`	Clears screen
`for (int i=0;i<foods.size();i++) {`	Displays food by looping through foods
`foods.get(i).display();`	Displays item in foods
`}`	Closes for-loop
`for (int i=0; i<segs.length;i++) {`	Displays segs of snake
`segs[i].display();`	Displays seg
`}`	Closes for-loop
`if (timeLimit<(millis()-timeStart)) {`	Determines elapsed time since sketch started and checks if greater than `timeLimit`
`endgame("Time.");`	If so, invokes endgame
`}`	Closes `if`
`}`	Closes draw
`void placefood() {`	Header for placefood
`for (int i=0;i<amountOfFood;i++) {`	for loop to build foods `ArrayList`
`foods.add(new Food(unit*int(random(width)/ unit),unit*int(random(height)/ unit)));`	Adds in a food object
`}`	Closes for-loop
`}`	Closes placefood

(*continued*)

Table 5-4. (*continued*)

`void buildfirstsegments(int n) {`	Header for `buildfirstsegments`; original snake is oriented horizontal, head to the right, and not at the boundaries
`int leftbd = unit*10;`	Determines left bound
`int rightbd = width-leftbd;`	Determines right bound
`int headx = unit*int(random(leftbd,rightbd)/ unit);`	Positions the head of snake between these horizontal bounds
`int heady = unit*int(random(leftbd,rightbd)/ unit);`	Using same bounds, positions head vertically
`Seg aseg;`	Used to hold each of the ordinary segments
`hseg = new HeadSeg(headx,heady);`	Creates new head segment
`segs = new Seg[n];`	Creates array of the indicated size and then assigns individual elements
`segs[0] = hseg;`	The first one is the head segment
`for (int i=1;i<n;i++) {`	Loop to make the successive segments; note that loop starts at `i` set to 1
`int nsegx = headx+(i*unit);`	Snake starts out horizontal, with head seg on the left
`int nsegy = heady;`	All these `seg` elements at same vertical position
`aseg= new Seg(nsegx,nsegy);`	Creates the Seg element
`segs[i] = aseg;`	Sets item in the `segs` array to reference the newly created Seg element
`}`	Closes `for`-loop
`}`	Closes `buildfirstsegments`
`void keyPressed() {`	Header for `keyPressed`

(*continued*)

Table 5-4. (*continued*)

`switch(keyCode) {`	Selects based on `keyCode`; note there is no action if the key is not an arrow key
`case UP:`	
`movesnake(0,-unit);`	Moves snake up the screen
`break;`	Leaves switch
`case DOWN:`	
`movesnake(0,unit);`	Moves snake down the screen
`break;`	Leaves switch
`case RIGHT:`	
`movesnake(unit,0);`	Moves snake to the right
`break;`	Leaves switch
`case LEFT:`	
`movesnake(-unit,0);`	Moves snake to the left
`break;`	Leaves switch
`}`	Closes switch
`}`	Closes `keyPressed` function
`void movesnake(int dx, int dy) {`	Header for `movesnake`; slides snake along
`int numOfSegs = segs.length;`	Current length
`int[] xpositions = new int[numOfSegs];`	Will hold current x positions in an array; will not use last value
`int[] ypositions = new int[numOfSegs];`	Will hold current y positions in an array; will not use last value
`for (int i=0;i<numOfSegs;i++) {`	Loop through segments
`xpositions[i] = segs[i].sx;`	Stores x coordinate
`ypositions[i] = segs[i].sy;`	Stores y coordinate
`}`	Closes `for`-loop

(*continued*)

Table 5-4. (*continued*)

`int newHeadx = xpositions[0]+dx;`	Determines new x coordinate for head segment
`int newHeady = ypositions[0]+dy;`	Determines new y coordinate for head segment
`segs[0].moveTo(newHeadx,newHeady);`	Moves first segment to calculated positions
`for (int i=1;i<numOfSegs;i++) {`	Loop through segs after the head
`segs[i].moveTo(xpositions[i-1],ypositions[i-1]);`	Moves into location previously held by seg in front
`}`	Closes loop
`for (int i=1;i<(numOfSegs-1);i++) {`	Checks for head segment colliding with any other segment, except last by looping through segments, except for the last
`if (closeEnough(newHeadx, newHeady, xpositions[i],ypositions[i])) {`	Checks if close enough, using stored positions
`endgame("Collision with self.");`	If `true`, invokes endgame, with appropriate message
`}`	Closes if `true` clause
`}`	Closes loop
`if ((newHeadx<0)||(newHeadx>(width-unit))||(newHeady<0)||(newHeady>(height-unit))) {`	Checks if head is out of bounds
`endgame("Out of bounds. ");`	If `true`, invokes endgame, with appropriate message
`}`	
`for (int i=foods.size()-1;i>=0;i--) {`	Iterates over the foods `ArrayList` backward; this is important because items are removed
`if (closeEnough(newHeadx,newHeady, foods.get(i).fx,foods.get(i).fy)) {`	Checks if close enough
`foods.remove(i);`	If `true`, remove is available for `ArrayList`

(*continued*)

Table 5-4. (_continued_)

`growSnake();`	And grows the snake
`}`	Closes `if true` clause
`}`	Closes loop
`}`	Closes movesnake method
`void growSnake() {`	Header for growSnake
`int numOfSegs = segs.length;`	Will examine last two segs; need to do this to determine what direction snake grows
`int lastx = segs[numOfSegs-1].sx;`	The next element is the same as the last in x or y, but these expressions always work; calculates x coordinate of last seg
`int lasty = segs[numOfSegs-1].sy;`	Calculates y coordinate of last seg
`int overx = segs[numOfSegs-2].sx;`	Calculates x coordinate of next to the last seg
`int overy = segs[numOfSegs-2].sy;`	Calculates y coordinate of next to the last seg
`int difx = lastx-overx;`	Calculates difference
`int dify = lasty-overy;`	Calculates difference
`int newx = lastx+difx;`	Uses values to calculate new x
`int newy = lasty+dify;`	Uses values to calculate new y
`Seg newseg = new Seg(newx, newy);`	Creates new Seg object
`segs = (Seg[])append(segs,newseg);`	Appends to segs (i.e., the snake)
`}`	Closes growsnake
`Boolean closeEnough(int x1,int y1,int x2,int y2) {`	Header for closeEnough
`return (dist(x1,y1,x2,y2)< margin);`	Returns the result of calculation
`}`	Closes closeEnough
`class Seg {`	Header for Seg class definition
`int sx;`	Horizontal location
`int sy;`	Vertical location

(_continued_)

Table 5-4. (*continued*)

`Seg (int x, int y) {`	Constructor for Seg
`sx = x;`	Set variable
`sy = y;`	Set variable
`}`	Closes constructor
`void display() {`	Header for display
`fill(0,250,0);`	Sets fill color
`rect(sx,sy,unit, unit);`	Draws rectangle
`}`	Closes display method
`void moveTo(int nx, int ny) {`	Header for moveTo; move to this position
`sx = nx;`	Sets new x coordinate
`sy = ny;`	Sets new y coordinate
`}`	Closes moveTo method
`}`	Closes Seg class
`class HeadSeg extends Seg {`	Header for HeadSeg, child class of Seg
`HeadSeg(int x, int y) {`	Constructor for HeadSeg
`super(x,y);`	Invokes parent constructor
`}`	Closes constructor
`void display() {`	Header for display for HeadSeg; the head segment is displayed with a circle on top of a rectangle
`fill(0,250,0);`	Sets color
`rect(sx,sy, unit, unit);`	Draws rectangle
`fill(0,0,200);`	Sets to blue
`ellipse(sx+.2*unit, sy+.2*unit, .60*unit,.60*unit);`	Draws circle
`}`	Closes display method
`}`	Closes HeadSeg class definition

(*continued*)

Table 5-4. (*continued*)

class Food {	Header for Food class
int fx;	x coordinate
int fy;	y coordinate
Food (int x, int y) {	Header for Food constructor
fx = x;	Set variable
fy = y;	Set variable
}	Closes constructor method
void display() {	Header for display method
fill(250,250,0);	Sets color for food
ellipse(fx+.1*unit,fy+.1*unit,.8*unit, .8*unit);	Draws circle
}	Closes display method
}	Closes Food class

Image Test Operation Overview

In this sketch, an image is presented to evoke a response from the player. Figure 5-6 shows the image, which was prepared by my son for my birthday and seems suitable for an image test. The image contains multiple instances of my granddaughter. The example provides a way for me to introduce the notion of access to and modification of an external file as well as a simple use of Regular expressions.

Figure 5-6. *Opening screen of image test*

After a specified amount of time, the player is given a chance to type in a response, as shown in Figure 5-7.

Figure 5-7. *Request for input for image test*

Unlike the key presses of the arrow keys in the snake sketch, players expect to type in text, see what is being typed character by character, and then press the Enter key to submit the complete response.

My sketch performs these tasks and then checks for the string 10, ten, or Ten in the response. If any of these strings are found, the response is marked as correct. A CSV file has been loaded, and a new row is added for this response. Table 5-5 shows the table at some point in my work. Notice that some rows have the Yes entry in the Correct column and some do not. The updated CSV file is available for use in the data subfolder.

Table 5-5. *Sample CSV File Opened in Excel*

Answer	Time stamp	Correct
I see a lot of Annikas	10/8/17 11:42	
10 Annikas in a tree	10/8/17 11:42	Yes
ten	10/8/17 11:43	Yes
How did you do this?	10/8/17 11:43	
A lot of girls	10/12/17 14:48	
ten girls	10/12/17 14:48	Yes
girls around a tree	10/12/17 14:51	
A lot of girls	10/12/17 14:51	
10 girls	10/12/17 14:51	Yes
Annika in a tree	12/3/17 9:15	
There are 10 Annikas	12/13/17 13:25	Yes
a lot of girls	12/13/17 13:25	
a lot of girls in a tree	12/13/17 13:26	

Implementing the Image Test

The new features of this sketch are handling of text input and the use of the Table data type with a CSV file. The sketch also makes use of Regular expressions. I will not go into detail on Regular expressions, except to say that they are exactly what you need to make a check on text.

Planning

The handling of text input is available in the Processing documentation and elsewhere online. The approach I took makes use of two character strings: myText and answer. The myText variable is changed at each key press. When the Enter key is pressed, the value of myText is assigned into answer. The draw function checks if answer is not empty.

Processing provides the Table data type. It is possible to create a Table within Processing, but I decided to create a file using Excel, save the file as a CSV file, and place it in the data folder. The sketch adds a row or multiple rows to the file. The program saves the file after each response.

The Regular expression function I use is match. The first parameter is the string to be examined, and the second holds the pattern. For this sketch, I set a variable

String correctanswers = "(10)|(ten)|(Ten)";

When my code uses this in match, the string will be checked for the presence of the string 10 or the string ten or the string Ten.

Often, I am too lazy to include the functionality of restarting a sketch, but I decided to do it this time. The user, test subject, or player action is to click the mouse. The response that I coded in mouseClicked was to make answer and myText each be the empty string and reset startTime using millis. Be warned that the restart coding can be more difficult than this. The relationship of functions is shown in Table 5-6.

Table 5-6. *Function Table for imageText*

Function name	Invoked by	Invokes
setup	Underlying Java program	
draw	Underlying Java program	storeAnswer
keyPressed	Underlying Java program	
storeAnswer	draw	
mouseClicked	Underlying Java program	

Program

The image test sketch has several global variables, as shown in the code in Table 5-7. These are critical for the communication among the functions.

Table 5-7. *Code for Image Test Sketch*

`Table results;`	Will hold table
`PImage picture;`	Will hold image
`int startTime;`	Set in `setup` or `mouseClicked`
`int duration = 4*1000;`	Time image is displayed
`float pictureWidth;`	For `aspectWoverH`
`float pictureHeight;`	For `aspectWoverH`
`float setHeight = 900;`	Sets height for image
`float computedWidth;`	Calculated from the `setHeight` and `aspectWoverH`
`float aspectWoverH;`	Calculated
`String prompt="What did you see? ";`	Instruction to player
`String myText = "";`	Added to in `keyPressed`
`String answer = "";`	Set when Enter is pressed
`String correctanswers = "(10)|(ten)|(Ten)";`	Regular expressions
`void setup() {`	Header for `setup`
`picture = loadImage("AnnikasInTree.jpg");`	Loads in image
`pictureWidth = picture.width;`	Sets `pictureWidth`
`pictureHeight = picture.height;`	Sets `pictureHeight`
`aspectWoverH = pictureWidth/ pictureHeight;`	Computes aspect ratio
`computedWidth = setHeight * aspectWoverH;`	Calculates `computedWidth`
`results = loadTable("results. csv","header");`	Reads in table from the CSV file in the `data` folder; the `"header"` indicates that there is a header row
`size(1000,1000);`	Sets window dimensions

(continued)

Table 5-7. (*continued*)

`startTime = millis();`	Used with current time and duration
`textSize(20);`	Sets `textSize`
`}`	
`void draw() {`	Header for `draw`
`background(0);`	Erases screen
`if ((millis()-startTime)<` `duration) {`	If still within duration
`image(picture,10,10,computedWid` `th,setHeight);`	Displays image at the computed dimensions
`}`	Closes `if`
`else{`	`else`
`text(prompt + myText,100,100);`	Asks for response
`if (answer.length()>0) {`	`keyPressed` builds up input in `myText`, stores in answer after Enter key is pressed, so if answer not empty
`storeAnswer();`	Stores answer as new row in the results table
`noLoop();`	Stops looping until `mouseClicked` restarts process
`}`	Closes if answer is not empty
`}`	Closes `else`
`}`	Closes `draw`
`void keyPressed() {`	Accepts keyboard input
`if (keyCode == BACKSPACE) {`	If Backspace is pressed
`if (myText.length() > 0 ) {`	If anything is already entered
`myText = myText.substring( 0 ,` `myText.length()- 1 );`	Takes out the last character
`}`	
`} else if (keyCode == DELETE) {`	If Delete is pressed

(*continued*)

Table 5-7. (*continued*)

`myText = "" ;`	Resets myText to empty
`} else if (keyCode == ENTER) {`	If Enter is pressed
`answer = myText;`	Sets answer to MyText

`} else if (keyCode != SHIFT &&`
`keyCode != CONTROL && keyCode`
`!= ALT) {`
	Checks for these three special keys

`myText = myText + str(key);`	Adds key to myText
`}`	Closes if testing for anything besides certain special keys
`}`	Closes keyPressed
`void storeAnswer(){`	Stores answer with a time stamp as new row in table
`String check = "";`	Sets check to empty string

`String ts =`
`month()+"/"+day()+"/"+year()+"`
`"+hour()+":"+minute()+":"+seco`
`nd();`
	Creates what I call the time stamp

`TableRow newRow = results.` `addRow();`	Adds new row, with two or three values set
`newRow.setString("Time` `Stamp",ts);`	Makes entry in the Time Stamp column
`newRow.` `setString("Answer",answer);`	Makes entry in the Answer column

`if`
`(match(answer,correctanswers)`
`!=null) {`
	If there is a match

`newRow.` `setString("Correct","Yes");`	Makes entry in the Correct column
`check = " Correct! ";`	Prepares for message
`}`	Closes if match

(continued)

Table 5-7. (*continued*)

`saveTable(results,"data/` `results.csv");`	Saves the table
`background(0);`	Clears screen
`text(check+"Click on screen to` `play again",200,200);`	Output message
`}`	Closes `storeAnswer`
`void mouseClicked() {`	Header for `mouseClicked` restarts the game by setting `startTime` as the current time and restarting looping
`myText="";`	Resets `myText`
`answer="";`	Resets `answer`
`startTime = millis();`	Sets `startTime` to now
`loop();`	Restarts looping; `draw` will be invoked
`}`	Closes `mouseClicked`

Things to Look Up

At some point, you should read about Regular expressions, as they are their own miniature and very powerful programming language.

You can read up on `Array` and `ArrayList`. Do some research on UNICODE.

There is considerable functionality in the use of the `Table` data type. For example, you can extract information from a `Table` constructed from a CSV file to control drawings and animations.

I suggested that you could change from milliseconds to seconds by dividing by 1,000. You can look up the `nf` function for formatting numbers.

How to Make This Your Own

You can replace the chicken and the feathers and perhaps add a background with your own artwork. You can alter the slingshot to be something else after you understand what needs to be set once the projectile takes off. You can add a scoring system. You can do research on ballistic motion, perhaps investigating how to model a torpedo.

You can make Snake a fancier game. For example, you can add food of different values or obstacles for the snake to avoid. It is also a good candidate for levels of play.

The image test can be changed by using your own initial image, with appropriate tests, as complicated as you can manage, for checking the answer. More generally, come up with your own ideas for posing questions, examining the responses, and using tables for recording results.

The dice game of craps might inspire you to expand on the game or use another dice game. Consider showing die faces.

What You Learned

This chapter covered ways Processing supports interactions, including mouse actions; single key presses, such as the use of the arrow keys; and multiple key presses for accepting pieces of text. The image test program demonstrated the use of a Table constructed from a CSV file. The sketch added a row to the Table and saved the Table, replacing the original file.

This was an introduction to Regular expressions. I hope you saw enough to investigate further either now or when you come across a possible use.

The snake and slingshot sketches demonstrated classes and inheritance, arrays and ArrayList, and calculations involving algebra and trigonometry. All three examples in this chapter demonstrate the use of logic. The image test should help your understanding of interactions we all have with computer technology.

What's Next

The next chapter features the use of transformations to produce an intricate pattern inspired by an origami model and changing an image to be grayscale. As an extra bonus, the image is acquired from the Web, providing a way to let users specify the image they want to use.

CHAPTER 6

Images and Graphics

Abstract

This chapter focuses on two examples, one with images and one with graphics. The first example displays an image, that is, a photograph, with instructions to press specific keys to modify the image in certain ways. The second example demonstrates the use of transformations for creating an origami-inspired flower design and can be considered graphics.

Note   The first edition of this book made use of a Processing function to access an image from a web address entered by the user. The exposition did include instructions on how to check if the operation failed, perhaps the address (URL) was mistyped or the file was not an image. The text provided a valid address on my faculty website that held the photo of my mother that you will see in use in the sketch. The administration at my college decided to stop hosting these websites! This experience—a website disappearing—is common! It is one reason that accessing online material is problematic. Another important reason, not applicable in this case, is that access can be without permission. In addition, Processing support is changing, and it appears to be more difficult to check for a bad image. I decided to go back to using images stored in the data folder. However, as I indicate in the "Things to Look Up" section, this is a topic to investigate and use appropriately.

© Jeanine Meyer 2022
J. Meyer, *Programming 101*, https://doi.org/10.1007/978-1-4842-8194-9_6

More on the Sketches

As has been my practice, I show screenshots from the featured examples before describing the critical Processing functions and programming techniques and then going over the implementations in detail. You have been introduced to `keyPressed`, `image`, and other basic Processing functions. These examples will show more uses of these functions and others. This spiral style of exposition starts off with two illustrations, both showing the sketches after actions by the user.

The image example demonstrates changing an image in different ways. Figure 6-1 shows a screen with two images; the lower one was produced using the Processing `filter` method with the GRAY option after the user pressed the g key. As you can see by reading the text on the screen, the choice is done using key strokes. (By the way, this meant that my normal method for screen capture had to be changed to using the Launchpad on my iMac.) You can see the results of pressing the other keys and sequences of keys later in the chapter.

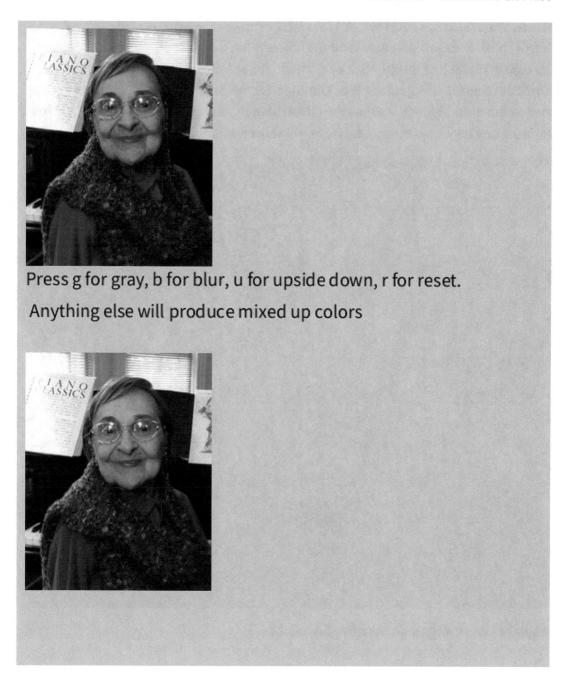

Figure 6-1. *Esther Minkin at piano: original and gray image*

The graphics example demonstrates the use of the translate and rotate functions with beginShape and endShape to produce a complex design made up of several layers of a hexagon shape. The inspiration for this was an origami model and is meant to be a flower. The sketch has some similarities with the make-a-polygon sketch in Chapter 2, but the basic hexagon shape used for the flower is not a regular polygon. The center of each flower is set by a mouse click by the user. The sketch does nothing to prevent the user from clicking on top of the text. The angle is determined by a calculation using the random function. Figure 6-2 shows the screen after the user has mouse-clicked five times. Pressing any key clears the screen. I also will show a variation of this sketch.

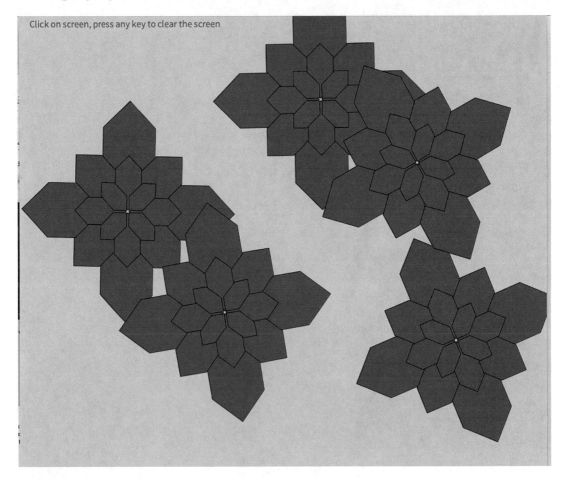

Figure 6-2. *Hexagon sketch after five clicks*

Programming Concepts

The general programming concepts I feature in this chapter include transformations of images, transformation of the coordinate system, drawing of shapes, and the use of the switch statement with char values.

Images As Arrays of Pixels

Images are encoded in different ways, for example, .png and .jpg. Processing accepts multiple formats.

Caution   When naming an image file, the case and spelling of the file extension matter. If the file you put in the data folder was flower.jpg, referring to it as flower. jpeg or flower.JPG will not work.

An image can be viewed as a set of picture elements known as *pixels*. A typical way to represent the color in a pixel and the default setting in Processing is the Red-Green-Blue-Alpha system. The *alpha* specifies the transparency. For this application, I ignore the alpha, but keep it in mind because you might want to use it for your own work.

Case Statement

You have seen the use of the switch statement to implement checking a specific variable for distinct values when variable is an integer. For the image transformation example, I use a char value. The value is obtained from the built-in variable key accessed in the keyPressed method. The char is a *primitive data type* as is the int data type. Keep in mind that String is not. My code checks for "g", "b", "u", and "r". For the case statement in the image sketch, I made use of the default option to produce an image with what I term mixed-up colors if the user presses anything other than the four choices.

Pixel Processing

Processing provides functions for producing arrays for the whole window or for an individual PImage. If original is the PImage holding the result of the loadImage function, then original.loadPixels(); sets original.pixels to be a one-dimensional array holding the information for each pixel. The size of the array is original.width * original.height. It is not necessary for this sketch, but there is a formula for getting to the element in the pixels array corresponding to the pixel at row r, r going from 0 to 1 less than original.height, and column c, c going from 0 to 1 less than original.width. The formula is

```
i = c + r*original.width;
```

The information for each pixel is in an object of data type `color`. It is possible to extract the red, green, and blue (along with alpha, which is not used here) using functions `red`, `green`, and `blue`. A formula exists and was used in the first edition of this book for producing a grayscale version of an image. However, Processing now provides the `filter` method for accomplishing this using GRAY as a parameter and the parameter BLUR to produce a blurred image. I use the individual pixel values for producing an upside down version of the image and one with mixed-up colors.

The beginShape and endShape Vertex Functions

Processing provides functions to draw shapes, and this is what I use to draw the basic hexagon. An advantage to using these functions as opposed to drawing lines as I demonstrated with the polygon sketch is that the fill and stroke settings can define the colors for the border and the internal parts of the drawing. There are several variations for beginShape and endShape. I used the default for `beginShape` and `endShape(CLOSE)`. This meant that I specified six vertices to define a hexagon.

Changing the Coordinate System

In Processing and other programming languages, all drawing is done in terms of a coordinate system. You have seen this already, starting from the first example with the Daddy logo. Processing provides a way to save the current coordinate system, make changes to the coordinate system, do some drawing, and, at some point, restore the last coordinate system saved. One type of change uses the `translate` function, and another uses the `rotate` function. I describe `rotate` and `translate` operations in the context of explaining the implementation of the origami flower sketch. In this sketch, I want to draw three hexagons, going from bigger to smaller, and, being a typical (lazy) programmer, I want to use the same code. This is accomplished by changing the coordinate system.

The functions used for saving and restoring coordinate systems are `pushMatrix` and `popMatrix`. The names make sense if you realize that the coordinate systems are defined by operations involving matrices and that saving the current coordinate system means placing it on a stack. The terminology for stacks is last in, first out (LIFO).

If my code sets up a coordinate system I call A and then does a push, does something to set up the B coordinate system, does some drawing, and then pushes B on the stack, when I want my code to put the coordinate system back to what it was before I made the transformations setting up B, I could use the pop function. I could then do something to set up C. If I wanted to go back to what it was before I set up A, I would invoke the pop operation twice. Examine and experiment with the hexagons sketch and then your own projects and this will become clear and something you can use.

Hue-Saturation-Brightness Color Mode

Processing and some other programming languages and tools provide an alternative to the Red-Green-Blue method for specifying color. The Hue-Saturation-Brightness mode, as the terms imply, provides a way to specify the color, as defined along what is called the color wheel; the strength or purity of the color; and the lightness and darkness. Some say this is a more natural way than RGB. However, I and others are so familiar with RGB, that any change is a challenge. The units for the three values can be set when specifying color mode. The default is 0 to 360 for Hue, 0 to 100 for Saturation, and 0 to 100 for Brightness. In my variation of the hexagons, my code varies the hue and the saturation systematically. You can modify or add other changes to the basic design, including making a similar systematic change of the brightness.

Changing Image Sketch Overview

I decided to build a sketch in which the user would produce a second image of Esther Minkin transformed in some way. Figure 6-3 shows the initial screen.

Press g for gray, b for blur, u for upside down, r for reset.

Anything else will produce mixed up colors

Figure 6-3. *Opening screen for image sketch*

Though it looks like the original image along with the instructions is only displayed once, in fact, the draw function does all the work. My first try did not have this, and the results were messy for the text in the instructions. You can see this in the code table.

You have seen the results from typing a g for grayscale in Figure 6-1. Figure 6-4 shows the results of clicking "b" for blur.

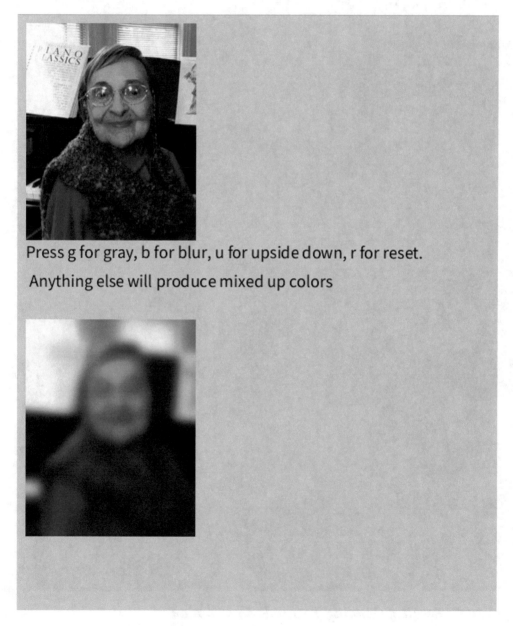

Figure 6-4. Screen after keying "b" for blur

Figure 6-5 shows the result from choosing the upside down option.

Press g for gray, b for blur, u for upside down, r for reset.

Anything else will produce mixed up colors

Figure 6-5. *Result of choosing the upside down option*

At some point in my programming this sketch, I realized that I had to decide if the options would be cumulative or not. I decided to make them cumulative. Typing "g" again does not have any effects, but typing "g" and then "b" has the results shown in Figure 6-6.

Figure 6-6. *Blurred grayscale image*

If the user then selected the upside down option, Figure 6-7 shows the results.

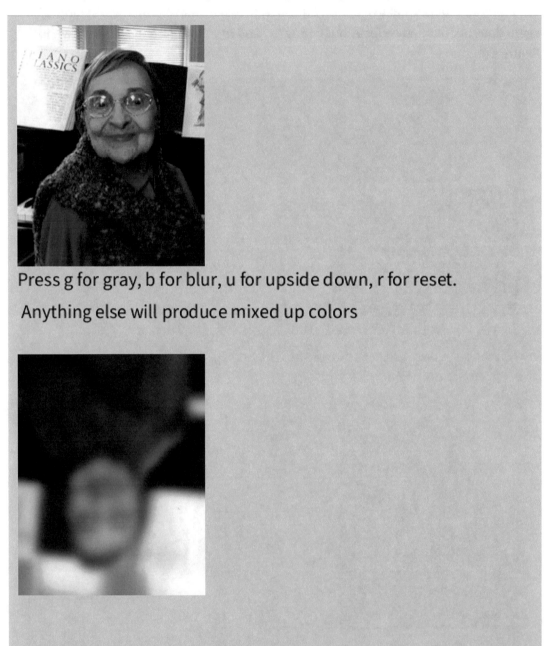

Figure 6-7. *Upside down, blurred, gray image*

There are other possibilities, including typing "u" twice, which does produce a right-sided image. However, I leave that exploration to the reader. The reset option produces a copy of the original image so cumulative effects start from the original image.

The last possibility is to decide if and what should be the transformation when the user types some other key. Do consider that one option is to do nothing. A variation of the "do nothing" is to not produce a new, transformed image, but let the user know that an unrecognized key was pressed.

I decided to produce something using the individual pixel values. This is shown in Figure 6-8.

Press g for gray, b for blur, u for upside down, r for reset.

Anything else will produce mixed up colors

Figure 6-8. *Default option of mixed-up colors*

Implementing the Image Transformations

My design decisions are strongly motivated by wanting to demonstrate programming techniques and Processing features. You should experiment with the code, perhaps adding new options and/or making different decisions on cumulative effects. You then can go on and use the techniques and the features in completely different sketches. Your decisions on issues such as cumulative effects and default values will depend on your goals and your audiences.

Planning

When I made the change from using an image on the Web to sticking with an image in the data folder, I realized that I needed to provide more options. I made use of the `filter` method for two changes and then decided to provide two more options, each making use of pixels. The presence of these distinct options meant that I did need to think about cumulative effects.

The sketch has a simple overall structure. The bulk of the action is in the keyPressed method. I make use of four PImage variables.

The relationship of the functions is shown in Table 6-1.

Table 6-1. *Functions in Image Changing Sketch*

Function name	Invoked by	Invokes
setup	Underlying Java program	
draw	Underlying Java program	
keyPressed	Underlying Java program	

Programming the Image Sketch

The program for the Image Sketch is explained in Table 6-2.

Table 6-2. *Image Changes Sketch*

`PImage original;`	Original image
`PImage changed;`	Changed image
`PImage buffer;`	Used for upside down
`int imgw;`	Width of image(s)
`int imgh;`	Height of image(s)
`Boolean secondImageAdded = false;`	Used to distinguish first display before any changes
`color mc;`	Used in the default option
`float redc;`	Used in the default option
`float greenc;`	Used in the default option
`float bluec;`	Used in the default option
`color[] choices = new color[3];`	Used in the default option for random choice
`int index;`	Used in the default option for random choice
`void setup() {`	Header for setup
`size(800,800);`	Sets the size of window
`textSize(20);`	Sets the size of text message giving instructions
`fill(0);`	Sets subsequent text to be black
`original = loadImage("esther.jpg");`	Loads image from data folder into original variable
`buffer = loadImage("esther.jpg");`	Loads same image into buffer variable
`changed = loadImage("esther.jpg");`	Loads same image into changed variable
`imgw = min(original.width,width);`	Sets imgw
`imgh = min(original.height,height);`	Sets imgh. Note this can change aspect ratio
`}`	Closes setup

(continued)

Table 6-2. (*continued*)

`void draw() {`	Header for draw
`  background(200);`	Erases window
`  image(original,10,10,imgw,imgh);`	Draws original
`  fill(0);`	Sets color for text

`  text("Press g for gray, b for blur,`
`u for upside down, r for reset.\n`
`Anything else will produce mixed up`
`colors",10,imgh+30);`
	Displays text. Note line break

`  if (secondImageAdded) {`	Checks to show changed image
`    image(changed,10,imgh+100,imgw,` `    imgh);`	Displays changed image
`  }`	Closes if true clause
`}`	Closes draw
`void keyPressed () {`	
`secondImageAdded = true;`	Used to always draw second image
`switch(key) {`	The switch uses the variable key
`  case 'g':`	Grayscale option
`    changed.filter(GRAY);`	Apply the GRAY filter to the changed image
`    break;`	Leaves switch statement
`  case 'b':`	Blurs option
`    changed.filter(BLUR,5);`	Changes image
`    break;`	Leaves switch statement
`  case 'r':`	Resets option
`    changed.copy(original, 0,0,` `    imgw,imgh,0,0,imgw,imgh);`	This restores the original image to the changed variable
`    break;`	Leaves switch statement
`  case 'u':`	Upside down option

(*continued*)

Table 6-2. (*continued*)

`changed.loadPixels();`	Must load the pixels
`buffer.loadPixels();`	The buffer will be changed entirely. This is to set up for pixel processing
`for (int i=0; i<changed.pixels.` `length;i++) {`	Goes through the whole image (changed)
`  buffer.pixels[changed.pixels.` `  length-1-i] = changed.pixels[i];`	Stores in buffer, starting from the end
`}`	Closes for-loop
`buffer.updatePixels();`	Updates pixels in buffer
`changed.copy(buffer,0,0,imgw,` `imgh,0,0,imgw,imgh);`	Now (and only now) copy over buffer into changed
`  break;`	Leaves switch statement
`default:`	The default option: user typed some other key
` original.loadPixels();`	Loads pixels
` changed.loadPixels();`	Loads pixels
`for (int i=0;i<original.pixels.` `length;i++) {`	Looking through original
`  redc = red(original.pixels[i]);`	Sets the red value
`  greenc = green(original.` `  pixels[i]);`	…green value
`  bluec = blue(original.pixels[i]);`	…blue value
`  choices[0] = color(redc,0,0);`	Sets up three values in choices, the 0th
`  choices[1] = color(0,greenc,0);`	…the first
`  choices[2] = color(0,0,bluec);`	…the second
`  index = int(random(3));`	Choose random value 0, 1, or 2

(continued)

Table 6-2. (*continued*)

`mc = choices[index];`	Sets that one to be the color
`changed.pixels[i] = mc;`	Set the ith element to the color mc
`}`	Closes for-loop
`changed.updatePixels();`	Updates pixels
`}`	Closes switch
`}`	Closes keyPressed

Origami Flower Graphic Overview

The second example draws a figure made up of hexagons wherever the user clicks on the screen. The graphic is inspired by the Origami Hydrangea by Shuzo Fujimoto. The operation of this sketch is straightforward. The player clicks on the screen, and the graphic image appears with the center at the location of the mouse and with a rotation randomly chosen in the range from 0 to PI/2 (90 degrees). The player can clear the window by pressing any key. Figure 6-2, earlier in the chapter, shows the window after five clicks. However, prompted by the technical reviewer, I have added a variation of this sketch, making use of the HSB mode. The variation has lost the connection to the origami model but does produce more complex graphic designs.

Planning

The flower design can appear to be a complex collection of lines. However, the design is easy, at least easier, to produce when it is viewed as a set of layers, with layers drawn on top of previous layers.

I decided that a layer in my sketch would consist of four hexagons, arranged in a cross. The hexagons in a layer are all the same size. For the next layer, the size is reduced. After examining the origami model and testing of code, I calculated that the reduction was by a factor of square root of 2.

Notice the small hole in the center of the flower. This does resemble the origami model, and I produced it in the sketch by the use of a fudge factor, which I put in a variable I named fudge. This was a late modification of the code.

Before starting the coding, I knew that my sketch would have a function for a single hexagon, a function for the four-hexagon, cross-like configuration I am terming a layer, and a function for the whole thing. I would code mouseReleased and keyPressed. I would obtain positioning and orientation by changing the coordinate system.

My code does not check if the mouse position at the click was such as to make some of the flower cover the instructions. Similarly, the code does not check if any lines are outside the window.

Implementing the Origami Flower Sketch

The challenge to implementing the origami sketch, assuming understanding of how to program the response to a mouse event such as mouseReleased and a keyPress event, and a general idea about transformations, is not a programming challenge. This is after determining the organization of the flower design in terms of layers. I say this not to say it is easy or difficult, but to point out that problem-solving occurs before and during coding.

With my general plans in mind, I figured out how to draw a single hexagon. I knew that it needed to be a function with parameters indicating the location and the size. Early in the programming, I decided the orientation of the base hexagon would be based on a random expression, but done outside the drawing of the hexagon. Here is the function for the basic hexagon, which I named hexShape. I put in the comment to remind myself of the meaning of the parameters.

```
void hexShape(float cx, float cy, float hexSize) {
    //cx and cy are center of circle for which this is
    //an inscribed NOT regular hexagon.
    beginShape();
    vertex(cx+hexSize,cy);
    vertex(cx+hexSize*.5,cy-hexSize*.5);
    vertex(cx-hexSize*.5,cy-hexSize*.5);
    vertex(cx-hexSize,cy);
    vertex(cx-hexSize*.5,cy+hexSize*.5);
    vertex(cx+hexSize*.5,cy+hexSize*.5);
    endShape(CLOSE);
}
```

Notice that beginShape is a function call. It does not indicate the start of a clause, and there are no brackets. However, I do indent one space because that makes sense for me. The built-in CLOSE parameter to endShape produces a line from the last vertex to the first. The use of beginShape and endShape meant that the pinkish color would appear inside the hexagons. I tested hexShape as soon as I wrote it.

The next step was planning that a function named hexLayer would call the hexShape function four times. This calls for a for-loop. In the body of the loop, I would include a translate and then a rotate transformation. Figure 6-9 shows the result of a translate operation.

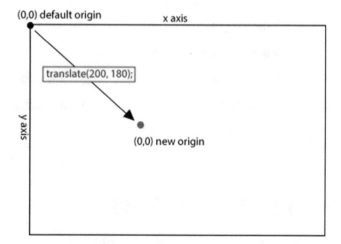

Figure 6-9. *Action of translate*

A rotate operation changes the orientation of the axes. A rotate transformation always is at the current coordinate system origin, so the translate is critical. The hexCombo function performs a rotation based on a calculation using random. Please note that the hexagon has symmetry such that rotating it by 90 degrees produces the same design.

My code has pushMatrix at the start of the body of the for-loop and then popMatrix at the end of the body. The fudge variable is used to slightly alter the location of the hexagon. The alteration is always in the same dimension (x) and direction (positive) because the rotation changes what that is for each hexagon drawn by hexShape. Again, I tested hexLayer as soon as I wrote it. See the code table for code that is commented out. I strongly urge you to do this when testing this sketch and in similar circumstances in your own work.

Finally, hexCombo invokes hexLayer four times, with the size passed to hexLayer shrinking by being divided by a factor of sqrt(2). Once again, I tested this as soon as I wrote it.

Table 6-3 shows the relationship of the functions for the hexagons sketch.

Table 6-3. *Function Table for Hexagons*

Function name	Invoked by	Invokes
setup	Underlying Java program	
draw	Underlying Java program	
mouseReleased	Underlying Java program	hexCombo
keyPressed	Underlying Java program	
hexCombo	mouseReleased	hexLayer (four times)
hexLayer	hexCombo	hexShape (four times)
hexShape	hexLayer	

Programming the Origami Flower

I did not copy over all the comments in my sketch but did include a few in setup with comments on the comments. Do go back to the polygons sketch in Chapter 2 and note the similarities. The code is shown in Table 6-4.

Table 6-4. *Hexagons Sketch*

`float fudge = 3;`	Defined to produce the hole in the center
`void setup() {`	Header for setup
`size(1000,900);`	Set the dimensions of window
`fill(200,0,100);`	Set color
`textSize(18);`	Set bigger text
`text("Click on screen, press any key to clear the screen",20,20);`	Display instructions

(continued)

Table 6-4. (*continued*)

//hexShape(220,120,200);	Consider keeping this and removing the // to see what is produced and doing the equivalent for your own designs
//hexLayer(400,400,200);	Consider keeping this and removing the // to see what is produced
//hexCombo(800,500,200);	Consider keeping this and removing the // to see what is produced
}	Close setup
void draw() {	Header for draw function, which is required to enable mouse and key events
}	Close draw
void mouseReleased() {	Header for mouseReleased
hexCombo(mouseX,mouseY,200);	Draw combo at mouse location
}	Close mouseReleased
void hexCombo(float cx, float cy, float startSize) {	Header for hexCombo
float curSize = startSize;	curSize starts off as startSize
translate(cx,cy);	Translate to cx,cy
rotate(random(HALF_PI));	Rotate based on random factor
hexLayer(0,0,curSize);	Do one layer
pushMatrix();	Save coordinate system
rotate(PI/4);	Rotate PI/4
curSize = curSize/sqrt(2);	Shrink curSize
hexLayer(0,0,curSize);	Do one layer
rotate(PI/4);	Rotate PI/4 again
curSize = curSize/sqrt(2);	Shrink curSize
hexLayer(0,0,curSize);	Do one layer

(*continued*)

Table 6-4. (*continued*)

`rotate(PI/4);`	Rotate PI/4 again
`curSize = curSize/sqrt(2);`	Shrink curSize
`hexLayer(0,0,curSize);`	Do one layer
`popMatrix();`	Restore coordinate system
`}`	Close hexCombo
`void hexLayer(float cx, float cy,float layerSize) {`	Header for hexLayer
`float pctrx, pctry;`	Used in call for hexShape
`float hexSize = layerSize;`	Set using parameter
`fill(200,0,100);`	Set fill (not necessary)
`for (int i=0;i<4;i++){`	Loop to draw four hexagons
`pushMatrix();`	Save coordinate system
`translate(cx,cy);`	Move the coordinate system cx horizontally and cy vertically
`rotate(HALF_PI*i);`	Rotate calculated amount (0, PI/2, PI, and 3*PI/2)
`pctrx =.5*hexSize+fudge;`	Add fudge factor to x position
`pctry = 0;`	Set y
`hexShape(pctrx,pctry, .5*hexSize);`	Draw hexagon
`popMatrix();`	Restore coordinate system
`}`	Close for-loop
`}`	Close hexLayer
`void hexShape(float cx, float cy, float hexSize) {`	Header for hexShape
`beginShape();`	Start shape
`vertex(cx+hexSize,cy);`	Rightmost vertex

(*continued*)

Table 6-4. (*continued*)

`vertex(cx+hexSize*.5,` `cy-hexSize*.5);`	Working around counterclockwise
`vertex(cx-hexSize*.5,` `cy-hexSize*.5);`	Working around counterclockwise
`vertex(cx-hexSize,cy);`	Leftmost vertex
`vertex(cx-` `hexSize*.5,cy+hexSize*.5);`	Continuing working around
`vertex(cx+hexSize*.5,` `cy+hexSize*.5);`	Continuing working around
`endShape(CLOSE);`	Close shape, connecting first and last vertices
`}`	Close hexShape
`void keyPressed() {`	Header for keyPressed
`background(200,200,200);`	Erase window

`text("Click on screen,`
`press any key to clear the`
`screen",20,20);`
	Display instructions

`}`	Close keyPressed

Programming the Hexagon with HSB Color Mode

This variation uses the same approach of layers. However, within the hexLayer function, a variable used to set the saturation is decreased by a fixed amount. At some point, it is reset back to 100. Similarly, within the keyPressed function, a variable used to set the hue is decreased by a fixed amount, and at some point, this variable is reset to 360. Figure 6-10 shows the window after a few clicks.

Figure 6-10. *Resulting screen after multiple mouse clicks*

Figure 6-11 shows the window after several pressing of keys and then the user clicked the mouse a few more times. The sketch has shown several color changes.

Click on screen, press any key to clear the screen

Figure 6-11. *Resulting screen after key presses and mouse clicks*

The code for the sketch is shown completely in Table 6-5. It does resemble the original version. I did add another layer, the topmost and the smallest. I also issue a println to show the changing saturation values and hue values in the console window.

Table 6-5. *Hexagons Varying the Colors Using HSB Sketch*

`float fudge = 3;`	Defined to produce the hole in the center
`int hueValue = 360;`	Initial value of hue. This is red
`int satValue = 100;`	Initial value of saturation. This is the highest value
`int brightValue = 100;`	Initial value of brightness. This is the highest value
`void setup() {`	Header for setup method
`size(1000,900);`	Sets window size
`fill(200,0,100);`	This uses the default RGB color mode
`textSize(18);`	Sets text size
`text("Click on screen, press any key to clear the screen",20,20);`	Displays text on the screen
`colorMode(HSB,360,100,100);`	Switches colorMode to HSB, setting the high values
`}`	Closes setup
`void draw() {`	Header for draw
`}`	Closes draw
`void mouseReleased() {`	Header for mouseReleased
`hexCombo(mouseX,mouseY,200);`	Draws the combo design
`}`	Closes mouseReleased
`void hexCombo(float cx, float cy, float startSize) {`	Header for hexCombo
`float curSize = startSize;`	Sets the current size
`translate(cx,cy);`	Translates to cx and cy. These will be the mouse coordinates
`rotate(random(HALF_PI));`	Rotates by random factor
`hexLayer(0,0,curSize);`	Draws first layer
`pushMatrix();`	Saves coordinate system

(*continued*)

Table 6-5. (*continued*)

`rotate(PI/4);`	Rotates quarter turn
`curSize = curSize/sqrt(2);`	Adjusts curSize
`hexLayer(0,0,curSize);`	Draws second layer
`rotate(PI/4);`	Rotates quarter turn
`curSize = curSize/sqrt(2);`	Adjusts curSize
`hexLayer(0,0,curSize);`	Draws third layer
`rotate(PI/4);`	Rotates quarter turn
`curSize = curSize/sqrt(2);`	Adjusts curSize
`hexLayer(0,0,curSize);`	Draws fourth layer
`rotate(PI/4);`	Rotates quarter turn
`curSize = curSize/sqrt(2);`	Adjusts curSize
`hexLayer(0,0,curSize);`	Draws fifth layer–one more than first sketch
`popMatrix();`	Restores original coordinate system
`}`	
`void hexLayer(float cx, float cy,float layerSize) {`	Header for hexLayer
`float pctrx, pctry;`	Used in calculations
`float hexSize = layerSize;`	Sets hexSize
`fill(hueValue,satValue,brightValue);`	Sets color using HSB system
`for (int i=0;i<4;i++){`	For loop to display the four hexagons making up the layer
`pushMatrix();`	Saves the coordinate system
`translate(cx,cy);`	Translate
`rotate(HALF_PI*i);`	Rotates based on i value
`pctrx =.5*hexSize+fudge;`	Positions horizontally (in new coordinate system)
`pctry = 0;`	Positions vertically

(*continued*)

Table 6-5. (*continued*)

`hexShape(pctrx,pctry,.5*hexSize);`	Draws the hexagon
`popMatrix();`	Restores previous coordinate system
`}`	Closes for-loop
`satValue = satValue-15;`	Modifies the saturation by subtracting 15. The 15 is arbitrary
`if (satValue<15) satValue = 100;`	Checks if saturation is lower than 10; if so, sets it to 100
`println("satValue is ",satValue);`	Displays new value in console window. This is to see the values
`}`	Closes hexLayer
`void hexShape(float cx, float cy, float hexSize) {`	Header for hexShape
`beginShape();`	Starts the shape
`vertex(cx+hexSize,cy);`	Rightmost vertex
`vertex(cx+hexSize*.5,cy-hexSize*.5);`	Working around counterclockwise
`vertex(cx-hexSize*.5,cy-hexSize*.5);`	Working around counterclockwise
`vertex(cx-hexSize,cy);`	Leftmost vertex
`vertex(cx-hexSize*.5,cy+hexSize*.5);`	Continuing working around
`vertex(cx+hexSize*.5,cy+hexSize*.5);`	Continuing working around
`endShape(CLOSE);`	Closes shape, connecting first and last vertices
`}`	Closes hexShape

(*continued*)

Table 6-5. (*continued*)

`void keyPressed() {`	Header keyPressed
`colorMode(RGB,255,255,255);`	Sets colorMode back to RGB
`background(200,200,200);`	Clears window
`fill(0);`	Sets fill to black for the text
`text("Click on screen, press any key to clear the screen",20,20);`	Displays instructions
`colorMode(HSB,360,100,100);`	Sets colorMode to BSH
`hueValue = hueValue-40;`	Decrements hue (change color)
`if (hueValue <40) {` `hueValue = 360;}`	If too low, resets to top value
`satValue = 100;`	Sets satValue
`brightValue = 100;`	Sets brightValue
`println("hueValue now ",hueValue);`	Displays in console window
`}`	Close keyPressed function

Under the Covers

What are PImages? They are not exactly objects. There is no new operator used. This gave me some hints that something different is going on. The following did not work for getting what I called a backup image:

```
backup = original;
```

Changing the original by changing the pixels array caused both PImages to change. The same thing happened when I used these two statements:

```
original = loadImage(..)
backup = loadImage(...)
```

Instead, the approach that did work was to use createImage to create a new PImage and then use PImage.copy.

Java does not support the `color` data type. You may have discovered this already when reading error messages. Variables of date type `color` are referred to as having data type `int`.

If you are porting Processing code over into Java, you do need the Processing libraries, and you can use the `color` function. You can change a statement such as

```
color cl = color(200,100,100);
```

to

```
int cl = color(200,100,100);
```

Things to Look Up

The examples in this chapter are RGB and HSB. The `colorMode` function can change how the RGB ranges are specified or change from the RGB to the hue, saturation, brightness (HSB) system. You will need to know this if you are working with HSB when using another tool to prepare images. The HSB example demonstrates systematic changing of hue and saturation, and you can see how to do similar things with brightness. Look up and compare both of these ways to express color.

For this application, I used the `loadPixels` and `updatePixels` methods for `PImage` objects. There are functions that produce and update the `pixels` array for the whole display window, and that is what I used in my first sketch for this project. You can look up these functions and examine the sketches on the code source site.

There is a `copy` method for copying parts of one `PImage` to another `PImage` or even the same `PImage`, which could be useful. The sketch demonstrated GRAY and BLUR as parameters for filter. You can look up other filter type functions for images, such as `tint`.

The `beginShape` and `endShape` functions have several variations. Processing also supports Bezier and spline curves. These are ways to express curves using what are termed anchor points and control points. These can be used as curves or as borders of shapes. You can give all these features a quick look and then return when you think you have an application.

The following are remarks inspired by my original idea to use a remote URL. A possible reader response about error handling is to say that syntactic errors are caught by the programming language, that is, by the PDE, and semantic errors will be caught by proper testing. I am all for "proper" testing, but it may not be enough. Moreover, the issue for an example such as having the user enter a valid URL could produce problems even if the rest of the coding is fine. You do not want the program to stop but, instead, give the user another chance. One approach could involve using Regular expressions to check for a valid web address. However, a well-formed URL could still be invalid in that the file might not exist or no longer exist. Some sort of error checking is crucial. Checking for a value of NULL may work, but, perhaps, not soon enough. Processing does provide the *try-and-catch* option for detecting and catching errors. Any code that you believe might produce a runtime error is put in a clause prefaced by the term `try`. After this clause, a `catch` clause is used to hold the response. This does require knowing what error can occur. You can examine a sketch taking this approach in the code section.

How to Make This Your Own

For the image changes sketch, choose your own original image or images. You will need to be careful in the size of the image. If the original has height more than half the size of the window or width more than the width of the window, you can change it using the copy command. However, if the aspect ratio, ratio of width to height, is important to you, you need to compute the aspect ratio of the original image and use it in the calculations.

Make the changes in an image depend on something other than user input. Investigate other uses of filter and pixel manipulation.

For the graphics sketch, design your own shape and then put shapes together, making use of transformations. You will see more uses of transformations when we get to 3D.

Please do study and modify the HSB variation to explore other uses of this color mode. You will only become familiar with it when you use it.

You can use images together with graphics that you (your code) create. For example, the following idea occurred to me when I learned about the `blur` parameter. Using mouse events, have your user (and at this point, I feel I should give the user a better name) indicate a rectangle on top of an image. Apply blurring to just this portion of the image.

If your sketch allows the user to select more than one change, consider what is appropriate concerning cumulative changes.

What You Learned

The main lesson from the graphics examples was the demonstration of dividing a problem up into parts: combo, layer, and hexagon. This may not be obvious and certainly varies with the problem. However, if you are open to dividing a task into subtasks, you will become a proficient programmer.

You learned ways to manipulate images (`PImage` objects). These included the use of `filter` and `PImage.pixels`. You can explore other facilities in Processing for manipulating images.

You saw another use of the `switch` statement, namely, the use of `char` values for the cases.

You also learned ways to manipulate (transform) the coordinate system to produce drawings, specifically drawings making use of `beginShape` and `endShape`. The transformations can be used for anything displayed in the window, including images and text and rectangles, lines, and ellipses.

In the spirit of making lemonade out of lemons, the calamity that occurred when I realized that the website holding my mother's image was gone was worth discussing. The Web does change. If and when you construct sketches (or programs in any computer language), you need to be aware of the dependencies.

What's Next

The next chapter presents more on files, with a focus on the construction of a program to produce a holiday card. The card consists of an image and a message in a chosen font. For this example, you will learn how to get a file, such as an image file, from the local computer. The sketch selects a random set of fonts from those available on the local computer, and the user selects one of the fonts for the card. Finally, the card maker types a short message. The image and message appear, and the card maker has the option to save the window (i.e., the card) in the data folder of the sketch. The general programming concepts include the use of fonts, invoking the file management system on the local computer so the user can select a file, defining a subclass `FontButton` for the `Button` class you already saw, and taking a screenshot of the Processing window and saving it as an image file in the sketch.

CHAPTER 7

Using Files for Making a Holiday Card

Abstract

This chapter explains how to build a sketch that lets the user, to give a better name: the card maker, prepare a holiday greeting card with an option to save the card in the sketch folder for printing, adding handwritten notes, and eventually send to family and friends. If and when the card maker chooses to save a card, a camera shutter sound is played. The final result is shown in Figure 7-1. The photograph included is of our backyard last January when there was considerable snow partially covering up and knocking over a statue. You can see that the card is suitable for writing a note. If the card maker saves the results, it can be printed out in the usual way.

The card maker chooses from a set of fonts available on the local computer and chooses an image file available on the local computer. A small program that accesses the names of all the fonts available on the local computer is described by itself. The functionality of playing a sound and finding a file on the local computer is each provided using libraries, collections of programs that are not part of the basic Processing environment but potentially available.

© Jeanine Meyer 2022
J. Meyer, *Programming 101*, https://doi.org/10.1007/978-1-4842-8194-9_7

Enjoy the Season.

Figure 7-1. *Final holiday card*

Programming Concepts

The general programming concepts for this chapter include files, libraries, fonts, setting up callbacks, and the idea of providing feedback to user actions.

Files

I looked up the definition of files and found several different ones. I urge you to do the same and decide which ones resonate with you. Here is my definition: Files are entities that hold information, that persist, and are independent of the Processing program. The term "persist" means that a file remains on your local computer even after you have exited Processing and even turned the computer off. This should not be an abstract concept at this point. In several previous chapters, you learned how to access image files and a CSV file, all of which had been uploaded to the sketch folder. The CSV file became a Table object. For the CSV file, you also learned how to modify, namely, add a row, to the table and then save it. This means you replaced the original with an updated CSV file. In Chapter 6, you saw how to write code to access a file on the Web, with guidance for how to detect the error situation of an address being bad. This chapter describes how to provide the user with the option to look for a file on their own computer, the local computer, and use it in the sketch. I also describe how to access the files defining fonts available on the local computer and use some of these in the program. You will learn how to take a screenshot to save the whole window, called a frame, in the sketch folder. The examples in this chapter show other programming techniques, including the use of sound. Incorporating sound also involves files: the sound file used to simulate a camera shutter and the programs that implement the playing of sound in the sound library. Most programming languages have facilities for handling files.

Libraries

Libraries are collections of programs beyond the standard built-in facilities of the specific programming language that can be accessed, with some minimal procedures and coding. It is appropriate to ask why everything is not included all the time. For Processing, for example, why isn't everything included in the PDE? The answer is that it would slow down the translation (compilation) process. In addition, new libraries are added all the time. For the holiday card example, I need to include a Java library for doing the file input/output operations, and I need a sound library for implementing the playing of sound.

Fonts

When we use a word processing program, we can make use of different fonts. Fonts deserve more attention than I generally can manage. I hesitate to pretend you are asking another question, but here it is: Where are the fonts? For the most part, the fonts are not "in" the word processing program or any one tool, but resident as files on the local computer, available for all the programs to use. The not-so-good news is that a different set of fonts might be available on other computers. You can run a program I will describe to see a complete list of the fonts available on *your* computer.

Callbacks

When the programmer defines a mouseClicked function, this act sets up the response when the underlying Java program detects that the mouse button has been clicked. Using more general terms, an *event handler* has been designated for the mouse click event. The terminology is different, but the results are the same for setting up a response to the user designating a file. The coding will be shown in the "Processing Programming Features" section. The programmer specifies a function, which is called setting a *callback*.

Feedback to Users

The make-a-card application provides the card maker the ability to take a screenshot and save it to the sketch folder. I decided to play an old-fashioned camera shutter sound when this happens. This did give me the excuse to use the sound library, but it also serves the important function of providing feedback to the user. You need to decide if and when and how to let your users know what is going on.

Processing Programming Features

I describe acquiring and using the library for sound and then the library for obtaining a local file. This should serve as an introduction, although I must point out that each library is different. You will need to research all the available capabilities. I also include here my reuse of the Button class I defined for an earlier example and my definition of a subclass I named FontButton.

Use of the Sound Library

The PDE has procedures for making use of libraries. If you click Sketch on the PDE toolbar, then select Import Library ... , a drop-down menu appears including Sound. Select on Sound and the sound library code in the form of class definitions will be available to you. The statement import processing.sound.*; is placed in the code. The statement brings in all the files, indicated by the * symbol, in the sound subfolder in the Processing library.

When I created the make card sketch, I went to an old sketch, created some time ago, invoked the Sketch/Show Sketch folder, opened up its data folder, and selected and used the mouse to drag the file camera-shutter-click-01.wav to the new sketch. This had the effect of putting a copy of the sound file in the make card sketch. The original file did not leave the old sketch! I then typed in the import statement myself. These actions meant that I did not need to use the import library procedure. However, I later returned to Sketch/Import Library …/Add Library to see what I had installed. I noticed that the sound library was an older version. It still worked for my application, but I clicked to perform an update.

To use the sound capabilities, I wrote a declaration statement for a global variable:

```
SoundFile shutter;
```

In the setup function, I included the statement

```
shutter = new SoundFile(this,"camera-shutter-click-01.wav");
```

This creates a new object of the class SoundFile. The constructor for SoundFile takes two parameters. The first, this, might seem mysterious. It associates the new object with the current object, which is the Processing program, a PApplet object. The second parameter is the name of the file in the data folder that I copied over from a previous sketch.

The last step in my relatively simple use of sound for this sketch is determining when I want the sound to be played. At this point in the code, I include the statement

```
shutter.play();
```

That is how it is done. You can find or make your own .wav files for this purpose.

Making and Saving an Image of the Current Window

The saveFrame function takes a screenshot of the current window and saves it as an image file. You can use placeholders in the name so that you can take multiple images. The statement

```
saveFrame("snaps/card####.png");u
```

will assign numbers to the #### so that distinct files are stored in a folder named snaps within the sketch folder. You can save the images in various image file formats: .png, .jpg, .tif, .tga, and so on. You do need to be very careful about how frequently your code does this, though, because each call is producing a file.

Use of Java Input/Output Library

Certain libraries, such as sound, are developed and maintained by the Processing Foundation, and others are designated as contributed by the larger Processing community. Others can be added by a procedure described in the Processing documentation, and still others, such as the library used for obtaining a file from the local computer, are available simply by typing in the import statement directly:

```
import java.io.File;
```

This import statement brings in the File class located in the io folder of the java library.

Processing provides a function called selectInput, which I invoke in the setup function:

```
selectInput("Select an image", "imageChosen");
```

This function makes use of the java.io.File class. The first parameter is a prompt that might appear but does not remain visible. What does happen is that the user is presented with Finder or its equivalent for accessing the file system to select a file. The second parameter, "imageChosen", is the name of the function I have written to respond to the user selecting a file. It is what I described as the *callback* function. I do not describe all of the function here because you will see it in the programming section. Here are the header and the first couple of lines:

```
void imageChosen(File f) {
    if(f.exists()) {
        original = loadImage(f.getAbsolutePath());
        ...
```

To be a callback function for the actions initiated by selectInput, the parameter specified in the header must be of data type File. An object of data type File has a method named exists, and it is invoked to indicate if the file does exist and can be used to load the image. If the card maker did not open a file, the f.exists() call would return false. Note also there is another method in use, getAbsolutePath. The file can be but presumably is not in the data folder for the sketch and so needs a complete path. The rest of imageChosen does the usual manipulation of an image before displaying it in the usual way. I also make use of a Boolean variable okay to check in another function if it is okay to proceed.

Subclasses

I required buttons for my user interface and decided to use the Button class I had developed for earlier examples, specifically the jigsaw puzzle. My code creates one button for each of the three fonts my code chooses for presentation to the card maker. However, these are special buttons, so I decided to define a subclass of Button, which I call FontButton.

I could have made use of parallel structures to hold the font but decided that the proper thing to do was to make the font, rather, the PFont, one of the variables defined in the class definition and to change to the PFont when displaying the button. I achieve this by defining FontButton as a subclass of Button. Here is the definition of the FontButton class:

```
class FontButton extends Button {
    PFont ft;
    FontButton (int x,int y,int bwid,int bht,color c, String lab,
    PFont fta)
{
    super(x,y,bwid,bht,c,lab);
    ft = fta;
}
void display() {
    textFont(ft);
    super.display();
    }
}
```

Note the one additional variable, ft. The FontButton constructor invokes the constructor for Button using the term super. It then uses the parameter fta to set ft. The display method for FontButton uses ft in a call to textFont to set the font and then invokes the display for the Button, using the expression super.display(). If I want to change how buttons look, I can change the code in the display method for Button with the knowledge that the display method for FontButton sets the font for any subsequent text but does not do anything else.

Show Fonts Sketch Operation Overview

For you to examine the fonts available on whichever computer you are using, I describe a program that acquires a list of the fonts and then reveals random choices at each mouse click in the window. The sketch displays the names of the fonts in the console window as shown in Figure 7-2.

```
showFonts | Processing 3.3.5

                                                            Java ▼

  showFonts  ▼
4 size(800, 600);
5 fill(255,0,0);
6 fontList =  PFont.list();
7  println(fontList);
8 }
```

Skia-Regular_Black-Condensed Skia-Regular_Black-Extended
Skia-Regular_Bold Skia-Regular_Condensed Skia-Regular_Extended
Skia-Regular_Light Skia-Regular_Light-Condensed
Skia-Regular_Light-Extended SnellRoundhand SnellRoundhand-Black
SnellRoundhand-Bold Stencil SukhumvitSet-Bold SukhumvitSet-Light
SukhumvitSet-Medium SukhumvitSet-SemiBold SukhumvitSet-Text
SukhumvitSet-Thin Superclarendon-Black Superclarendon-BlackItalic
Superclarendon-Bold Superclarendon-BoldItalic Superclarendon-Italic
Superclarendon-Light Superclarendon-LightItalic Superclarendon-Regular
Symbol Tahoma Tahoma-Bold TamilMN TamilMN-Bold TamilSangamMN
TamilSangamMN-Bold TeamViewer8 TeluguMN TeluguMN-Bold TeluguSangamMN
TeluguSangamMN-Bold Thonburi Thonburi-Bold Thonburi-Light Times-Bold
Times-BoldItalic Times-Italic Times-Roman TimesNewRomanPS-BoldItalicMT
TimesNewRomanPS-BoldMT TimesNewRomanPS-ItalicMT TimesNewRomanPSMT
Trattatello Trebuchet-BoldItalic TrebuchetMS TrebuchetMS-Bold
TrebuchetMS-Italic TwCenMT-Bold TwCenMT-BoldItalic TwCenMT-Italic
TwCenMT-Regular Verdana Verdana-Bold Verdana-BoldItalic Verdana-Italic
Waseem WaseemLight Webdings Weibei-SC-Bold Weibei-TC-Bold
Wingdings-Regular Wingdings2 Wingdings3 YuGo-Bold YuGo-Medium
YuMin-Demibold YuMin-Medium YuppySC-Regular YuppyTC-Regular
ZapfDingbatsITC Zapfino

  >_ Console   ⚠ Errors

Figure 7-2.   *Console showing names of some of fonts*

The sketch provides a way for users to see what a randomly selected font looks like by clicking in the window. The screenshot shown in Figure 7-3 shows some of the actual fonts on screen. Reacting to a mouse click and making a random choice should be familiar to you.

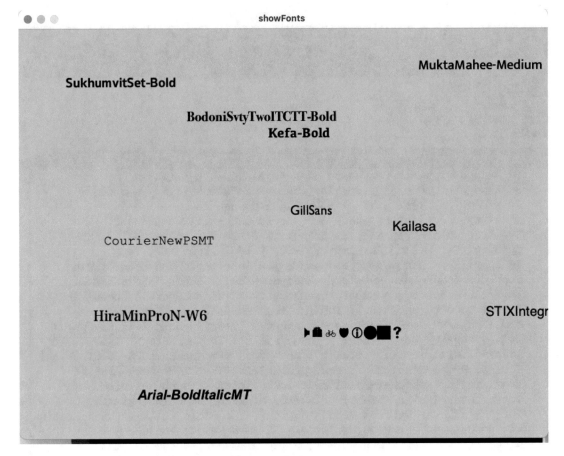

Figure 7-3. *Window after many mouse clicks*

Implementing the Show Fonts Sketch

The implementation is fairly straightforward, given the function PFont.list. However, it does give me an opportunity to describe something I have not mentioned before: *class methods*. These are methods that apply to the PFont class as a whole and not individual PFont objects. It is properly called a method and not a function. The list method does what I have promised: it generates an array of String objects, each the name of a font available on the local computer. The println function prints the whole array on the console, requiring several lines.

Responding to the user pressing the mouse button should be familiar to you. I write code in the mousePressed function. The code makes use of random to get an index into the fontList array. I use createFont to create the font selected and then textFont to make this the current font. Finally, I use text to place the name of the font at the location specified by mouseX and mouseY. This is an exercise that distinguishes between the thing and the name of the thing, something computer scientists tend to do. See the "Under the Covers" section to find out what happens to the fonts.

Programming the Show Fonts Sketch

This sketch is short enough that I will dispense with the "Planning" section and the function relationship table and go straight to the code, shown in Table 7-1.

Table 7-1. *Show Fonts Sketch*

`String[] fontList ;`	Array to hold names of fonts
`PFont myfont;`	Set and used in mousePressed; note that this could be a local variable
`void setup() {`	Header for setup
`size(800, 600);`	Set the dimensions of window
`fill(255,0,0);`	Set color (for text) to red
`fontList = PFont.list();`	Obtain the names of all the available fonts
`println(fontList);`	Print on console
`}`	Close setup
`void draw() {`	Header for draw, defined to enable mouse events
`}`	Close (empty) draw
`void mousePressed() {`	Header for mousePressed
`int ch = int(random(0,fontList.length));`	Make a random selection of a font; need to make it an integer
`myfont = createFont(fontList[ch],20);`	Create a font corresponding to the one chosen; set size
`textFont(myfont);`	Set newly created font as the current font
`text(fontList[ch],mouseX,mouseY);`	Display text, name of the font at mouse location
`}`	Close mousePressed

Make Card Sketch Operation Overview

You have seen a screenshot of the completed make card sketch, Figure 7-1. Figure 7-4 shows the screen when the card maker is presented with a choice of fonts.

Figure 7-4. *Example of make card interface*

Figure 7-5 is a screenshot taken on my computer at the start of the card-making process. You are seeing folder names and file names on my computer. Your screen would look different. The Finder program (and on a PC, this would be the equivalent file system program) starts. Its window has partially blocked the Processing sketch window.

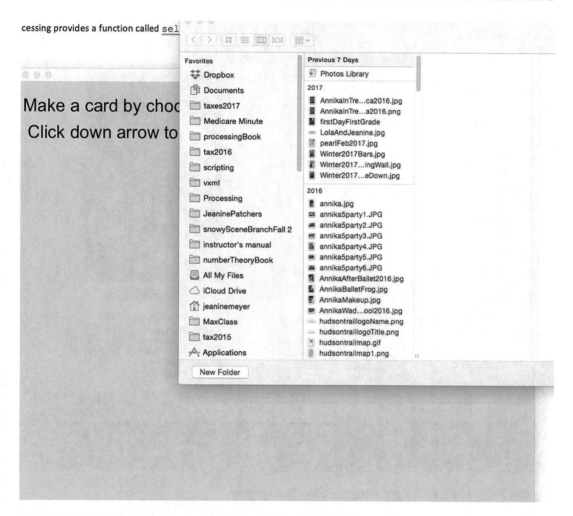

Figure 7-5. *Screenshot at start of make card sketch*

The next step is to find a suitable image. The card maker can examine several image files. Figure 7-6 shows my actions looking for a picture to use. I selected a picture of my mother and myself on the *Clearwater*, a boat built to encourage support for environmental causes, including cleaning up the Hudson River. The next step is to click Open in the lower right corner. This takes control back to the Processing sketch and produces Figure 7-7, which is the equivalent of Figure 7-4. Notice that a different set of three fonts have been chosen.

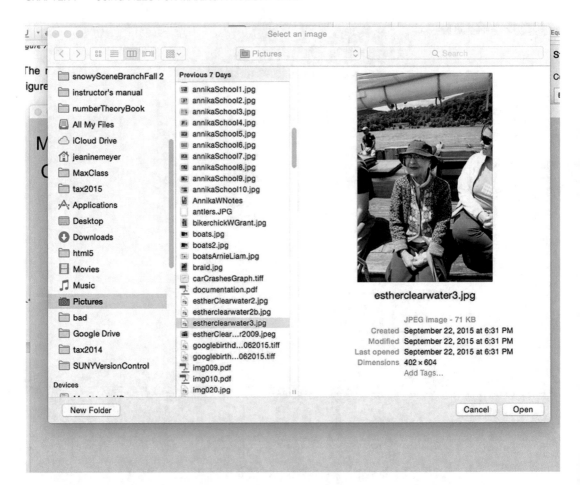

Figure 7-6. *Esther and Jeanine on the Clearwater*

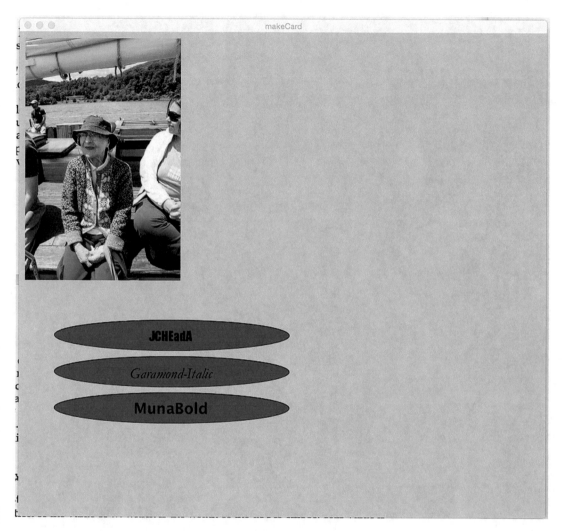

Figure 7-7. *Font buttons*

After clicking on one of the font buttons, the card maker gets a screen like Figure 7-8. After typing in a message, the final card appears, like the example shown in Figure 7-1.

Figure 7-8. *Card maker now types in a message*

The card maker has the option of clicking on the down arrow to take a snapshot of the entire Processing window and then saving it to the sketch folder. Figure 7-9 shows two windows, with one showing the whole sketch. The sketch folder contains two subfolders and two PDE files:

- snaps subfolder

- makeCard.pde

- Button.pde

- data subfolder

The Button.pde file contains the Button class definition that I chose to copy into its own tab. I refer you again to the Processing documentation for the use of tabs.

In Figure 7-9, the window on top on the right shows an image file that has been saved.

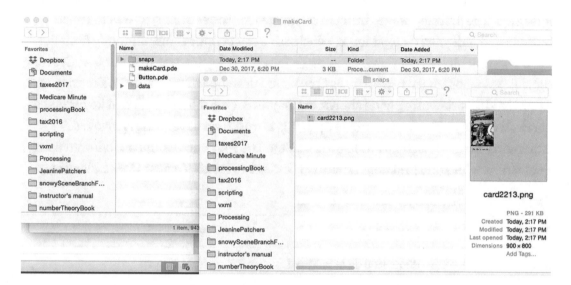

Figure 7-9. *Screenshot showing image saved in sketch folder*

Implementing the Make Card Sketch

This example was inspired by the holiday season as well as the goal of showcasing the use of files on the local computer and the use of libraries. I leave it to you, the reader, to build on the example and to make use of the features in interesting ways.

Planning

The operations required to enable the card maker to make a card are as follows:

- Allow the card maker to select a picture (image file) on the local computer.

- Prepare a set of three fonts from which the card maker can choose one from the fonts available on the local computer.

- Accept the card maker's font selection.

- Allow the card maker to write a message.

- Allow the card maker the option of saving the card to the snaps subfolder of the sketch folder.

I decided to take the easy path by building the card in the fixed sequential order indicated. The first step was to bring in an image file. The second step was to create buttons that indicated distinct fonts. I decided to select three fonts randomly from the large set available. The card maker selects a font. The last step was to input text. Creating the buttons would make use of the Button class I developed for Chapter 4. Entering text would be supported using code shown in Chapter 5. One difference is that keyPressed checks if the key is the Down arrow key. If this is true, then saveFrame is invoked. Otherwise, the getTextInput function is called. The sequence would be followed using Boolean variables and functions, such as f.exists to check if a file f does indeed exist.

Table 7-2. *Functions for Makecard.pde*

Function	Invoked by	Invokes
setup	Underlying Java program	selectInput
buildFontButtons	Draw	FontButton constructor, display
Draw	Underlying Java program	buildFontButtons, displayAll
displayAll	draw	
imageChosen	Callback set by call of selectInput in setup	
mouseClicked	Underlying Java program	
keyPressed	Underlying Java program	getTextInput

I did copy the Button class definition from Chapter 4 and paste it into a new tab. A new tab is created by clicking on the arrow toward the top of the PDE window and selecting the new tab option. A small window will appear giving you a field to enter the name. Using tabs is not required but is a frequent practice for class definitions or just to divide large programs into smaller pieces. This produces a separate PDE file, as was shown in Figure 7-9. Figure 7-10 shows the Button tab, scrolled down to show the definition of FontButton.

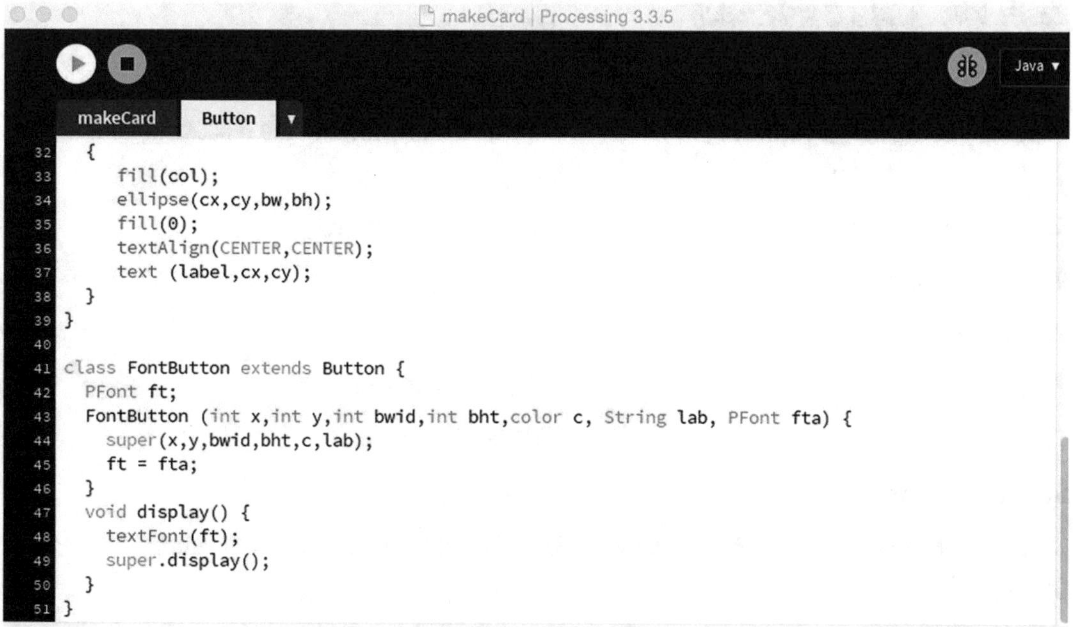

```
32   {
33       fill(col);
34       ellipse(cx,cy,bw,bh);
35       fill(0);
36       textAlign(CENTER,CENTER);
37       text (label,cx,cy);
38   }
39 }
40
41 class FontButton extends Button {
42   PFont ft;
43   FontButton (int x,int y,int bwid,int bht,color c, String lab, PFont fta) {
44     super(x,y,bwid,bht,c,lab);
45     ft = fta;
46   }
47   void display() {
48     textFont(ft);
49     super.display();
50   }
51 }
```

Figure 7-10. *Screenshot of Processing showing FontButton class definition*

Programming the Make Card Sketch

The program for the make card sketch is shown in Table 7-3. Remember that you must include the Button and FontButton code, shown in Figure 7-10. You can go back to Chapter 4 for comments on each line of the Button class. I give my usual advice: Do not read it from start to finish. Use the function relationships, shown in Table 7-2, to guide you.

Table 7-3. *Make Card Sketch*

`import java.io.File;`	Bring in one class, File, from the java.io library
`import processing.sound.*;`	Bring in all the classes in the processing.sound library
`SoundFile shutter;`	Will hold the sound clip
`PImage original;`	For the image
`float imgw;`	Width of the image
`float imgh;`	Height of the image
`float aspect;`	Calculate aspect ratio
`String[] fontList;`	List of fonts
`String[] myListOfFontNames = new String[3];`	List of the three fonts selected randomly
`PFont chosenFont;`	For the current font
`FontButton[] fontButtons = new FontButton[3];`	For the three buttons
`Boolean fontButtonsBuilt = false;`	Will indicate the phase of operations
`String prompt="Your message: ";`	Used in inputting the message text
`String myText = "";`	Used in inputting text
`String answer = "";`	Used in inputting text
`String message = "";`	Holds the complete, inputted text
`PFont firstFont;`	Set to Arial, used for initial instructions
`Boolean okay = false;`	Will be set to true when image file is selected and image loaded
`void setup()  {`	Header for setup
`size(900,800);`	Set the dimensions of window
`shutter = new SoundFile(this,"camera-shutter-click-01.wav");`	Load the sound

(continued)

Table 7-3. (*continued*)

firstFont = createFont ("Arial-Black",30);	Create the font
textFont(firstFont);	Set font for instructions
fill(0);	Set text color to black
text("Make a card by choosing a picture, then a font, then a message.\n Click down arrow to take a snap. Reload to try again.",10,50);	Display instructions; the \n forces a line break
fontList = PFont.list();	Read in names of all fonts on local computer
selectInput("Select an image", "imageChosen");	Invoke thread to let user find a file; set imageChosen as the callback
}	Close setup
void buildFontButtons() {	Header for buildFontButtons
for (int i=0;i<3;i++) {	Loop to set up three buttons
int ch = int(random(0,fontList. length));	Make random choice
PFont ft = createFont(fontList[ch],25);	Create the font
myListOfFontNames[i] = fontList[ch];	Store the name
fontButtons[i] = new FontBut ton(260,500+i*60,400,50,col or(200,0,100), fontList[ch],ft);	Create the button and store in array by invoking constructor
fontButtons[i].display();	Display the button just created
}	Close for-loop
}	Close buildFontButtons

(*continued*)

Table 7-3. (*continued*)

`void draw() {`	Header for `draw`
`if (okay) {`	Initially `false`, set to `true` in `imageChosen`
`if (original!=null) {`	Extra check to be sure file does exist
`background(200);`	Clear window
`image(original,10,10,imgw,imgh);`	Display image
`if (!fontButtonsBuilt) {`	Now check if font buttons are built
`buildFontButtons();`	Build font buttons
`fontButtonsBuilt = true;`	Set Boolean to `true`
`noLoop();`	Stop looping
`}`	Close if font buttons need to be built
`else {`	`else` (font buttons are built, move on to getting text for the message)
`text(prompt+myText,100,imgh+100);`	Display prompt plus whatever has been typed in
`if (answer.length()>0) {`	If answer set (done in `getTextInput`)
`message = answer;`	Set message
`displayAll();`	Display image and message
`}`	Close `if`
`}`	Close `else`
`}`	Close `if original!=null`
`}`	Close `if okay`
`}`	Close `draw`
`void displayAll() {`	Header for `displayAll`
`background(200);`	Clear window
`image(original,10,10,imgw,imgh);`	Draw image
`text(message,30,imgh+50);`	Display message
`noLoop();`	Stop looping
`}`	Close `displayAll`

(*continued*)

Table 7-3. (*continued*)

`void imageChosen( File f ) {`	Header for `imageChosen`
`if( f.exists() ) {`	Check if f is valid
`original = loadImage(` `f.getAbsolutePath() );`	Load image using absolute path; this image is not in the data subfolder
`imgw = original.width;`	Prepare for calculation to make image smaller; set `imgw`
`imgh = original.height;`	Set `imgh`
`aspect = imgw/imgh;`	Calculate aspect ratio
`imgh = min(imgh,400);`	Resize as needed
`imgw = imgh * aspect;`	Won't change if `imgh` did not change
`background(200);`	Clear window
`image(original, 10,10,imgw,imgh);`	Display image
`okay = true;`	Set Boolean
`}`	Close if f exists
`}`	Close `imageChosen`
`void mouseClicked() {`	Header for `mouseClicked`
`for (int i=0;i<3;i++) {`	Loop through all the buttons
`if (fontButtons[i].` `isOver(mouseX,mouseY)) {`	Is mouse over this one?
`chosenFont = fontButtons[i].ft;`	Set `chosenFont`
`textFont(chosenFont);`	Make this current font
`textAlign(LEFT);`	Set alignment
`break;`	Leave for-loop
`}`	Close if `isOver`
`}`	Close for-loop
`loop();`	Restore looping
`}`	Close `mouseClicked`

(*continued*)

Table 7-3. (*continued*)

`void getTextInput() {`	Header for `getTextInput`
`if (keyCode == BACKSPACE) {`	Backspace case
`if (myText.length() > 0) {`	Only do something if there has been text
`myText = myText.substring(0,` `myText.length()-1);`	Remove last character
`}`	Close `if` text
`} else if (keyCode == DELETE) {`	Close `if` backspace and check if delete
`myText = "" ;`	Remove all text
`} else if (keyCode == ENTER) {`	Close `if` all text and check for enter
`answer = myText;`	Set answer; this will stop entry
`}`	Close `if enter`

`else if (keyCode != SHIFT &&`
`keyCode != CONTROL`
`&& keyCode != ALT) {`
	Check for not being these special keys

`myText = myText + str(key);`	Add in this key
`}`	Close check for not specials
`}`	Close `getTextInput`
`void keyPressed() {`	Header for `keyPressed`
`if (keyCode == DOWN) {`	Check if `keyCode` is DOWN arrow
`shutter.play();`	Make noise
`saveFrame("snaps/card####.png");`	Save the frame
`}`	Close `if` down
`else {`	`else`
`getTextInput();`	Check for text
`}`	Close `else`
`}`	Close `keyPressed`

Under the Covers

The imagery of "under the covers" might not quite fit the point I want to make here. A Processing sketch (i.e., our code) is running on a local computer with other code, including Java code and programs that make up the operating system. It is operating system programs that perform tasks such as interacting with files. Similarly, the definitions of fonts are files that reside on the local computer.

Java provides ways of defining and running what are termed *threads of execution*, or *threads* for short. The notion is that the programmer can set up distinct sequences of programming statements. Threads can be executed concurrently if there are multiple processors or in what is termed pseudoconcurrency. Their use must be managed so that problems do not arise, such as data being accessed before it is ready or changes made out of the anticipated order. In the example here, the program does not do anything until the callback established by the selectInput call has loaded an image.

When I introduced the topic of local variables and global variables in Chapter 1, I said that "local variables go away" when the function exits. This is not completely accurate. It is true that the values in the local variables are not available for use outside the function or if and when the function is invoked again, the values do not persist. However, the space taken up by the variables is not immediately reclaimed. Java has what is called *garbage collection*, a process in which values that are in use are marked. Values are marked if they are pointed to or referenced by global variables or variables in running functions. Think about the showFonts program. The mousePressed function creates a font and assigns it to the variable myFont. If myFont had referenced another font, set in the previous call of mousePressed, the space taken up by the old font would not be marked as in use. Values marked are moved into one area so that Java has room to keep going. The garbage collection is invoked automatically. By the way, garbage collection is done in its own thread. Although it is true that storage and memory are plentiful in modern computing, it still can be the case, especially on mobile devices, that space taken up and not released causes problems. These are termed *memory leaks*.

Things to Look Up

Explore other libraries. Libraries provide considerable functionality. However, there can be problems with individual libraries and with incompatibilities between and among libraries. For example, the current recommendation found in online sources is to use monaural sound files, not stereo, with the sound library. This is easy to do with the camera shutter sound featured here.

Understand the differences between `createFont` and `loadFont`.

Independent of the mechanics of fonts, I urge you to investigate the uses of different types of fonts in terms of communication and aesthetics. Do keep in mind that less is more. Just because you can use a large number of distinct fonts does not mean you should.

Look up Java threads and Java garbage collection.

How to Make This Your Own

It could be that we take the clutter of windows on our computer screens for granted and think nothing of the Finder window partially covering the Processing sketch window. It did bother me. One approach is to not go immediately to the file finder, but display the instructions and have a button for each of the tasks. This also could be part of an important enhancement to allow do-overs for each of the steps.

Enhance the sketch by adding new features to the card design. For example, you could make it possible for the card maker to add multiple pictures.

Independent of making a card, design your own programs that include providing users, players, or makers the ability to include their own images or their own tables of information.

What You Learned

You learned how to access files on the local computer such as image files and, also, the very specific files holding fonts. Providing your user with the ability to access a file on the local computer required the use of a Java library.

You learned how to take a screenshot of the current window and save it in the sketch folder using `saveFrame`. The naming system provides a way to save multiple images.

To let the user know that something did happen as a result of a certain action, in this case, a key press, you learned how to play a sound using a `.wav` file, which also required the use of a library.

You continued to learn about classes and subclasses.

What's Next

The next chapter features an example incorporating video clips. This also requires the use of a library. A critical aspect of the example is not just playing a single video clip by itself, but combining display and manipulation of videos with manipulation of images and drawings.

CHAPTER 8

Combining Videos, Images, and Graphics

Abstract

This chapter features a family collage sketch. The critical programming concepts are playing a video clip and handling video together with images and rectangles. The rectangles represent the category of graphics. The distinct types of items are defined using classes and subclasses.

In addition to introducing the use of video, this chapter and its example can be viewed as another lesson on classes. You can go back to Chapter 4 and review the bouncing things example. The code for repositioning of the pieces by mouse actions has some similarities to creating a line and then moving an image on the line example in Chapter 4.

The source code material includes an extra example, a demonstration of using line drawing on canvas *or* an image *or* a video for directions for an origami model. Illustrations are given as a teaser.

Programming Concepts

This section provides general background on video and the notions of shallow vs. deep copying. I then move to the details of how video is handled in Processing and more on classes and subclasses.

J. Meyer, *Programming 101*, https://doi.org/10.1007/978-1-4842-8194-9_8

Video

Digital video files come in a variety of formats, just like images. It should be easy to accept that a considerable amount of data is involved, potentially a full image for every frame of the video. Some formats perform compression across frames as well as within frames. The term *codec* is used for the software or hardware device used for encoding and decompressing video. There are trade-offs to make between quality of the video and size of the file. There also are differences in the speed of going from the stored, digital format to presentation on the screen. It also can be important to ask if the video is to be streamed or acquired all at once. Regarding quality of the image, you might need to think about whether this video is to be viewed on a small screen, like a phone; a typical computer monitor; a high-definition TV; or projected on a large screen for viewing by a big audience.

Copying a Video

A general concept in computing is *shallow copying* vs. *deep copying*. It relates to the issue of whether your code is dealing with a value or a reference to a value. These issues arise in all programming languages and are not confined to working with videos or images. If your code copies the reference, it will be to the same value. In my first version of the collage, my `duplicate` method of the class I named `MovieItem` copied the reference to the `Movie` object. Therefore, the method produced two items in the window playing the same movie, frame by frame. I decided that I wanted the `duplicate` operation to produce a new, distinct copy of the video. With this approach, Annika does a round with herself. We can think of the movies being at different points in the reel. I did this by implementing a deep copy. You can examine the code in the "Program" section.

Processing Programming Features

The critical Processing programming features are video and more on classes and subclasses.

Video

Processing provides a library for handling videos. We need to go to the toolbar and click Sketch/Add Library... and select Video. This will put the following line into your code:

```
import processing.video.*;
```

The main class in this library is called Movie. A Movie object is created using the new operator and the Movie constructor. A typical setting of a Movie variable would look something like the following:

```
myMovie = new Movie(this, "snowman.mov");
```

where snowman.mov is a file that has been placed in the data folder of the sketch. The this term refers to the PApplet defined for the sketch and is one of the few situations in which we need to think about the Java program being created. When you get to the "Implementing the Family Collage Sketch" section, you will see the Movie constructor in use.

The methods I use for the family collage in addition to the constructor, Movie, are loop, pause, stop, and jump. In addition, I must include the following function in my sketch:

```
void movieEvent(Movie m) {
    m.read();
}
```

This is invoked whenever a Movie object has a new frame available. Think of the Movie as running in a parallel thread and letting my Processing sketch know when there is something happening. This is exactly like our providing a body for setup, draw, mouseClicked, and so on. Finally—and it is important to realize that I have not gotten to it yet—the current frame of the video needs to be displayed in the Processing window. I define a class I named MovieItem as a subclass of a class named Item. (There also is an ImageItem subclass.) Each of these classes has a display method. Object variables include variables for specifying the horizontal and vertical coordinates and the width and the height. The display of the Movie is done using the image function:

```
void display() {
    image(imovie, xpos, ypos,iwidth,iheight);
}
```

where the video is displayed and the dimensions of the display are dependent on the variables (xpos, ypos, iwidth, and iheight) set and maintained by my code.

You can use what you learned in previous chapters to access a video on the Web or ask the user to identify a video on the local computer. Do keep in mind that videos can be quite large, so you do need to make sure the video is fully loaded before attempting to use it. Do also read about obtaining streaming video, including video from webcams and other cameras.

Now what I have written about the use of the Movie class has a lot of detail. I hope you can appreciate that most of the implementation of video is done for us within the code of the Library.

Classes and Subclasses

My initial objectives for my family collage are to be able to move each item by dragging with the mouse, duplicate an item, and delete an item. I then realized that sometimes items get under other items, so I wanted a way to move an item to the top. I also decided that I wanted to be able to pause and restart a video. As I have written, I also decided to treat a duplicate of a video as a distinct entity. My implementation has the Item class and the ImageItem and MovieItem subclasses. I use a tab to hold all the class definitions. I name the tab definitions, which means that the sketch folder has a PDE file named Definitions.pde. The Item class is simply a rectangle. All the items are stored in an array.

In addition to the constructor methods, the methods are isOver, removeIt, display, move, duplicate, restart, and pauseMovie. Because of how I invoke the methods, which you will see in the code, I need to define all methods in the parent class. The restart and pauseMovie methods in the Item class are empty.

The example demonstrates the power of classes and subclasses to share the coding that is alike across classes and supply distinct coding when required.

Under the Covers

Reinforcing what has been said, videos are large, complex entities, and Processing (Java) handles them as such, playing each video independently of everything else in its own thread. The image function used for static images is used to display the current frame of a video. The function movieEvent is invoked by the underlying Java program in the same way that mousePressed, mouseReleased, mouseDragged, and keyPressed are invoked. The parameter to movieEvent indicates which Movie object had the event, so the call in the body of movieEvent to m.read(); responds to the event by updating the Movie with the available frame. If the event was something other than the arrival of a new frame, the last frame would be reread. Note that the one function handles all Movie objects.

Because videos are large, it can be critical to make sure that videos no longer in use are treated in such a way that garbage collection can reclaim the space. For the family collage sketch, this meant that I wrote code to assign the value null to the variable referencing the video when the user chose to delete it.

Family Collage Operation Overview

The use of the family collage to reposition, create new items, and remove items is suggested in Figure 8-1, showing the initial look of the collage, and Figure 8-2, which shows the window after some changes have been made. The user clicks and drags to move an item around the screen. To fully appreciate the sketch, you need to run the code to see the videos playing and to observe dragging items, duplicating (copying) items, and deleting items. As already mentioned, video can be paused and restarted from the beginning.

collage5

c for copy, d for delete, t for move to top, p for pause video, r for restart.

Figure 8-1. *Opening window for family collage*

The image with the little girl at the table is a frame of a video clip that is being played. This frame was captured when I used the Grab utility to get the screenshot. The collage starts off with the video clip, two static images, and two rectangles. Each of the items can be repositioned. It also is possible to copy any item, move the copy around, and delete any item. The video clip can be paused and restarted.

Figure 8-2 shows a screen after I, as the user, made some modifications. There are two different copies of the same movie (Annika singing the snowman song from *Frozen*) that started at different times and, therefore, are at different places.

Figure 8-2. Collage after some manipulation

You also should take note of the two rectangles at the upper left corner, as one is slightly offset from the other. My duplicate method creates the second item slightly offset from the position of the original.

Implementing the Family Collage Sketch

Once you understand how videos work, I claim that the implementation is straightforward and based on what you already know about classes and subclasses and mouse events for dragging.

Planning

I decided to have the different types of items in my collage implemented as subclasses of an Item class and to store all Item objects in an array. Because I was providing a way to move items around, I needed to erase the window and redisplay everything: all the items and the instructions. Methods to display an item would be present in each class. Processing provides the ArrayList construct, which you read about in the snake example in Chapter 5, with its own remove method. However, I chose to use a standard array to hold all the Item objects, mainly to show that it was possible to write a function for removing an element, which I did in the removeFromItemsArray, using two for-loops.

Each Item has object variables indicating the horizontal and vertical coordinates. The move method performs an incremental move. The change amounts are calculated using mouseX-pmouseX and mouseY-pmouseY.

The inclusion of video items meant that I needed to design a MovieItem class, which would contain a Movie variable. Table 8-1 shows the functions defined in the collage6 tab. Some of these functions do invoke methods of the classes defined in the definitions tab. Note that I use the modifier *appropriate* for those methods that are overridden in the subclass definitions. The move, isOver, and the move method defined in the Item class (the parent class) are not overridden.

Table 8-1. *Function Table for* `collage6` *Tab*

Function	Invoked by	Invokes
setup	Underlying Java program	`Item, ImageItem, MovieItem`
draw	Underlying Java program	Appropriate `display` method
overWhich	`mousePressed`	`isOver`
keyPressed	Underlying Java program	`overWhich, swapThem,` appropriate `duplicate, removeIt, restart, pauseMovie`
swapThem	`keyPress`	
removeFromItemsArray	`removeIt`	
mousePressed	Underlying Java program	`overWhich`
mouseDragged	Underlying Java program	`move`
mouseReleased	Underlying Java program	
movieEvent	Underlying Java program	The `read` method for a `Movie`

Programming the Family Collage Sketch

Table 8-2 lists the code and descriptions for the `definitions` tab, which is the class definitions for `Item`, `ImageItem`, and `MovieItem`. Table 8-3 lists the code for the main program, which is held in the `collage6` tab. Note that the `Item` class serves as the class definition for the rectangles and also as the parent class for `ImageItem` and `MovieItem`. I do realize that these might seem long, but the individual functions are fairly short. Remember that you do not have to and should not read it from start to finish but move around, using the function relationship table (Table 8-1) to guide you. You also can download and use the online source code and just return here when you have a question.

Table 8-2. *Code for Class definitions*

`class Item {`	Header for `Item`
`float xpos;`	Horizontal coordinate can change
`floatypos;`	Vertical coordinate can change
`float iwidth;`	Width
`float iheight;`	Height
`int cred;`	Redness
`int cgreen;`	Greenness
`int cblue;`	Blueness
`Item(float x,float y,float w,float h,int red,int green, int blue) {`	Header for `Item` constructor
`xpos = x;`	Sets initial horizontal coordinate
`ypos = y;`	Sets initial vertical coordinate
`iwidth = w;`	Sets width
`iheight = h;`	Sets height
`cred = red;`	Sets redness
`cgreen = green;`	Sets greenness
`cblue =blue;`	Sets blueness
`}`	Closes constructor
`Boolean isOver(float x,float y) {`	Header for `isOver` method
`return ((x>xpos)&&(y>ypos)&&(x<(xpos+iwidth))&&(y<(ypos+iheight)));`	Returns the result of calculation against four sides
`}`	Closes `isOver`
`void removeIt(int i) {`	Header for `removeIt`
`removeFromItemsArray(i);`	Removes from the `Items` array
`}`	Closes `removeIt`
`void display() {`	Header for `display`

(continued)

Table 8-2. (*continued*)

`fill(cred,cgreen,cblue);`	Sets the color
`rect(xpos,ypos,iwidth,iheight);`	Draws rectangle
`}`	Closes display
`void move(float dx,float dy) {`	Header for move
`xpos +=dx;`	Incrementally adjusts xpos
`ypos +=dy;`	Incrementally adjusts ypos
`}`	Closes move
`void duplicate() {`	Header for duplicate
`Item copy;`	For the copy
`copy = new Item(xpos+10, ypos+10,` `iwidth,iheight,cred,cgreen,cblue);`	Creates new Item, offset position
`items = (Item[]) append(items,copy);`	Adds to Items array
`}`	Closes duplicate
`void restart() {`	Header for restart
`}`	Closes empty method
`void pauseMovie() {`	Header for pauseMovie
`}`	Closes empty method
`}`	Closes Item class definition
`class MovieItem extendsItem{`	Header for MovieItem subclass of Item
`Movie imovie;`	iMovie references the Movie object
`String movieFileName;`	Holds movie file name, used by duplicate
`PApplet paref;`	Holds reference to the PApplet, used by duplicate
`MovieItem (float x,float y,float w,` `float h,String mfn, PApplet par ) {`	Constructor

(*continued*)

Table 8-2. (*continued*)

`super(x,y,w,h,255,255,255);` `//sets up white rectangle`	Calls parent constructor to set base variables
`imovie = new Movie(par,mfn);`	Sets reference to the `Movie`
`movieFileName = mfn;`	Sets the name of file
`paref =par;`	Sets reference to `PApplet`
`imovie.loop();`	Starts the movie
`}`	Closes constructor
`void removeIt(int i) {`	Header for `removeIt`
`imovie.stop();`	Stops the movie
`imovie = null;`	Extra precaution to remove the link to movie, for garbage collection
`super.removeIt(i);`	Calls parent method
`}`	Closes `removeIt`
`void duplicate() {`	Header for `duplicate`
`Itemcopy;`	Will hold the copy
`copy = new MovieItem(xpos+10, ypos+10, iwidth,iheight,movieFileName,paref);`	Creates the `MovieItem`; this will start the new `Movie`. Note reference to the `paref`
`items = (Item[]) append(items,copy);`	Adds to `items`
`}`	Closes `duplicate`
`void display() {`	Header for `display`
`image(imovie, xpos, ypos,iwidth,iheight);`	Draws in window the current frame
`}`	Closes `display`
`void restart() {`	Header for `restart`
`imovie.jump(0);`	Goes to first frame
`imovie.loop();`	Starts movie
`}`	Closes `restart`

(*continued*)

Table 8-2. (*continued*)

`void pauseMovie() {`	Header for pauseMovie
`imovie.pause();`	Pause (uses the method of Movie object)
`}`	Closes pauseMovie
`}`	Closes MovieItem class definition
`class ImageItem extends Item {`	Header for ImageItem
`PImage myImage;`	Reference to PImage
`String filename;`	File name, used by duplicate
`ImageItem (float x,float y,float` `w,float h, String imagefilename) {`	Header constructor
`super(x,y,w,h,255,255,255);` `//sets up white rectangle`	Calls parent constructor to set base variables
`filename =imagefilename;`	Saves file name
`myImage = loadImage(imagefilename);`	Sets PImage
`}`	Closes constructor
`void duplicate() {`	Header for duplicate
`Item copy;`	For copy
`copy = new ImageItem(xpos+10, ypos+10,` `iwidth,iheight,filename);`	Creates new ImageItem, offset
`items = (Item[]) append(items,copy);`	Adds to Items array
`}`	Closes duplicate
`void display() {`	Header for display
`image(myImage, xpos,` `ypos,iwidth,iheight);`	Draws image
`}`	Closes display
`}`	Closes class definition

As noted earlier, Table 8-3 shows the code for the main tab, labeled `collage6`. I kept the name so I could let you know that my program went through several revisions.

Table 8-3. *Code for collage6*

`import processing.video.*;`	Imports video library
`MovieItem myMovieItem;`	Used by `setup`
`Item[] items = {};`	Will hold all the items, starts out empty
`Item curItem = null;`	Will hold the item being dragged
`void setup() {`	Header for `setup`
`size(1000, 1000);`	Sets window
`Item myItem1 = new Item(10,30,100,200,250,0,200);`	Creates rectangle item
`items = (Item[]) append(items,myItem1);`	Adds to `items`
`Item myItem2 = new Item(500,800,200 ,100,0,100,100);`	Second rectangle
`items = (Item[]) append(items,myItem2);`	Adds to `items`
`myMovieItem = new MovieItem(250,200,300,200,"snowman. mov",this);`	Creates `MovieItem`, including creating `Movie`, starting `Movie`. This refers to the PApplet
`items= (Item[]) append(items,myMovieItem);`	Adds to `items`
`ImageItem myImage = new ImageItem (10,500,205,154,"pigtails1.JPG");`	Creates first `ImageItem`
`items = (Item[]) append(items,myImage);`	Adds to `items`
`myImage = new ImageItem(600,300, 300,400,"climbing.jpg");`	Creates second `ImageItem`
`items = (Item[]) append(items,myImage);`	Adds to `items`
`}`	Closes `setup`

(continued)

Table 8-3. (*continued*)

`void draw() {`	Header for `draw`
`background(255);`	Erases window

`text("c for copy, d for delete, t`
`for move to top, p for pause video,`
`r for restart.",`
`5,20);`
	Outputs the instructions

`for (int i=0; i<items.length;i++){`	Loop through `items`
`items[i].display();` `//use appropriate method`	Displays each item
`}`	Closes for-loop
`}`	Closes `draw`
`int overWhich() {`	Header for `overWhich`. The function determines the first item the mouse is over
`for (int i=0; i<items.length;i++) {`	Loop through items
`if (items[i].isOver(mouseX,mouseY))` `{`	Is it over the item
`return i;`	Returns the index (exit function)
`}`	Closes `if true` clause
`}`	Closes the `for`-loop
`return -1;`	Did not exit function in the `for`-loop, so return -1
`}`	Closes `overWhich`
`void keyPressed() {`	Header for `keyPressed`
`int i;`	Will hold the return value of `overWhich`
`i = overWhich();`	Invokes `overWhich`
`if (i < 0) {`	If negative, means not over any item
`return;`	Return; no action
`}`	Closes `if true` clause

(*continued*)

Table 8-3. (*continued*)

`else {`	Else
`switch(key) {`	Switch depending on letter pressed
`case 'c':`	
`items[i].duplicate();`	Copies item at `ith` position and adds to `items` array
`break;`	Leaves switch
`case 'd':`	
`items[i].removeIt(i);`	Deletes `ith` element from `items` array
`break;`	Leaves switch
`case 't':`	
`swapThem(i,items.length-1);`	Swaps the item with the last; that is, the topmost
`break;`	Leaves switch
`case 'r':`	
`items[i].restart();`	Restarts the item
`break;`	Leaves switch
`case 'p':`	
`items[i].pauseMovie();`	Pauses the item
`break;`	Leaves switch
`default:`	
`println("invalid key pressed");`	Shows up on console
`break;`	Leaves switch (not strictly necessary because this is the last)
`}`	Closes switch
`}`	Closes `else` clause
`}`	Closes `keyPressed`
`void swapThem(int j,int k) {`	Header for `swapThem`; general function, although only used to swap with the topmost item

(continued)

Table 8-3. (*continued*)

`Itemtemp;`	Needs a placeholder
`temp = items[j];`	Sets `item` at j
`items[j] = items[k];`	Swaps in `item` at k
`items[k] = temp;`	Sets `item` at k
`}`	Closes `swapThem`
`void removeFromItemsArray(int i) {`	Header for `removeFromItemsArray`
`Item[] tempitems = new Item[items.length-1];`	Creates new array, size one less than the size of current `Items` array
`for (int k = 0; k<i;k++) {`	For loop up to item to remove
`tempitems[k] = items[k];`	Copy over kth item
`}`	Closes loop
`for (int k=i+1;k<items.length;k++) {`	For loop starting after item to remove
`tempitems[k-1] = items[k];`	Copy over kth item
`}`	Closes loop
`items =tempitems;`	Sets `items` to the array just created and populated
`}`	Closes `removeFromItemsArray`
`void mousePressed() {`	Header for `mousePressed`
`int i;`	Will hold the index of item
`i = overWhich();`	Find out if on any item
`if (i>=0) {`	If this is a valid item
`curItem = items[i];`	Sets `curItem`
`}`	Closes `if true` clause
`}`	Closes `mousePressed`
`void mouseDragged() {`	Header for `mouseDragged`
`float dx;`	Will hold incremental x amount

(*continued*)

Table 8-3. (*continued*)

`floatdy;`	Will hold incremental y amount
`if (curItem!=null) {`	Only do this if `curItem` is set
`dx = mouseX- pmouseX;`	Calculates horizontal change
`dy = mouseY- pmouseY;`	Calculates vertical change
`curItem.move(dx,dy);`	Sets `curItem` to move these amounts
`}`	Closes `if` clause
`}`	Closes `mouseDragged`
`void mouseReleased(){`	Header for `mouseReleased`
`curItem = null;`	Sets `curItem` to `null`, which means no more dragging
`}`	Closes `mouseReleased`
`void movieEvent(Movie m) {`	Header for `movieEvent`
`m.read();`	Reads the next frame for the specified `Movie`
`}`	Closes `movieEvent`

Things to Look Up

You can and should read the documentation on the use of video. This would include a video in a file and videos captured from cameras. If you have a webcam on your computer, you can investigate how to include it in a sketch.

How to Make This Your Own

Add other types of items, including drawings, perhaps what you made for Chapter 1.

Inspired and instructed by the last two chapters, incorporate ways for collage makers to access image files and video files on their own computers or on websites.

The collage example given here, by allowing multiple copies of the one video, results in Annika singing a round with herself. If you decide to allow more than one movie, either by uploading the video file(s) to the data folder or providing the capability of the collage maker adding videos dynamically, you might want to address the issue of too much sound. One approach I took for a program using JavaScript was to specify a sound level for each video. However, there now are policies involving autoplay of video on the Web that made me opt for muting audio on my collage program.

You can incorporate video controls. Perhaps you want the restart operation to continue playing where the video was paused.

Here is an extra example from me. I have included in the code section a sketch that shows directions for folding an origami model, the kissy fish. This came about when I was working in a different language, JavaScript, and new features were added to incorporate line drawings and video. It occurred to me that origami directions consist of a sequence of steps and there may a different format that is best for each distinct step. Most of the steps in my example are shown as line drawings, each constructed dynamically, in the style of standard origami diagrams. For example, see Figure 8-3, which uses a dashed line and an arrow to indicate the next fold. The skinny, solid lines indicate the crease lines made by past folds.

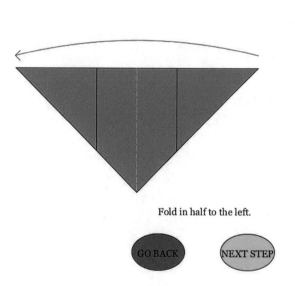

Figure 8-3. *Step in making kissy fish*

Certain steps are shown as photographs, because I thought photographs were best at communicating what was going on in the folding procedure. Figure 8-4 shows the model before a step I call throat surgery.

Stick your finger in its mouth and move the inner folded material to one side

Figure 8-4. *Step before throat surgery*

Figure 8-5 shows the model after throat surgery.

origamifish

Throat fixed.

Figure 8-5. *Model after throat surgery*

Finally, there are two steps that I decided needed to be shown using video. Figure 8-6 shows a frame from one of the two videos, showing how to operate the model.

Talking fish.

Figure 8-6. *Video showing kissy fish in operation*

Thus, the sketch demonstrates the use of graphics, image, and video. The reason I omitted extensive coverage of this example was not because I felt the programming was too difficult, but because of the complexity of the algebra and trigonometry required for the line drawings and origami is my interest and, possibly, not yours. You are welcome to try it out and examine the coding. The origami directions sketch might inspire you to think about a process you know that consists of steps where you can decide what the best way is to convey each individual step: a drawing made dynamically, an image, a video, or perhaps an audio file or something else.

Review previous examples and think about incorporating video clips, perhaps as an initial, splash type of opening screen, or as a response to some action. Perhaps you can make your chicken fly off if hit by the slingshot.

What You Learned

This chapter introduces incorporating video into your sketches. The `Movie` object, or, more precisely, a reference to the `Movie` object, was a variable in a class. The use of classes and subclasses demonstrated the object-oriented approach that provides a way to be consistent about what code can be shared and what must be different in dealing with a set of things.

What's Next

The next chapter describes the implementation of the paper-and-pencil game, Hangman. I provide two approaches. In one, the player enters letters by typing keys on the keyboard. In the other, a button is provided for each letter. My intention is to encourage you to realize that there generally are multiple ways to implement something even as simple and familiar as this game. For my sketch, I make use of a very small word list provided as a CSV file in the data folder. I use some of my favorite words and discuss scaling up.

CHAPTER 9

Word Guessing Game

Abstract

The focus for this chapter is a game of guessing a word one letter at a time. It resembles several such games. The computer program will take the role of the player that chooses the secret word. The number of guesses, or, as this version counts, the number of letters that are not in the secret word, can be fixed ahead of time and is hard-coded in my sketches. You can think of this as the number of allowed wrong moves. An alternative approach is to have the player propose the number of guesses, wrong guesses, or have a time limit. My programs demonstrate the allowed number of remaining using a circle that goes from green to red. This provides an excuse to explain two specific Processing features.

More on the Sketches

Typical practices in guessing letters are to either write out the letters guessed or write out the whole alphabet and cross out each letter as it is guessed. I decided to create two implementations to demonstrate different programming features. The first one, shown in Figure 9-1, represents an implementation of the game in which the player tries letters using the letters on the keyboard. Keeping track of letters guessed is left to the player. The figure shows that the player can make six more incorrect tries before losing the game. That is, when the display shows 0, the player can try one more letter. However, if that letter fails—is not in the secret word—the player loses.

© Jeanine Meyer 2022
J. Meyer, *Programming 101*, https://doi.org/10.1007/978-1-4842-8194-9_9

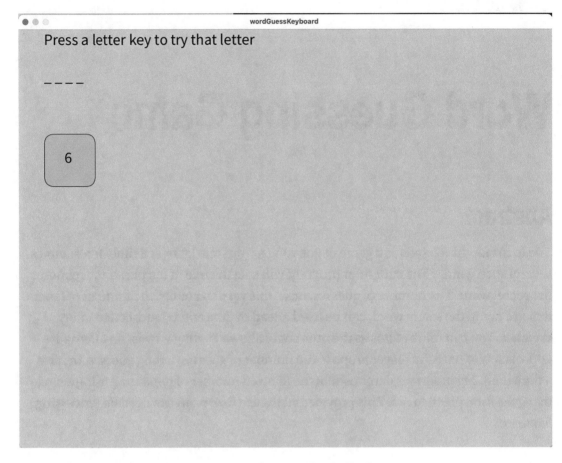

Figure 9-1. *Window with secret word, using keyboard*

In the second implementation, I supply buttons for each letter and remove the button once it has been used. To be fully accurate, my code covers up the button so it is not visible and sets a Boolean variable to indicate that this button has been removed.

Figure 9-2 shows the window of the implementation using buttons for each letter. Notice that the g button is missing and that is the button that I pressed. This implementation does not let the player make the mistake of trying a letter not in the secret word a second time, so this implementation changes the game. The existence of these two implementations gives you a chance to think about what is the same and what is different between the two implementations in terms of the user interface.

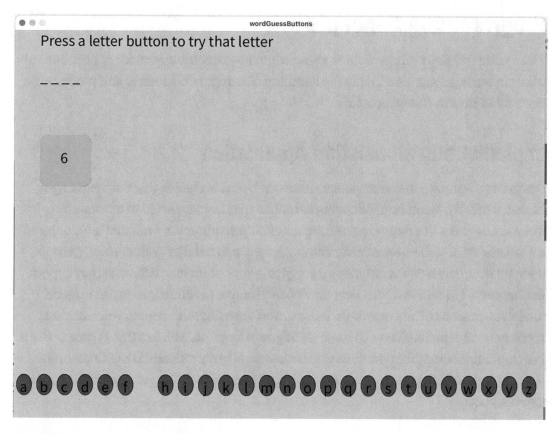

Figure 9-2. *Window with letter keys*

The implementation using Buttons uses the Button class that you saw in a previous chapter, with one modification. This demonstrates reusing code and is very, very common.

The secret words are chosen at random from a list contained in a CSV (comma-separated value) file in the data folder. My word list has only five words. They are carefully chosen to include words that check aspects of the programming and help me play the game while I am testing the program. It often makes sense to do the initial development with a smaller list. The word list can be replaced simply by changing the file in the data folder; no change is required in the code. This is called scaling up. Not all scaling up operations are that simple.

Programming Concepts

This section suggests things to think about when implementing familiar applications and issues in testing. I mention briefly the handling of strings of characters and producing a circle filled in with changing colors.

Implementing an Existing Application

Designing a known paper-and-pencil game can be more challenging than you might expect. Similarly, it can be challenging to build a new implementation of something that already exists in a computerized form. When you automate a manual task, or build a new version of something already computerized, you need to evaluate and, perhaps, trade off using the new capabilities vs. supplying your audience with what they expect. In Chapter 8, I provided a brief overview of an example for directions for an origami model making use of line drawings, images, and video. In this chapter, you will read about two implementations of a basic word guessing game. The fact that I came up with two implementations that produce games that are slightly different is not uncommon. It would be useful to perform testing to see how people, including young children and parents, react.

Testing and Scaling Up

Building a computer application involves testing! For games and related activities, you do not want to struggle with playing the game while building the game. My implementation of each implementation made use of a word list supplied as a file in the data folder. I did not need to wait to put together a final list while testing the logic of either sketch. Instead, I made a list of just five words. The number 5 does not appear in my code. Instead, my code reads in the Table and constructs an array of String objects. Besides being words that I like, the words I used are of different lengths so I know immediately or after guessing one letter what the word is without modifying the code that makes a random choice. Some of the words have letters that appear more than once, so I could verify that my code does the correct thing. I can be confident that my sketches will work with the longer lists.

Testing might not be so easy; code might need to be modified. For example, in more complex applications, I might want to replace a random choice to test specific logical paths through the code. This is something to think about on a case-by-case basis. Bigger and more complex systems, especially systems that change frequently, could require the development of a testing suite or an automated system for testing, not requiring human interaction.

I did not include a final word list in the code available with the source code, but I can tell you my approach. I searched and found online lists that were supplied for spelling bees for different grades. It was easy to download and convert such a list to a CSV file. For each case, you might need to think about what is an appropriate source for the data. It probably is not a list of your favorite words. You also should consider the alternative of going to the Web for a new list each time you run the program. For this game, the list of words does not have to be complete in any sense. However, for a game in which the player gets to pick, the list should be large.

For the Word Game sketches, my code extracts the words and prepares a String array. The code does a lot of work at the start, when users generally are relatively patient as opposed to taking a small amount of time for each game. If what you determine to be the appropriate data source is very large, this might not be the proper decision.

Most, if not all, programming languages provide functions for examining and manipulating strings of characters. You do need to check on what is available. You also need to be careful about strings of characters vs. single characters.

Displaying the State of the Game

The reader may have guessed, or knew from the game has it appeared in the first edition, that my original word game showed the state of the game by a sequence of pictures. My approach for this edition was motivated by my wish to show off certain features of Processing. I decided to go from green light to red light (without going to yellow in-between. I leave that to the reader). My implementation made use of the map and lerpColor functions.

The map function is used with any two ranges of numbers plus a number representing something in the first range. The function returns the corresponding number in the second range. Suppose you are a teacher and gave a quiz of 30 problems, with 1 point apiece. Suppose the number of problems correct was held in the variable score. You could use

```
grade = map (score,0,30,0,100);
```

to get a grade out of 100.

The lerpColor function (LERP stands for linearly interpolate) uses two colors and a number (float) and calculates an integer that can be interpreted as a color between the two colors. The code

```
float inter = map(wrongs,0,maxTries,0,1);
color c = lerpColor(greenC, redC, inter);
fill(c);
```

is used to set the fill value for a circle to be displayed. The variables greenC and redC have been set to be green and red. The variable wrongs holds the number of wrong guesses at letters in the secret word, and the variable maxTries holds the number of wrong guesses allowed. The number of wrong guesses to go is shown against the specified color background. The player is allowed one more guess after the number reaches 0.

Displaying Text

Displaying text over and over on a static background can produce degraded text. One fix is to use a call to background, and this often is required. An alternative approach is to draw a rectangle first and put the text on top of it. The fill for the rectangle can be what would have been used in background so it does not appear. I wrote a function displayTextsBackground to be invoked when needed.

Processing Programming Features

The treatment of the word list is essentially the same as the data file kept and updated in the image test sketch described in Chapter 5. One key difference is that the file is not modified. My code brings in the file as a Table and then sets (populates) an array of String objects in the setup function. My code also sets a variable, numwords, to hold the number of words. Doing this once at the start saves a small amount of time later when making the choice. The choice of word to be the secret word is done in the keyPressed function and uses the random function.

Note

The number of elements in an array named myArray is myArray.length. The number of characters in a string named myString is myString.length(). The first length is a variable; the second is a method. To use entities in this example, the number of words in the array wordlist is wordlist.length. Because I set the variable numwords in setup, you won't see this in the program. The number of letters in the secret word, held in the variable secret, is secret.length(). I set wlen to this value. Processing will catch errors you might make regarding length, and you will catch on. It is not something you would be expected to work out for yourself.

Examination and manipulation of the secret word are done using built-in String methods. The length method returns the length of the secret word, required to set the variable blanks to a combination of the underline (_) and the blank characters. When the player has made a guess, the method charAt is used within a for-loop that iterates through each of the characters in the secret word. In one implementation, the for-loop is in the keyPressed function; in the other, it is in the mousePressed function.

When the player guesses a letter that is in the secret word, the blanks String is changed to show the guessed letter. My function is more general than it needs to be, accepting as parameters a base String, parameter name base; a String representing that to be inserted, parameter name sub; an integer indicating the place of the insertion, parameter place; and an integer indicating the number of characters removed, parameter remove. The function makes use of the substring String method. This method provides a way to extract a piece of a string using index values. A call of substring(myString,a,b) extracts the string from position a, with 0 corresponding to the first character, up to, but not including, b. This is another programming feature that you can and will get accustomed to if you give yourself time. It also is helpful to try small examples.

Note also that the base here will be the blanks String, which has two characters for every character in the secret word. The call of replace is blanks = replace(blanks,letterpicked+" ",i*2,2);.

The function is

```
String replace(String base,String sub,int place,int remove){
    String prior = base.substring(0,place); //before insert
    String after = base.substring(place+remove); //after
    return prior+sub+after;
}
```

Notice that the `replace` function does not change the `base` but returns the new string.

Operation Overview

Both sketches start with what is termed a splash window or screen, shown in Figure 9-3. Having this extra window made it easier to program restarting with a new secret word. Of course, an improved splash window could be more interesting.

Figure 9-3. *Opening window for both implementations*

You have seen what the next windows look like for the two implementations in Figure 9-1 and Figure 9-2. Figure 9-4 shows another game in process. The player has correctly guessed an *m* but tried three other letters, resulting in the murky color that is a specific point between green and red.

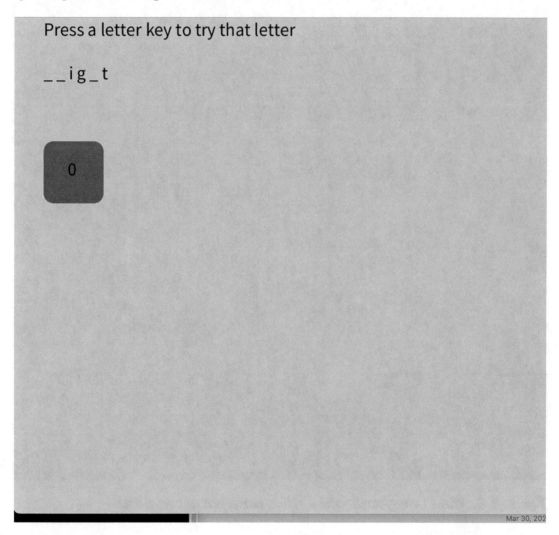

Figure 9-4. *Word Game with buttons after several moves*

Switching to the game without buttons, the player has used the keyboard, correctly picked three letters, but picked several wrong letters, as shown in Figure 9-5.

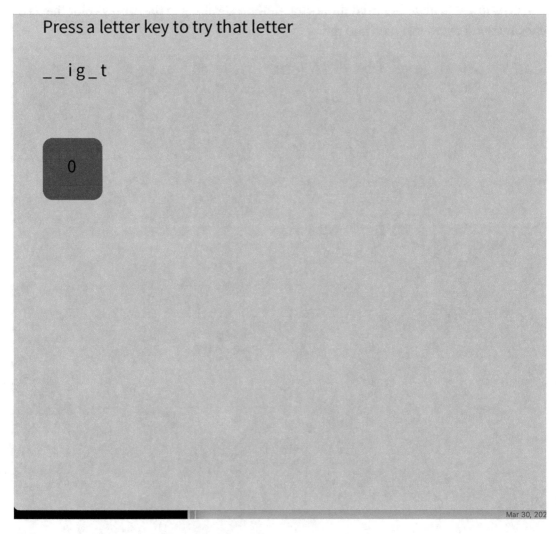

Figure 9-5. *Word Game, keyboard version, close, but not yet a loss*

Figure 9-6 shows a winning game.

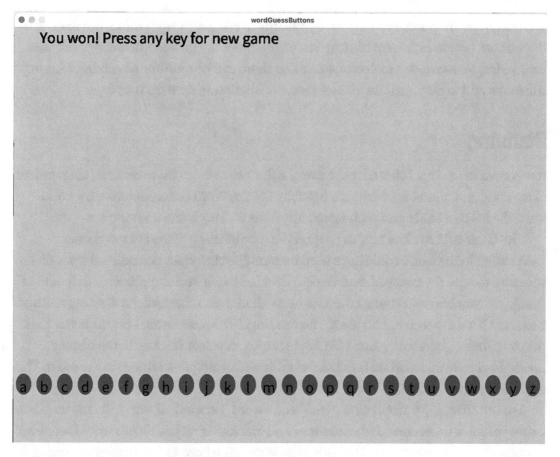

Figure 9-6. *A win in the Word Game with buttons*

Pressing any key starts a new game. I have nothing in the code that prevents the same word from being selected during a session. It is something to consider adding to the sketches. The longer the word list, though, the less likely that secret words will be repeated often.

If you have multiple windows open on your desktop and you move among the different programs, you could have the experience of pressing a key for a program such as these with no response. There are a lot of possibilities, but there is a good chance that the operating system is not sending the key event information to the program you want to use. Your program needs to have the focus, and some other program has it instead. The focus will go to a program by clicking its window. This is common when users have numerous applications open.

Implementing the Word Game Sketches

The examples for this chapter do not require me to design an application, but instead to think about how to represent the features of guess-a-word games. I decided to produce the two implementations to demonstrate that there can be multiple possibilities in such situations and to demonstrate different ways of obtaining input from a player.

Planning

It was clear to me that I should make use of a file for the word list to make it independent of the code and, therefore, easily changeable. For the Word Game sketches, my code loads the file as a Table and then extracts the words to populate a String array.

The letter Button class for this chapter is a modification of the Button classes used earlier in the text. I could have used the same Button class and defined a parallel structure to hold the removed attribute but decided that a better approach was to add to the object variables and change the isOver method. I also changed the display method because I liked my rectangular design for the single-character letter buttons better than the ovals for longer labels. Note: I did not include a check of removed in the display method because this method is only invoked when all alphabet buttons are present. This decision can be debated.

For the changing presentation of the secret word, I started off with a String variable, named blanks, that consists of underlines and blanks. Using just blanks would not work because they all run together. String methods are used both for examining the secret word, held in the variable secret, and modifying the variable blanks.

The tables showing the functions and their relationships show the main differences between the two implementations. Table 9-1 shows the functions and relationships for the Word Game using the keyboard. It is, as you should expect, simpler. The main action is in keyPressed. Actually, keyPressed is invoked for the key press that starts off the application plus the game play.

Table 9-1. *Function Table for the Word Game Using the Keyboard*

Function	Invoked by	Invokes
setup	Java program	
draw	Java program	displayTextwBackground
keyPressed	Java program	advance, replace, displayTextwBackground
replace	keyPressed	
advance	keyPressed	displayTextwBackground
displayTextwBackground	draw,keyPressed, advance	

The functions table for the Word Game using letter buttons is shown in Table 9-2. You will see that several functions are invoked in only one place. Here, keyPressed is used for starting the application. The mousePressed function does the work during the playing of the game.

Table 9-2. *Functions Table for the Word Game with Buttons*

Function	Invoked by	Invokes
setup	Java program	
draw	Java program	displayTextwBackground
keyPressed	Java program	advance, showButtons, keyPressed
mousePressed	Java program	whichLetter, replace, advance, resetAlphabetButtons, showButtons, drawTextwBackground
replace	mousePressed	
advance	mousePressed	resetAlphabetButtons, displayTextwBackground
setupAlphabetButtons	setup	Button
resetAlphabetButtons	mousePressed, advance	Directly changes removed

(continued)

Table 9-2. (*continued*)

Function	Invoked by	Invokes
showButtons	keyPressed, mousePressed	Button.display
whichLetter	mousePressed	Button.isOver
Button	setupAlphabetButtons	
isOver	whichLetter	
display	showButtons	
displayTextwBackground	draw, mousePressed,advance, keyPressed	

Programming the Word Game Sketches

The two sketches are essentially the same, differing mainly in the treatment of the letter buttons. However, one issue did arise and was pointed out to me by the technical review. The Buttons version of the game did not allow the player to guess the same letter more than one time. The keyboard version did. My original implementation could be tricked by a sly player selecting the same correct letter over and over. The keyboard version required an extra check to determine if the player truly had guessed all the letters.

The code for the Word Game using the keyboard is shown in Table 9-3. It is long, but as I have written before, do not read it from start to finish. Use the functions table and examine individual lines of code.

Table 9-3. *Word Game Using Keyboard Program*

`String[] wordlist;`	Will hold all the words
`Table words;`	Table for loading in words
`int numWords;`	Set to be number of words
`Boolean chosen = false;`	Will change when secret word is selected
`String secret;`	Current secret word
`String blanks = "";`	Will hold blanks and the guessed letters
`int wlen;`	Length of secret word

(*continued*)

Table 9-3. (*continued*)

`int wrongs;`	Number of wrong guesses
`int nGuessed;`	Number of guesses
`String msg = "Press any key to start";`	Starting message
`color bgcolor = 200;`	Background color
`int msgstart = 50;`	Horizontal start of messages
`int maxTries = 7;`	Number of wrong answers allowed. Can still win on the 8th try
`color greenC = color(0,255,0);`	Green color
`color redC = color(255,0,0);`	Red color
`void setup() {`	Header for setup
`  size(1050,800);`	Set the dimensions of window
`  textSize(30);`	Set text size
`  words = loadTable("words.csv");`	Bring in word file
`  numWords = words.getRowCount();`	Set the number of words
`  wordlist = new String[numWords];`	Create array of appropriate size
`  for (int i = 0;i<numWords;i++) {`	For loop to populate the array
`    wordlist[i] = words.getString(i,0);`	Extract word from table
`  }`	Close for-loop
`  background(bgcolor);`	Set the color of window
`}`	Close setup
`void draw() {`	Header for draw
`  if (!chosen) {`	If secret word is not chosen
`  displayTextwBackground();`	Display msg
`  }`	Close if
`}`	Close draw

(*continued*)

Table 9-3. (*continued*)

`void displayTextwBackground() {`	Header for displayTextwBackground
`fill(bgcolor);`	Prepare to draw invisible rectangle
`noStroke();`	No stroke
`rect(0,0,width, 60);`	Draw rectangle to be under msg
`fill(0);`	Set text color to black
`text(msg,msgstart,30);`	Display text
`}`	Close displayTextwBackground
`void keyPressed() {`	Header for keyPressed
`if (!chosen) {`	No word chosen
`msg = "Press a letter key to try that letter";`	Set msg
`displayTextwBackground();`	Display text on top of invisible rectangle
`secret = wordlist[int (random(numWords))];`	Choose random word from wordlist
`wlen = secret.length();`	Set wlen with length
`chosen = true;`	Set chosen Boolean
`blanks = "";`	Start the preparation of blanks
`wrongs = 0;`	Initialize wrongs
`nGuessed = 0;`	Initialize nGuessed
`for (int i=0;i<wlen;i++) {`	For loop to set blanks
`blanks = blanks + "_ ";`	Two characters for each letter
`}`	Close for-loop
`fill(0);`	Set fill to black
`textAlign(LEFT);`	Set alignment
`text(blanks,msgstart,100);`	Display blanks
`}`	Close if not chosen

(*continued*)

Table 9-3. (*continued*)

`else {`	Else clause—secret has been set
`char letterpicked = key;`	Set letterpicked. Note: data type is char
`Boolean found = false;`	The found variable starts as false
`for (int i=0;i<wlen;i++){`	For loop going through secret
`if (secret.` `charAt(i)==letterpicked) {`	If ith char is equal to letterpicked
`found = true;`	Set found to true
`blanks = replace(blanks,` `letterpicked+" ",i*2,2);`	Modify blanks
`nGuessed++;`	Increment nGuesses
`}`	Close if clause
`}`	Close loop through all letters in secret
`if (found) {`	If letter is found (could be set multiple times)
`fill(bgcolor);`	Set fill to background color
`noStroke();`	No stroke
`rect(0,60,width,80);`	Draw a rectangle to erase that section of the window
`fill(0);`	Set fill now to black
`textAlign(LEFT);`	Set alignment
`text(blanks,msgstart,100);`	Display the modified blanks
`}`	Close if found
`else {`	Else bad guess
`wrongs++;`	Not found means increment wrongs
`advance();`	Show advanced color and count
`}`	Close else
`if ( (nGuessed>=wlen)&&` `(checkIfDone() {`	Check if all letters are guessed
`background(bgcolor);`	Set background color

(*continued*)

Table 9-3. (*continued*)

`textAlign(LEFT);`	Set alignment
`msg = "You won! Press any key for new game";`	New message
`chosen = false;`	Set chosen back to false
`displayTextwBackground();`	Display msg
`nGuessed = 0;`	Set nGuessed back to 0
`wrongs = 0;`	Set wrongs back to 0
`}`	Close if all letters are guessed
`}`	Close else for not chosen
`}`	Close keyPressed
`String replace (String base, String sub, int place, int remove) {`	Header for replace
`String prior = base. substring(0,place);`	Extract substring before the insertion
`String after = base. substring(place+remove);`	Extract substring after the insertion
`return prior+sub+after;`	Return new string
`}`	Close replace
`boolean checkIfDone() {`	Header for checkIfDone
`for (int i=0;i<blanks. length();i++) {`	Iterate through the blanks string
`if (blanks.charAt(i)== '_') {`	Check for the presence of a blank
`return false;`	If found, return false: still work to do
`}`	Close if true clause
`}`	Close for-loop
`return true;`	Return true: no blanks in the blanks string

(*continued*)

Table 9-3. (*continued*)

`}`	Close checkIfDone
`void advance() {`	Header for advance
`if (wrongs>maxTries) {`	Check if too many wrong guesses
`    background(bgcolor);`	Set background
`    textAlign(LEFT);`	Set alignment
`    msg = "You lost! Press any key for new game";`	Set msg to indicate loss
`    chosen = false;`	Reset chosen to false
`    displayTextwBackground();`	Display msg
`    nGuessed = 0;`	Reset nGuessed to 0
`    wrongs = 0;`	Reset wrongs to 0
`}`	Close clause for end of game
`else {`	Else game continues
`// update display`	Make rectangle holding number of wrong guesses be a specific color in range from green to red
`float inter = map (wrongs,0,maxTries,0,1);`	inter will be proportion from 0 to 1
`color c = lerpColor(greenC, redC, inter);`	Use inter to get an intermediate color
`fill(c);`	Set fill with that color
`rect(msgstart,200,100, 100, 20);`	Draw rectangle
`fill(0);  //set color of text for the number be black`	Set fill to black
`textAlign(LEFT,CENTER);`	Set alignment
`text(str(maxTries-wrongs), msgstart+40,200+40);`	Display the number of wrong answers allowed
`}`	Close clause
`} //ends advance`	Close advance

The program and description for the Word Game main coding with letter buttons are shown in Table 9-4. I have included a modified version of the Button class shown earlier. The modification of the Button class from that used in the previous chapter was to add the removed variable. This variable is used only in the isOver method. The button is immediately erased (covered over). The display method is only invoked at the start of a round.

Please note the similarities between the keyboard and the buttons programs.

Table 9-4. *Word Game with Buttons Program*

`String[] wordlist;`	Will hold all the words
`Table words;`	Table for loading in words
`int numWords;`	Will be set to the number of words
`Boolean chosen = false;`	Will change when secret word is selected
`String secret;`	Current secret word
`String blanks = "";`	Will hold blanks and the guessed letters
`int wlen;`	Length of secret word
`int wrongs;`	Number of wrong guesses
`int nGuessed;`	Number of guesses
`String msg = "Press any key to start";`	Starting message
`color bgcolor = 200;`	Background color
`int msgstart = 50;`	Horizontal start of messages
`int maxTries = 7;   //number of wrong answers allowed. Can still win on the 8th try.`	Number of wrong answers allowed. Can still win on the 8th try
`color greenC = color(0,255,0);`	Green color
`color redC = color(255,0,0);`	Red color
`Button[] buttons = {};`	Sets buttons array
`float padding = 8;`	Padding for buttons
`void setup() {`	Header for setup
`  size(1050,800);`	Sets the dimensions of window

(continued)

Table 9-4. (*continued*)

`textSize(30);`	Sets text size
`words = loadTable("words.csv");`	Brings in word file
`numWords = words.getRowCount();`	Sets the number of words
`wordlist = new String[numWords];`	Creates array of appropriate size
`for (int i = 0;i<numWords;i++) {`	For loop to populate the array
`  wordlist[i] = words.getString(i,0);`	Extracts word from table
`}`	Closes for-loop
`background(bgcolor);`	Sets the color of window
`setupAlphabetButtons();`	Sets alphabet buttons
`}`	Closes setup
`void setupAlphabetButtons() {`	Header for setupAlphabetButtons
`String alphabet =  "abcdefghijklmno` `pqrstuvwxyz";`	Holds alphabet
`int startx = 20;`	Starting horizontal position
`int starty = 680;`	Vertical position
`int buttonwidth = 30;`	Width of button
`int buttonheight = 40;`	Height of button
`int margin = 10;`	Space between buttons
`int spacing = margin + buttonwidth;`	Total space
`for (int i=0;i<alphabet.length();i++) {`	For loop for buttons

`  Button b = new Button(startx+i*spacing,`
`starty, buttonwidth, buttonheight,`
`color(200,0,0), str(alphabet.`
`charAt(i)));`
	Invokes Button constructor

`  buttons =  (Button[]) append` `(buttons,b);`	Adds new Button to buttons
`}`	Closes for-loop
`}`	Closes setupAlphabetButtons

(*continued*)

Table 9-4. (*continued*)

```void resetAlphabetButtons() {```	Header for resetAlphabetButtons
``` for (int i=0;i<buttons.length;i++) {```	For loop
``` buttons[i].removed = false;```	Resets removed object variable to false
``` }```	Closes for-loop
```}```	Closes function
```void showButtons() {```	Header for showButtons
``` for (int i=0;i<buttons.length;i++) {```	For loop
``` buttons[i].display();```	Invokes display method
``` }```	Closes for-loop
```}```	Closes function
```char whichLetter (int x, int y) {```	Header for whichLetter
``` for (int i=0;i<buttons.length;i++) {```	For loop checking buttons
``` if (buttons[i].isOver(x,y)) {```	Invokes isOver method
``` return (buttons[i].label.``` ``` charAt(0));```	At a hit, returns the letter
``` }```	Closes if
``` }```	Closes for-loop
``` return ('?');```	Returns indication of not over any button
```}```	Closes function
```void draw() {```	Header for draw
``` if (!chosen) {```	If secret word is not chosen
``` displayTextwBackground();```	Displays msg
``` }```	Closes if
```}```	Closes draw

(*continued*)

Table 9-4. (*continued*)

`void displayTextwBackground() {`	Header for displayTextwBackground
`fill(200);`	Prepares to draw invisible rectangle
`noStroke();`	No stroke
`rect(0,0,width, 60);`	Draws rectangle to be under msg
`fill(0);`	Sets text color to black
`text(msg,msgstart,30);`	Displays text
`}`	Closes displayTextwBackground
`void keyPressed() {`	Header for keyPressed
`if (!chosen) {`	No word chosen
`msg =  "Press a letter button to try that letter";`	Sets msg
`displayTextwBackground();`	Displays text on top of invisible rectangle
`secret = wordlist[int(random(numWords))];`	Chooses random word from word list
`wlen = secret.length();`	Sets wlen with length
`chosen = true;`	Sets chosen Boolean
`blanks = "";`	Starts the preparation of blanks
`wrongs = 0;`	Initializes wrongs
`nGuessed = 0;`	Initializes nGusses
`for (int i=0;i<wlen;i++) {`	For loop to set blanks
`blanks = blanks + "_ ";`	Two characters for each letter
`}`	Closes for-loop
`fill(0);`	Sets fill to black
`textAlign(LEFT);`	Sets alignment
`text(blanks,msgstart,100);`	Displays blanks
`advance();`	Displays status
`showButtons();`	Shows the alphabet buttons

(*continued*)

Table 9-4. (*continued*)

`}`	Closes if not chosen
`}`	Closes keyPressed
`void mousePressed() {`	Header for mousePressed
`char letterpicked = whichLetter` `(mouseX,mouseY);`	Invokes whichLetter
`if (letterpicked=='?') { return;}`	If no letter button was pressed, no action
`Boolean found = false;`	Initializes found to false
`for (int i=0;i<wlen;i++){`	For loop going through secret word
`if (secret.charAt(i)==letterpicked) {`	Checks ith letter
`found = true;`	Sets found to true
`blanks =  replace(blanks,` `letterpicked+" ",i*2,2);`	Modifies blanks
`nGuessed++;`	Increments nGuessed
`}`	Closes if
`}`	Closes for-loop
`if (found) {`	If found in word at least once
`fill(bgcolor);`	Erases old blanks, starting with fill
`noStroke();`	No stroke
`rect(0,60,width,80);`	Draws rectangle over area
`fill(0);`	Now sets fill to black
`textAlign(LEFT);`	Align
`text(blanks,msgstart,100);`	Displays blanks
`}`	Closes if
`else {`	Else bad guess
`wrongs++;`	Increments wrongs
`advance();`	Change display
`}`	Closes else

(*continued*)

Table 9-4. (*continued*)

`if (nGuessed>=wlen) {`	Checks if all letters are guessed
`background(bgcolor);`	Erases whole window
`textAlign(LEFT);`	Sets alignment
`msg =  "You won! Press any key for new game";`	Sets msg
`resetAlphabetButtons();`	Resets buttons (resets removed variables)
`showButtons();`	Shows alphabet buttons
`chosen = false;`	Resets chosen
`displayTextwBackground();`	Displays the msg
`nGuessed = 0;`	Resets nGuessed
`wrongs = 0;`	Resets wrongs
`}`	Closes clause checking if game won
`}`	Closes mousePressed
`String replace(String base, String sub,int place,int remove){`	Header for replaced used to update blanks
`String prior =  base.substring(0,place);`	Extracts part of string prior to change
`String after =  base. substring(place+remove);`	Extracts part of string after the changed part
`return prior+sub+after;`	Constructs new string
`}`	Closes replace
`void advance() {`	Header for advance
`if(wrongs>maxTries) {`	Checks for loss
`background(bgcolor);`	Erases whole windows
`textAlign(LEFT);`	Sets alignment
`msg = "You lost! Press any key for new game";`	Sets msg

(*continued*)

Table 9-4. (*continued*)

`resetAlphabetButtons();`	Resets buttons (resets removed variables)
`chosen = false;`	Resets chosen
`displayTextwBackground();`	Displays msg
`nGuessed = 0;`	Resets nGuessed
`wrongs = 0;`	Resets wrongs
`}`	Closes clause determining loss
`else {`	Starts else
`float inter = map(wrongs,0,` `maxTries,0,1);`	inter will be proportion from 0 to 1
`color c = lerpColor(greenC, redC,` `inter);`	Uses inter to get an intermediate color
`fill(c);`	Sets fill with that color
`rect(msgstart,200,100, 100, 20);`	Draws rectangle
`fill(0);`	Sets fill to black
`textAlign(LEFT,CENTER);`	Sets alignment
`text(str(maxTries-wrongs),` `msgstart+40,200+40);`	Displays the number of wrong answers allowed
`}`	Closes else clause
`}`	Closes advance
`//Button class`	
`class Button {`	Header for Button class
`int cx,cy;`	Horizontal and vertical positions
`int bw, bh, bwsq, bhsq;`	Width, height, and calculated values used in isOver
`color col;`	color
`String label;`	Holds the letter of the alphabet
`boolean removed;`	Will be set to true after letter is tried

(*continued*)

Table 9-4. (*continued*)

`Button (int x,int y,int bwid, int bht,` `color c, String lab)  {`	Button constructor
`cx = x;`	Sets object variables, x position
`cy = y;`	y position
`bw = bwid;`	Width
`bh = bht;`	Height
`bwsq = bw*bw;`	Calculates for isOver
`bhsq = bh*bh;`	Calculates for isOver
`col = c;`	Sets color
`label = lab;`	Sets label
`removed = false;`	Initial value of removed
`}`	Closes Button
`boolean isOver(int x,int y)  {`	Header for isOver method
`if (removed) return (false);`	Returns false—can't be over a removed button
`float disX = cx - x;`	Start of calculation
`float disXsq = disX * disX;`	Continues calculation
`float disY = cy - y;`	Continues calculation
`float disYsq = disY * disY;`	Continues calculation
`float v = (disXsq / bwsq) +` `(disYsq/bhsq);`	Completes calculation
`if (v<1) {`	isOver is true …
`removed = true;`	Marks button as removed
`fill(bgcolor);`	Sets fill to background color
`stroke(bgcolor);`	Turns off stroke
`ellipse(cx,cy,bw+8,bh+8);`	Draws ellipse to erase button

(*continued*)

Table 9-4. (*continued*)

`    return (true);`	Returns true
`  }`	Closes check for isOver
` else {`	else
`    return (false);`	Returns false
`  }`	Closes else clause
` }`	Closes isOver method
` void display()  {`	Header for display method
`//display only invoked at start of a round`	No need to check removed variable
`  fill(col);`	Sets fill
`  ellipse(cx,cy,bw,bh);`	Draws ellipse
`  fill(0);`	Sets fill to black
`  textAlign(CENTER,CENTER);`	Sets alignment
`  text (label,cx,cy-2);`	Draws text, positioned within ellipse
`  textAlign(LEFT);`	Resets alignment
` }`	Close of display method
`}`	Close of Button class

Things to Look Up

Look up String methods.

Look up treatment of tables, formed from comma-separated values, and think about how you can use them with other applications.

Research how text is formed, including the use of transparent pixels to produce smooth borders on the letters.

Study methods for manipulating colors, such as filtering using TINT or GRAY.

How to Make This Your Own

Build on my green-to-red idea or do something different to indicate the state of the game. You may consider using images or making line drawings.

Do the research to find suitable word lists online. You might want to use the URL method of bringing in the file or files, though this can be problematic as well as unethical if it is using something without permission.

For the implementation using the keyboard, display the letters of the alphabet that have been played.

Change what happens with a loss by showing the whole secret word, with the guessed letters a different color than the unguessed letters. Similarly, you may give a winner the chance to see the complete word.

Keep score over one session using global variables, or update a CSV file kept in the data folder.

Define levels of play that access different word lists and have different displays.

Create or acquire suitable video clips or audio clips to play on a win or a loss.

Move on to other guessing games. Invent your own.

What You Learned

In this chapter, you saw another use of a CSV file and two different ways to support player input: the keyboard and letter buttons. The fact that how to implement a simple word guessing game is not obvious is more common than you might imagine. You read about the possibilities of developing and initial testing with a small data set. You saw manipulation of String objects and calculations involving colors. The letter Button class is similar, although not identical, to the Button class used in previous chapters. This can be termed partial reuse of programming.

What's Next

The next and final chapter is an introduction to drawing in 3D. Working in 3D is a challenge. Doing your own experimenting will help your understanding. Both featured examples show the use of 2D images with 3D objects. One example shows a ball, wrapped in a 2D image, apparently rolling around in 3D. The other example will include an explanation of how to detect when a specified time has elapsed. The source code includes extra examples, introduced briefly in the text.

CHAPTER 10

3D

Abstract

This last chapter is an introduction to the 3D capabilities of Processing. Just as Processing provides ways to draw in the plane, we can build a sketch with objects that are rendered in space, that is, three dimensions. It is important to recall that once things have been drawn in the Processing window, any notion of how the pixels were colored is not maintained. That is why the coding has to keep track of food items and snake segments and rock, slingshot, and chicken, drawing them again as required. Processing does not provide a 3D modeling system, but the facilities provide considerable power. With that in mind, in this chapter, we'll review programming and Processing concepts and then focus on two 3D sketches.

The first is an animation in which a ball wrapped in the Spanish flag rolls around a wading pool at the Alhambra (Figure 10-1).

© Jeanine Meyer 2022
J. Meyer, *Programming 101*, https://doi.org/10.1007/978-1-4842-8194-9_10

Figure 10-1. *Ball with Spanish flag rolling around the Alhambra*

The second example is a cube, with pairs of photos of Annika's dance recital on opposing sides (Figure 10-2). The cube can be rotated and builds on a sketch described in the Processing documentation. This can be fully appreciated only by running the program.

Figure 10-2. *Rotating cube*

As with everything in programming, it is essential for your understanding that you experiment: Copy the simple sketches in the documentation and make changes, download or copy the examples in this book and make changes, and create your own sketches. I include extra sketches with the source code. See later in the chapter for screenshots of a dreidel (a top that spins and slows down) and a representation of the solar system, with nine planets rotating round the sun, including Pluto, although that makes for an even greater challenge.

Programming Concepts

Representation of 3D on the flat computer screen requires what is termed *rendering*. The 3D objects in Processing are collections of flat *faces*, in certain contexts called *facets*, made up of *edges* and *vertices* (corners) and information on what is the inside vs. the outside of the object. The locations of the vertices are specified using three values for the x, y, and z axes, analogous to x and y coordinates for 2D. In Processing, the standard orientation for the z axis is coming out of the plane of the screen. That is, values for the z dimension increase moving toward us; the default zero z position is at the screen; and values are more negative moving away from us. Although I could, with confidence, make the statement that most programming tools use the origin in the upper left corner, the upside-down arrangement that Processing uses for 2D work, 3D tools differ on the orientation of the three dimensions. Processing uses a left-handed coordinate system, whereas some languages and tools use a right-handed coordinate system.

The task of the renderer is to determine how the object is projected onto the screen to be viewed by the user. This often involves calculating when all or portions of edges and faces are blocked by other faces. This is known as the hidden line or hidden surface removal problem. The calculations use the eye, gaze location (the point in space that the eye is looking at), type of projection (standard perspective or something else), and, sometimes, lighting. Default settings mean that programmers might not need to specify everything to produce results.

Processing and other tools provide a set of primitive 3D shapes along with ways for programmers to construct their own shapes. Spheres are provided as faceted polyhedrons, with the standard setting providing so many facets that they appear round to us. Transformations, such as shown in 2D, are provided.

Processing Programming Features

The first piece of code that signals to Processing that we want to use 3D is the `size` statement. The line `size(500,740,P3D);` specifies the dimensions of the Processing window and indicates the use of the 3D renderer. Processing provides two 3D primitives: sphere and box. The `sphere` takes one parameter, the radius of the sphere. The `box` takes one or three parameters; using one produces a cube, and using three specifies the three sizes of the three dimensions of the box. The location of the `sphere` or the box is at the current origin of the coordinate system, which starts in the upper left corner. The result of the following sketch is shown in Figure 10-3.

```
void setup() {
    size(800,600,P3D);
    sphere(200);
}
```

Figure 10-3. *Sphere drawn at origin in upper left*

I have more to say about the sphere, but first, let's take the common first step of moving the origin to the center of the window.

```
void setup() {
    size(800,600,P3D);
    translate(width/2, height/2, 0);
    sphere(200);
}
```

The code has changed the original origin in the x and y dimensions, but not in z dimensions. This demonstrates the critical aspect of 3D in Processing: drawing is done by setting the origin.

The lines on the sphere mark the facet lines (Figure 10-4). This is a polyhedron with many flat sides, enough to fool our eye into seeing a sphere. The lines are governed by the setting of stroke and the interior of the faces by the setting of fill.

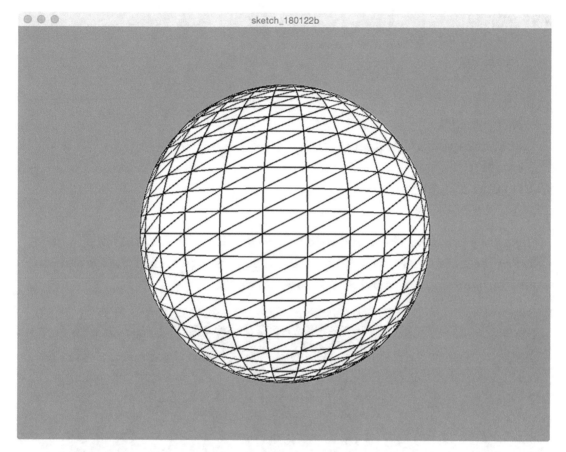

Figure 10-4. Sphere at translated origin

Other transformations, such as rotateX, rotateY, rotateZ, and scale, change what we see in the window. The use of scale can change a sphere into an ellipsoid with different dimensions. You can change the number of facets using sphereDetail, and you can turn off seeing the facets using noStroke. This also removes all edges, which might or might not be what you want.

My next example demonstrates the use of the camera function along with fill and noFill. The first step is to write the setup function and include a call to noFill. The draw function erases the window, as you have seen many times before, and invokes translate to move the drawings to the center of the window. The effects of translate and any other transformation go away after each call of draw and must be repeated.

Using noFill will show you so-called wire frame objects. There is no hidden line removal; all we see are the edges. The following code for setup and draw draws two boxes.

```
void setup() {
    size(800,600,P3D);
    noFill();
}
void draw() {
    background(200);
    translate(width/2,height/2,0);
    box(30);
    box(100,150,200);
}
```

This code produces what is shown in Figure 10-5. The two boxes are not obvious. Consider the inner square: if I held up a fully 3D cube right in front of one eye and you closed the other eye, you would see a square, not a cube.

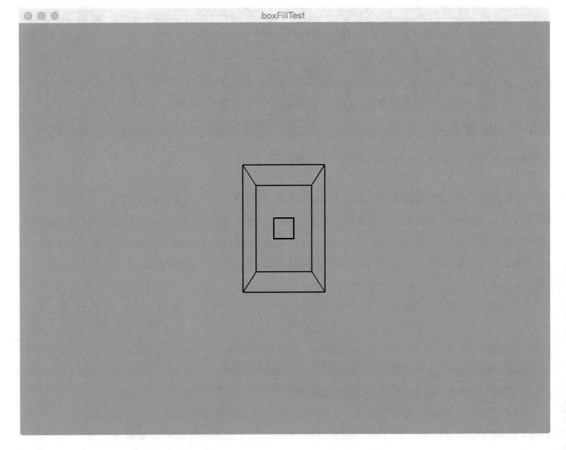

Figure 10-5. *Box within a box*

Now, I show a definition for mouseDragged in which I use the camera function to change the position of the eye to be the current mouse coordinates on the window. You are familiar with providing code for the mouse event functions and making use of mouseX and mouseY. I do not change the other values controlled by the camera function. More accurately, I restate the default values. These include the z location of the eye, the gaze point, and the orientation. My one-eyed camera person is not tilting their head.

```
void mouseDragged() {
    camera(mouseX, mouseY, (height/2.0) / tan(PI*30.0 / 180.0), width/2.0,
height/2.0, 0, 0, 1, 0);
}
```

Providing this capability for interaction means that the user gets a much greater sense of the 3D nature of the drawing. Figure 10-6 shows the box within box drawing with the only change being the modified eye position.

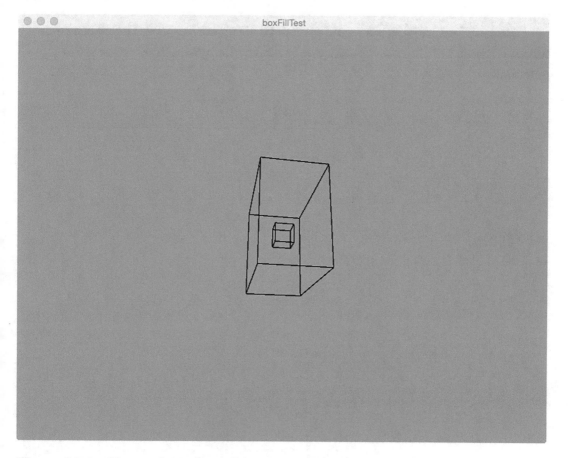

Figure 10-6. *Changed window after mouse dragging*

Finally, I decided I wanted to toggle back and forth between having fill and not having fill, that is, hidden lines removed vs. wire frame. To do this, I declared a global variable noFillB and wrote a keyPressed function.

```
boolean noFillB = true;
void keyPressed() {
    if (noFillB) {
        fill(255);
        noFillB = false;
    }
    else {
        noFill();
        noFillB = true;
    }
}
```

Figure 10-7 shows what we would consider a 3D object in space. The fill has been turned back on. The inner box is completely hidden along with three edges of the outer box.

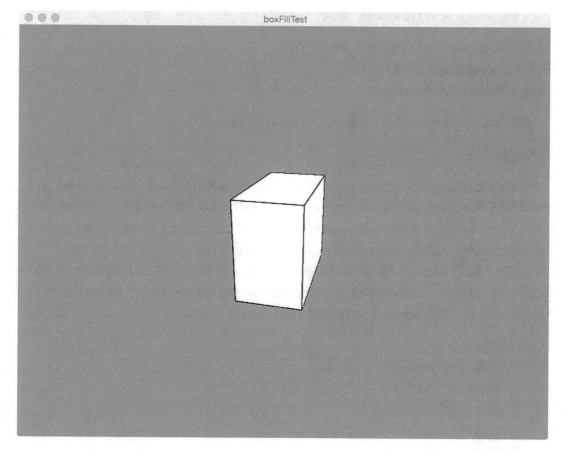

Figure 10-7. *Hidden lines removed*

Processing provides texture facilities to put images on 3D shapes. The documentation provides examples of making a 2D map of the world the texture on the sphere. For the rolling ball example, I decided to use the Spanish flag. The first step is to declare a global variable of type PShape.

```
PShape ball;
```

Create the shape in the setup function:

```
PImage design = loadImage("flag.png");
ball = createShape(SPHERE,10);
ball.setTexture(design);
```

To draw the shape in the window at the current origin, I use

```
shape(ball);
```

Recall the hexagons drawn as part of the origami model in Chapter 6. Processing provides a way to create custom shapes in 3D as well as 2D. The vertices are specified using three numbers. It is possible to set the fill for these shapes, as demonstrated by the following code that I have taken from my dreidel example (look ahead to Figure 10-10). The code here, all in setup, draws four triangular sides for the base of the top. Figure 10-8 shows a screenshot. Notice that the vertex mentioned first in the set of vertices starting with beginShape and ending with endShape repeats to close the shape.

```
void setup() {
        size (600,600,P3D);
        translate(width/2, height/2,0);
        noStroke();
        scale(100);
    fill(100,100,0);
    //bottom triangle from each of the 4 sides to center point
    beginShape();
        vertex(-1,1,1);
        vertex(-1,1,-1);
        vertex(0,2,0);
        vertex(-1,1,1);
    endShape(CLOSE);
    fill(100,0,0);
    beginShape();
        vertex(1,1,1);
        vertex(1,1,-1);
        vertex(0,2,0);
```

```
        vertex(1,1,1);
    endShape(CLOSE);
    fill(0,100,0);
    beginShape();
        vertex(-1,1,-1);
        vertex(1,1,-1);
        vertex(0,2,0);
        vertex(-1,1,-1);
    endShape(CLOSE);
    fill(0,0,100);
    beginShape();
        vertex(-1,1,1);
        vertex(1,1,1);
        vertex(0,2,0);
        vertex(-1,1,1);
    endShape(CLOSE);
}
```

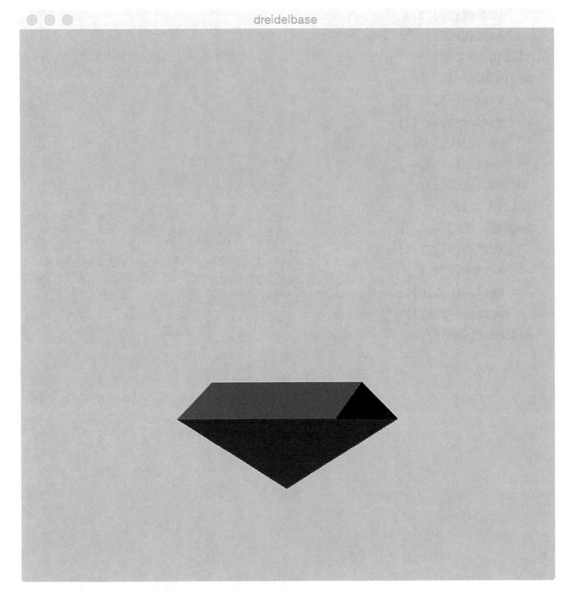

Figure 10-8. *3D shape, colored using* `fill`

The code for the dreidel base applied colors using `fill` in the standard way. An alternative is to put what is called texture on a 3D shape by specifying the position in space of the 3D object and the corresponding position in a 2D image. This requires five numbers. Following the example in the Textured Cube in the Processing documentation,

I use the technique of specifying the vertices using unit values and scale the object to be bigger using the scale function. You will find the entire sketch code in the "Program" section for the rotating cube example.

Processing also provides ways of specifying lighting for the scene. It appears that just using the single statement lights(); does improve the look of many sketches involving 3D. The statement must be in the draw function or some other function invoked for each frame, because the settings are reset at each invocation of draw.

I urge you to experiment with the primitives and transformations. I do caution you to proceed at a slow pace, though, as I did in the example with the two boxes. If you change where an object is located and change one or more of the camera parameters and apply rotations, it will not be easy to understand what is going on. If an object such as a sphere is very small, it might appear as a black ball as opposed to a faceted sphere. Making a snowman is a good place to start. You can find a snowman consisting of three spheres and a snowman on a box in the source code. The facets produce a crystal-like effect that fits the idea of a snowman.

Under the Covers

The rendering of 3D scenes into output on the 2D display is called the 3D graphics rendering pipeline. Today, much of the computation is done using special graphics processing units (GPUs) with much parallel computation. The increase in computer speed over the years has been considerable, but the demands from the gaming and movie industries also have increased, so this still is an area of research and development.

Rolling Ball at Alhambra Operation Overview

In the first sketch, the ball rolls down the left side, across the back, up the right side, and then goes back down the right side, across the back from right to left, and up on the left side (Figure 10-1). I do call this a cheap trick: the background is a 2D image from a postcard that I purchased at the Alhambra in Granada, Spain. I term this sketch a cheap trick because of the use of the 2D image from the postcard. Please do keep in mind that the size of the image had to match the size of the Processing window. The ball uses the Processing *texture* feature to appear to be wrapped in the Spanish flag. The 3D space is superimposed on the background.

The rolling ball at the Alhambra starts in motion. Pressing any key toggles back and forth between stopping and starting. The stop-and-start feature was added later by declaring a global variable, moving, and putting all the coding in the draw function within an if (moving) statement. After I did this, it was much easier for me to produce a screenshot of the sketch with the Spanish flag displayed as I wanted.

Implementing the Rolling Ball at Alhambra

Having been to the Alhambra and possessing the postcard, I decided to produce a sketch that superimposes the movement of a ball against the picture. The program just grew after that, with wrapping the ball in the Spanish flag to show the rotating and providing the stop-and-start feature.

Planning

The first task for the rolling ball was to determine the turning points, and this was done by trial and error. I wrote a sketch that made the postcard picture the background and then drew a sphere at each guessed location. This was an instance of what is termed *throw-away code*, and you need to be willing to do it. The next task was developing the movement back and forth over the three sides of the reflecting pool. I realized that the coordinates change in z or x. More exactly, the change is decreasing in z, then increasing in x, then increasing in z, then (turning around) decreasing in z, decreasing in x, and increasing in z. I was satisfied with this as an adequate example for my classes. However, when I was writing this book, I decided to do more.

Moving an object in 3D in Processing requires resetting of the origin. If the origin of a sphere is the center, then rotating the sphere on itself is easy once I decide along which axis I want to do the rotation. This creates a new challenge: My code can rotate the sphere, but how to make it visible that the ball is rotating if it is simply a sphere? The answer is to put something on the sphere using the texture facilities. I made use of an image of the Spanish flag. Note that it has file extension png.

I came to the realization that the path was made up of six segments, not three: going down the left side, across from left to right at the back, coming up the right side, going down the right side, across from right to left at the back, and coming up the left side. I used a switch statement in a function I named rotateAndDraw to handle the cases corresponding to the segments.

I put in the stop-and-start facility to give the user something to do, but then I became a happy user because, as I have said, it made it easier to get the screenshot I wanted. My first thought was to use noLoop to stop the action, but I decided that a Boolean would be better. The relationship of the functions is shown in Table 10-1.

Table 10-1. *Function Table for Rolling Ball*

Function	Invoked by	Invokes
setup	Underlying Java program	
draw	Underlying Java program	forwardtravel, backwardtravel
forwardtravel	draw	rotateAndDraw
backwardtravel	draw	rotateAndDraw
keyPressed	Underlying Java program	

Programming the Rolling Ball at Alhambra

The global variables include the values defining the turning points, Boolean (true–false) values, often called *flags,* the PImage for the background and the PShape for the ball, and the message giving instructions. I note that forwardtravel and backwardtravel could have been part of draw, but this way made sense to me. Table 10-2 shows the code.

Table 10-2. *Program for Rolling Ball*

PImage bg;	This is the image from the postcard showing the Alhambra
float x,y,z;	Used to indicate the parameters of translate to position the origin to draw the ball
float xstart = 150;	The leftmost x position
float xend = 330;	The rightmost x position
float ylevel = 400;	The constant y level; that is, the height
float zstart = -50;	The farthest away z position
float zend = 450;	The closest z position

(continued)

Table 10-2. (*continued*)

`boolean forward = true;`	Indicating forward motion or not
`float a=0;`	The a stands for angle; this is used for rotating the ball, initialized to 0
`PShape ball;`	Will hold the ball, with its texture
`boolean moving = true;`	Used to indicate movement or not
`String msg = "Press any key to stop or restart.";`	Instructions
`void setup() {`	Header for setup
`size(500,740,P3D);`	Set the dimension of window and 3D
`noStroke();`	Turn off stroke
`sphereDetail(15);`	Set the amount of detail (faceting)
`bg = loadImage("alhambra.jpg");`	Load postcard image
`PImage design = loadImage ("flag.png");`	Load Spanish flag image
`ball = createShape(SPHERE,10);`	Create a shape
`ball.setTexture(design);`	Give it texture; that is, wrap the flag around the sphere
`background(bg);`	Set initial background
`x = xstart;`	Initialize x
`y = ylevel;`	Initialize y
`z = zend;`	Initialize z
`textSize(20);`	Set text size for instructions
`}`	Close setup
`void draw() {`	Header for draw
`if (moving) {`	Only do something if moving is true
`background(bg);`	Erase the window and redraw background
`fill(0);`	Set color for clearing bottom of image

(*continued*)

Table 10-2. (*continued*)

`rect(0,700,500,40);`	Draw black rectangle
`fill(250,0,0);`	Set color for instructions message
`text(msg,100,720);`	Output instructions
`lights();`	Set lights
`if (forward) {`	If forward
`forwardtravel();`	Invoke forwardtravel
`}`	Close clause
`else {`	else
`backwardtravel();`	Invoke backwardtravel
`}`	Close clause
`}`	Close the if (moving) clause
`}`	Close draw
`void forwardtravel() {`	Header for forwardtravel
`if ((z>zstart)&&(x==xstart)) {`	Check if at first segment
`z--;`	Decrement z (move away)
`rotateAndDraw(1);`	Invoke rotateAndDraw with parameter 1
`}`	Close clause
`else { if (x<xend) {`	Check if at segment at back
`x++;`	Increment x
`rotateAndDraw(2);`	Invoke rotateAndDraw with parameter 2
`}`	Close clause
`else { z++;`	Increment z (move toward viewer)
`rotateAndDraw(3);`	Invoke rotateAndDraw with parameter 3
`if (z>zend) {forward = false;};`	If at the end, set forward to false
`}`	Close clause
`}`	Close clause
`}`	Close forwardtravel

(*continued*)

Table 10-2. (*continued*)

`void backwardtravel() {`	Header for `backwardtravel`
`if ((z>zstart)&&(x>=xend)) {`	If at fourth segment
`z--;`	Decrement z
`rotateAndDraw(4);`	Invoke `rotateAndDraw` with parameter 4
`}`	Close clause
`else { if (x>xstart) {`	If in back segment
`x--;`	Decrement x (move to the left)
`rotateAndDraw(5);`	Invoke `rotateAndDraw` with parameter 5
`}`	Close clause
`else { z++;`	Increment z, now moving toward viewer
`rotateAndDraw(6);`	Invoke `rotateAndDraw` with parameter 6
`if (z>zend) {forward = true;};`	If at end, set `forward` to `true`
`}`	Close clause
`}`	Close clause
`}`	Close `backwardtravel`
`void rotateAndDraw(int p) {`	Header for `rotateAndDraw`; parameter will indicate the segment and therefore what gets rotated positively or negatively
`a=a+PI/10;`	Increment a (the angle)
`translate(x,y,z);`	Position origin at `x,y,z`; these have been set previously
`switch(p) {`	Switch on the parameter
`case 1:`	First segment, going down the left
`rotateX(a);`	Rotate around x axis
`break;`	Leave switch
`case 2:`	Second segment, going from left to right at the back

(continued)

Table 10-2. (*continued*)

`rotateZ(a);`	Rotate around z axis
`break;`	Leave switch
`case 3:`	Third segment, coming up the right
`rotateX(-a);`	Rotate around x axis, negatively
`break;`	Leave switch
`case 4:`	Fourth segment, going back down the right, away from viewer
`rotateX(a);`	Rotate around x axis
`break;`	Leave switch
`case 5:`	Fifth segment, going at the back right to left
`rotateZ(-a);`	Rotate around z axis, negatively
`break;`	Leave switch
`case 6:`	Sixth segment, coming back up the left side
`rotateX(-a);`	Rotate around x axis, negatively
`break;`	Leave switch
`}`	Close switch
`shape(ball);`	Draw the ball
`}`	Close `rotateAndDraw`
`void keyPressed() {`	Header for `keyPressed`
`moving = !moving;`	Toggle the `moving` Boolean; using `!`, which is logical not, changes `true` to `false` and `false` to `true`
`}`	Close `keyPressed`

Rotating Cube Operation Overview

The example, shown in Figure 10-2, is based on the Textured Cube described in the Processing documentation. I emphasize again that the sketch needs to be run to be appreciated. The user can rotate the cube using the mouse. Note that dragging the mouse to the right or left causes the cube to be rotated around the y axis. Dragging the mouse up or down the screen causes the cube to be rotated around the x axis. If the mouse is dragged diagonally, it is rotated along both axes.

I made the addition of having the cube rotate by itself after no action by the user after a specified amount of time. This is a nice, although perhaps creepy, effect, and it demonstrates a technique for handling the event of nothing happening.

Implementing the Rotating Cube

I include this as one of the featured examples because of my addition and because I felt it merited extra attention beyond what was provided in the documentation. The main Processing feature demonstrated is applying texture, in the form of images, to faces of a cube.

Planning

I decided to use three images for texture, each for the pair of opposing sides of the cube. Following the Textured Cube example, applying a texture (i.e., an image) to a portion of a 3D shape can be done using unit measurements as opposed to the exact pixel dimensions to relate a set of 3D coordinates (three numbers) to a set of 2D coordinates (two numbers). Each face of the cube is associated with one of the three images.

Two global variables are set up to hold the amount of rotation around the x axis (rotx) and the rotation around the y axis (roty). These values are set in one of two ways. If the user drags the mouse, the mouseDragged function is invoked. The calculation is done to set rotx using the difference between the previous x coordinate of the mouse, held in pmouseY, and the current x coordinate, held in mouseY. The calculation for roty is the difference between mouseX and pmouseY. Here is the code:

```
void mouseDragged() {
    float rate = 0.01;
    last = millis();
```

```
    rotx += (pmouseY-mouseY) * rate;
    roty += (mouseX-pmouseX) * rate;
}
```

A horizontal (x) movement will set off a rotation around the y axis, and a vertical (y) movement will set off a rotation around the x axis. The expressions involving the previous mouse positions are different because of the upside-down coordinate system. Do not take my word for this. Change mouseDragged and move the mouse and see what seems correct to you.

The rate variable determines how much moves of the mouse affect rotations. You can experiment with the value. Do keep in mind that the mouseDragged function is called at every frame, so you don't want small moves to lead to big rotations.

The line with millis relates to the second way the rotation variables are set. You can go back to Chapter 5 and review how a pause is implemented in the image test sketch. In the rotating cube example in this chapter, the rotation variables are set if the user does not do anything for a specified amount of time. The specified amount of time is held in the variable interval. The millis function returns the time in milliseconds since the sketch is started. The global variable last is set in setup to the value returned by millis()and in mouseDragged. In the draw function, the following if statement determines if enough time has elapsed since the user did something.

```
if ((millis()-last) > interval) {
    setRotation();
}
```

In English, the condition in the if statement asks if the difference between current time and the last time something happened is greater than interval. The setRotation function is the following:

```
void setRotation() {
    rotx += PI/400;
    roty += PI/400;
}
```

I could have put these two statements in the if clause, but I generally favor defining functions for distinct tasks.

To produce the cube, I modified the function in the Processing documentation in two ways. I gave the function three parameters for the three sets of opposite sides of the cube. Then I used beginShape(QUADS) and endShape() three times, referencing a different one of the parameters each time. I used the approach of defining the cube as occupying the space from -1 to 1 along the *x* axis, -1 to 1 along the *y* axis, and -1 to 1 along the *z* axis. The vertices of the images are indicated by (0,0), (1,0), (1,1), and (0,1). It is important to note two things. First, this is a very tiny cube. The reason we can see it is that there is a call to scale(200) before the TextureCube function is invoked. Second, there is some distortion of the images I use for this because they are not squares.

The function table for rotating cube is shown in Table 10-3.

Table 10-3. *Function Table for Rotating Cube*

Function	Invoked by	Invokes
setup	Underlying Java program	
draw	Underlying Java program	setRotation, TexturedCube
mouseDragged	Underlying Java program	
setRotation	draw	
TexturedCube	draw	

Programming the Rotating Cube

In Table 10-4, you will find the code for this sketch. I did copy the vertex calls in the TexturedCube function from the Processing documentation, but I did do my own fiddling around to convince myself they were correct. I suggest you do your own experimentation. You might end up making the images applied as textures be mirror images some of the time.

Table 10-4. *Program of Rotating Cube*

`PImage frog, flowers, makeup;`	For the three images
`float rotx = PI/4;`	Initial rotation around x axis
`float roty = PI/4;`	Initial rotation around y axis
`int last;`	Hold time last thing was done
`int interval = 6000;`	Amount of wait before rotation "by itself"
`void setup() {`	Header for `setup`
`size(1000, 1000, P3D);`	Set the dimensions of window and set up for 3D
`frog = loadImage("AnnikaFrog.JPG");`	Load `frog` image
`flowers = loadImage("AnnikaFlowers.` `JPG");`	Load `flowers` image
`makeup = loadImage("AnnikaMakeup.jpg");`	Load `makeup` image
`textureMode(NORMAL);`	Set normal texture mode
`last = millis();`	Initial setting of `last`
`}`	Close `setup`
`void draw() {`	Header for `draw`
`background(0);`	Erase window
`textSize(20);`	Set the text size

`text("Drag using mouse anywhere on`
`screen to rotate cube. If no action,`
`cube will rotate by itself.", 17,14);`
	Give instructions

`noStroke();`	No `stroke`
`translate(width/2.0, height/2.0,` `-100);`	Move origin to center and back away from viewer
`if ((millis()-last) > interval) {`	Has there been nothing happening for a long enough time?
`setRotation();`	Set the rotations
`}`	Close `if` clause

(continued)

Table 10-4. (*continued*)

`rotateX(rotx);`	Rotate around x whatever `rotx` is
`rotateY(roty);`	Rotate around y whatever `roty` is
`scale(200);`	Scale up (because cube defined is tiny)
`TexturedCube(frog,flowers,makeup);`	Invoke TexturedCube to draw the cube with the images
`}`	Close draw
`void setRotation() {`	Header for `setRotation`
`rotx += PI/400;`	Increment `rotx`
`roty += PI/400;`	Increment `roty`
`}`	Close `setRotation`
`void TexturedCube(PImage tex1,` `PImage tex2, PImage tex3) {`	Header for TexturedCube; the parameters are the three images for opposing sides of the cube; the cube is 2 pixels by 2 pixels by 2 pixels
`beginShape(QUADS);`	Begin a shape, using the QUADS parameter indicating how the images will be applied
`texture(tex1);`	Use the first image; it will be applied to the faces of the cube that are at z equal to 1 and -1; these are the front face and the back face
`vertex(-1, -1,1, 0, 0);`	Connect the corners of the face to the corners of the image; the upper left corner of the face is connected to the top left corner of the image
`vertex( 1, -1,1, 1, 0);`	The upper right corner of the face is connected to the top right corner of the image
`vertex( 1,1,1, 1, 1);`	The bottom right corner of the face is connected to the bottom right corner of the image
`vertex(-1,1,1, 0, 1);`	The bottom left corner of the face is connected to the bottom left corner of the image

(*continued*)

Table 10-4. (*continued*)

	This still uses tex1; now applied to the back face; the x and y specifications will be opposite the previous set of images to display the images correctly
vertex(1, -1, -1, 0, 0);	Connect the corners of the face to the corners of the image; the upper right corner of the face is connected to the top left corner of the image
vertex(-1, -1, -1, 1, 0);	The upper left corner of the face is connected to the top right corner of the image
vertex(-1,1, -1, 1, 1);	The bottom left corner of the face is connected to the bottom right corner of the image
vertex(1,1, -1, 0, 1);	The bottom right corner of the face is connected to the bottom left corner of the image
endShape();	End the shape assigning the image as texture in two parts, for the two opposing faces
beginShape(QUADS);	Begin a shape, using the QUADS parameter indicating how the images will be applied
texture(tex2);	Use the second image; it will be applied to the faces of the cube that are at y equal to -1 and 1; these are the top face and the bottom face
vertex(-1, -1, -1, 0, 0);	Now the coordinate that stays the same is the y coordinate for the cube; it is at -1 for the first four (the top face) and then will be at 1 for the next four; the image vertex at 0,0 is at the cube vertex -1,-1,-1
vertex(1, -1, -1, 1, 0);	The image vertex at 1,0 is at the cube vertex 1,-1,-1
vertex(1, -1,1, 1, 1);	The image vertex at 1,1 is at the cube vertex 1, -1,1

(*continued*)

Table 10-4. (*continued*)

`vertex(-1, -1,1, 0, 1);`	The image vertex at 0,1 is at the cube vertex `-1, -1,1`
	Using the same image, `tex2`, the next four vertices describe the bottom face
`vertex(-1,1,1, 0, 0);`	The image vertex at 0,0 is at the cube vertex `-1,1,1`
`vertex( 1,1,1, 1, 0);`	The image vertex at 1,0 is at the cube vertex `1,1,1`
`vertex( 1,1, -1, 1, 1);`	The image vertex at 1,1 is at the cube vertex `1,1,-1`
`vertex(-1,1, -1, 0, 1);`	The image vertex at 0,1 is at the cube vertex `-1,1,-1`
`endShape();`	End the shape
`beginShape(QUADS);`	Begin a shape, using the QUADS parameter, indicating how the images will be applied
`texture(tex3);`	Use the third image; it will be applied to the faces of the cube that are at x equal to `-1` and `1`; these are the left and right faces
`vertex(-1, -1, -1, 0, 0);`	Now the coordinate that stays the same is the x coordinate for the cube; it is at `-1` for the first four (the left face) and then will be at `1` for the next four; the image vertex at 0,0 is at the cube vertex `-1,-1,-1`
`vertex(-1, -1,1, 1, 0);`	The image vertex at 1,0 is at the cube vertex `-1,-1,1`
`vertex(-1,1,1, 1, 1);`	The image vertex at 1,1 is at the cube vertex `-1,1,1`

(*continued*)

Table 10-4. (*continued*)

`vertex(-1,1, -1, 0, 1);`	The image vertex at 0,1 is at the cube vertex -1,1,-1
	Using the same image, `tex3`, the next four vertices describe the right face
`vertex( 1, -1,1, 0, 0);`	The image vertex at 0,0 is at the cube vertex 1,-1,1
`vertex( 1, -1, -1, 1, 0);`	The image vertex at 1,0 is at the cube vertex 1,-1,-1
`vertex( 1,1, -1, 1, 1);`	The image vertex at 1,1 is at the cube vertex 1,1,-1
`vertex( 1,1,1, 0, 1);`	The image vertex at 0,1 is at the cube vertex 1,1,1
`endShape();`	End the shape
`}`	
`void mouseDragged() {`	Header for `mouseDragged`
`float rate = 0.01;`	Used to scale the change in mouse positions
`last = millis();`	Set `last` to indicate time when something happened
`rotx += (pmouseY-mouseY) * rate;`	Increment `rotx`
`roty += (mouseX-pmouseX) * rate;`	Increment `roty`
`}`	Close `mouseDragged`

Things to Look Up

The Processing documentation provides a basic tutorial on 3D at `https://processing.org/tutorials/p3d/`. It includes a description of what it means to be a left-handed coordinate system and the diagram shown in Figure 10-9.

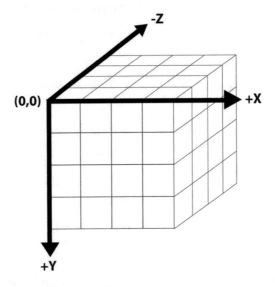

Figure 10-9. *Orientation of x, y, and z axes*

You will become comfortable with the coordinate system if and when you build on my examples and examples in the Processing documentation and when you design and build your own projects.

Investigate how to make custom shapes and how to apply textures. Review the use of transformations, especially using scale after creating a custom shape using unit dimensions.

Proceed slowly and study the different ways to use the camera function to change the various parameters for calculating the display and how to specify the different ways of lighting. At the risk of repeating myself, proceed step by step. If you change shapes and make transformations and change camera parameters all at once, you probably will get confused.

How to Make This Your Own

You certainly can do your own cheap tricks, making objects move against interesting flat backgrounds. You can use your own pictures for textures on rotating cubes or give the user the option to use images on the local computer or on the Web.

A good next challenge would be bouncing things in a five-sided box. You can decide if there is an invisible sixth side. Another challenge would be a shooter game, perhaps a version of slingshot.

One addition for the rotating cube could provide users a way to upload images from their own local computer. See Chapter 7 for background on how to do this.

I have provided additional examples in the source code section. These include a simple snowman consisting of just three spheres, the simple snowman on a box, the original rolling ball around the Alhambra, a dreidel, and a (crude) solar system.

The dreidel is shown in Figure 10-10. During Hanukkah, people play a gambling game. The player spins the dreidel, a top with four Hebrew letters. When it stops, the letter determines if the spinner takes the whole pot (often Hanukkah gelt, or foil-covered chocolate candy), half the pot, puts in one, or does nothing. In my sketch, the dreidel, made up of textured and colored 3D parts, spins and slows down after a random amount of rotation. There is an adjustment at the end so the final letter is facing directly forward, although I also print the result to the console. Spinning can be restarted using any key, and the mouse can be used to rotate the spinning or stationary dreidel around the x or y axes.

Figure 10-10. *Dreidel (spinning top)*

A student insisted that I include Pluto in a sketch of the solar system. I took this as a fine idea because of the challenge of depicting the Pluto object revolving in a different plane. However, a bigger challenge was that Pluto is very small relative to the other planets. The planets depicted are only very roughly proportional, with Pluto being the most out of proportion. A screenshot is shown in Figure 10-11. You need to look very closely to see the representation of Pluto.

Figure 10-11. Solar system (planets not in proportion)

What You Learned

This chapter was an introduction to 3D using Processing. You learned about the 3D coordinate system and transformations such as translations and rotations. You learned about the 3D primitives, applying texture, and creating custom 3D shapes. Objects are positioned by transformations of the coordinate system. What you learned to do in 2D can apply to the 3D domain. This applies to the mouseDragged event and the mouseX, mouseY, pmouseX, and pmouseY variables and using millis to insert a wait for something to happen.

What's Next

This is the last chapter! I hope this book was a satisfactory introduction to programming and the Processing language and it made you want to create your own sketches.

In the Appendix, I provide an introduction to p5js, a companion project by the Processing development community to provide a way to publish (disseminate) Processing sketches on the Web. That is, it is a way to use JavaScript with Processing functions. I offer three examples. The first is my familiar Daddy Logo. The second is a coin-toss type of application, alternating between two photos taken when we were in the Wall Street area in New York City. The third is a 3D helix that can be rotated just as the cube is rotated.

APPENDIX A

Introduction to p5.js

To quote from p5js.org, *p5.js is a JavaScript library for creative coding, with a focus on making coding accessible and inclusive for artists, designers, educators, beginners, and anyone else!*

By developing a library and tools, including a Web editor, the Processing community provides a way to produce projects for the Web. The p5.js effort is currently led by Qianqian Ye and evelyn masso and was created by Lauren Lee McCarthy.

The p5.js library and tools provide for JavaScript a similar entry that Processing provides for Java. In fact, if you go to `https://processing.org/`, you can find links to tools for using Processing functionality to Python and other programming languages.

In this Appendix, we will show you how to use the Web editor and ideas that you have learned in this book to make sketches in JavaScript, the programming language for websites. After this introduction, you may want to go further with p5.js. The next steps are to download the tools in order to create your sketches on your own computer, acquire webspace or turn your computer into a local server, and upload what you have produced. The p5js site has instructions, a large reference section, and videos. Note: The material on the p5js.org website does not presume prior knowledge of Processing or programming, but what you have learned about Processing and programming in general in this book will help you advance to building projects as complicated as your imagination and inspiration carry you.

As was my practice in the chapters in this book, I work using examples: the Daddy logo, a head/tail sketch I named Fearless Girls vs. the Bull, and a 3D construction I call Rainbow Helix.

Getting Started Using p5.js

The p5js project provides a Web editor and an environment that lets us create, run, and store sketches (programs). To put it another way, you can get started at programming without doing any downloads! Go to `https://p5js.org/` and click on Editor on the left or you can go directly to `https://editor.p5js.org/`

© Jeanine Meyer 2022
J. Meyer, *Programming 101*, https://doi.org/10.1007/978-1-4842-8194-9

Figure A-1 shows the opening screen. You can start using it immediately. However, to save your work, you do need to sign up, so I encourage you to do that. The panel on the left is for your code. The coding does resemble what you have been reading about in this book, namely, there is something called **setup** and something called **draw**. However, there are differences. Instead of specifying that each of these functions does not return a value by writing **void**, the definition of functions in p5.js requires us to write *function*. You next see what appears to be and is an invocation (function call) to **createCanvas**. This is what p5.js uses in place of **size**. In the definition of **draw**, you will see something familiar: a call to the function **background**. I encourage you to explore the rest of the Editor, including running the sketch by pressing on the arrow. The Web editor gives a name to sketches. This one is Abundant hip. You can modify what is here and add more code. Because I assume (I hope) you are familiar with programming in Processing, I will go on with the examples, but take as long as you want here. This template will appear when you click on File to get a pulldown menu and then click on New.

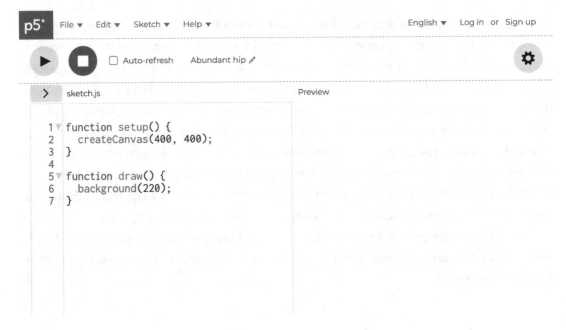

Figure A-1. Opening screen in editor

Overview of Examples

The Daddy Logo example is essentially the same as the Processing example featured in Chapter 1. It is a static drawing of two images. Figure A-2 is a screenshot of the Web editor, with the start of the code showing on the left in the panel labeled sketch.js and the result on the right in the panel labeled Preview. Notice the name daddyLogo appears next to a pencil. I changed what was there. It wasn't Abundant hip, but sometimes equally silly.

Figure A-2. *Screenshot for complete Daddy Logo*

After showing similar screenshots of the other two examples, I will describe the changes you need to make from Processing as presented in this book to p5js.

The Fearless Girls vs. the Bull is a coin-toss type of program. The Bull is a well-known statue near the New York Stock Exchange. The Fearless girl statue was nearby but has been moved. My granddaughter, also a fearless girl, is standing next to the statue. The sketch features the use of the functions *random* and *mouseReleased*. Just as in the example in Chapter 2, pressing and then releasing the mouse button causes one of two pictures to be shown. Figure A-3 shows an expanded screenshot of the editor. One aspect of this sketch is that it makes use of two image files. On the left you see a list of files, two of which refer to the images. The description of the implementation will describe how to upload the image files for use with the code.

Figure A-3. Sketch shows display of the Fearless Girls picture

The last example is new and is included here to show the use of classes and 3D. It also features the use of *mouseDragged* for moving the helix. Figure A-4 is a screenshot of the helix.

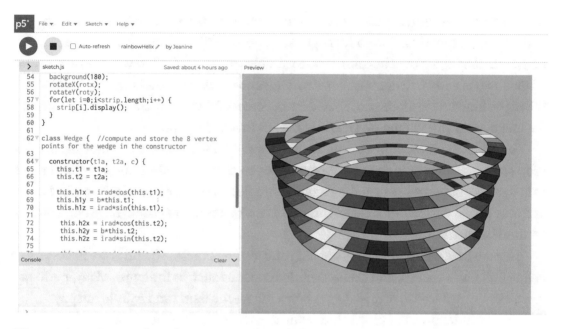

```
54    background(180);
55    rotateX(rotx);
56    rotateY(roty);
57    for(let i=0;i<strip.length;i++) {
58      strip[i].display();
59    }
60  }
61
62  class Wedge {  //compute and store the 8 vertex
        points for the wedge in the constructor
63
64    constructor(t1a, t2a, c) {
65      this.t1 = t1a;
66      this.t2 = t2a;
67
68      this.h1x = irad*cos(this.t1);
69      this.h1y = b*this.t1;
70      this.h1z = irad*sin(this.t1);
71
72      this.h2x = irad*cos(this.t2);
73      this.h2y = b*this.t2;
74      this.h2z = irad*sin(this.t2);
75
```

Figure A-4. *Screenshot showing rainbow helix*

The helix is constructed of flat shapes positioned in 3D. The definition of a class, used for the sections of the helix, is similar but with small differences from Processing code. I will make some general comments and then include tables for the coding for each example, with line-by-line explanations. My prediction is that you will not need to read the explanation for each line.

Implementing Daddy Logo

The p5.js language has functions and variables like other programming languages. Processing and many other programming languages are what is termed *strongly typed*. We, the programmers, need to specify the data type of each variable, each parameter to each function, and the return value for each function. What we get for our efforts is error messages that tell us if we are using something in a way that does not match how we defined it. JavaScript and p5.js (which is JavaScript with the addition of a library of Processing functions) are each NOT *strongly typed*. This does mean we don't get certain error messages. The benefit is that the initial programming is quicker. It is necessary to let (no pun intended) the editor know that something is a variable, and for that, p5.js requires us to use the word **let**. These statements are called *declarations*. Declaration statements can be used to initialize variables. However, some expressions must wait until the **setup** function. The daddyLogo sketch starts with declarations of *global variables*. The term *global* means that the variables maintain the last value set even after a function has ended. In contrast, *local* variables are declared and set within functions. When the function ends, the variables are not accessible, and any changes made within the function are not maintained if and when it is invoked again.

The sketch has definitions for **setup** and **draw**. As was the case in Processing, the Processing language uses **setup** as the name suggests: it generally is invoked first (I need to hedge here as you will see in the second example). The **draw** function is invoked over and over unless we include a call to **noLoop** to make this stop. (I could have done that for this sketch.)

As is the case with Processing, opening and closing brackets ({ and }) are necessary to define functions, classes, and clauses within functions such as for-loops. Many, perhaps most, errors are because of mistakes in bracketing. Processing and p5js do not pay attention to indenting, but proper indenting does help us, so try to use it.

As was the case in the daddyLogo in Processing, the definition of the daddy function allows the function to be used to draw different figures. I think of one as regular and the other as skinny. My purpose back in Chapter 1 and here is to demonstrate the advantages of variables and functions. The face is drawn using two ellipses with color the skintone value. The two ellipses overlap to form the peanut shape. The positioning and the sizes of the eyes, the mouth, and the two arcs representing the single hair are calculated from the parameters to daddy. Reminder: In p5js as well as Processing, horizontal values, referencing the x axis, increase moving from left to right. Vertical values, y axis, increase moving down the screen. This last is typical of most computer applications, but not what we are used to when creating graphs, so it does require an adjustment in our thinking.

Look over the code in the table. Use it to create your own drawings.

let ctrx = 100;	Horizontal value for 1st figure
let ctry = 160;	Vertical value for 1st figure
let faceWidth = 80;	Width for 1st figure
let faceHeight = 100;	Height for 1st figure
let skinnyFaceWidth = 60;	Width for 2nd figure

(continued)

`let skinnyFaceHeight = 130;`	Height for 2nd figure
`let eyeSize = 10;`	Eye size
`let skintone;`	Color for skin to be set in setup
`function setup()`	Header for setup function
`{`	
`  createCanvas(800,600);`	Set size of window
`  ellipseMode(CENTER);`	Parameters for ellipse will start in the center
`  skintone = color(255,224,189);`	Set color for faces. Please feel free to set the color
`}`	
`function draw()`	Header for draw function
`{`	
`  daddy(ctrx,ctry,faceWidth, faceHeight);`	Invoke daddy function with one set of parameters
`  daddy(3*ctrx, 2*ctry,skinnyFaceWidth, skinnyFaceHeight );`	Invoke daddy function with another set of parameters. Notice the modified parameters
`}`	
`function daddy(x,y, w, h)`	Header for daddy function. Parameters for position and dimensions
`{`	
`  noStroke();`	Turn off outlines
`  fill(skintone);`	Set color for fill
`  let eyeXoffset = int((15.0/80.0)*w);`	Calculate eye X offset as expression using w parameter

(continued)

`let eyeYoffset = int(.35*h);`	Calculate eye Y offset as expression using h parameter
`let mouthYoffset = int(.10*h);`	Calculate mouth Y offset as expression using h parameter
`let mouthWidth = int(.5*w);`	Calculate mouth width as expression using w parameter
`let mouthHeight = int(.3*h);`	Calculate mouth height as expression using h parameter
`let hairOffsetY = eyeYoffset*3;`	Calculate hair Y offset in terms of already-calculated eye offset
`let hairRadius = 3*eyeSize;`	Calculate hair arc radius in expression of eye size
`ellipse(x,y,1.2*w,h);`	Draw part of face
`ellipse(x,y-h/2,w,h);`	Draw part of face
`stroke(0);`	Now set stroke to black
`fill(0);`	Set fill to black
`ellipse(x-eyeXoffset,y-eyeYoffset,eyeSize,eyeSize);`	Draw left eye
`ellipse(x+eyeXoffset,y-eyeYoffset,eyeSize,eyeSize);`	Draw right eye
`noFill();`	Turn off fill
`arc(x,y-hairOffsetY,hairRadius,hairRadius,-PI/2,PI/2);`	Draw the lower part of single hair
`arc(x,y-hairOffsetY-hairRadius,hairRadius,` `hairRadius,PI/2,PI*3/2);`	Draw the upper part of single hair
`stroke(240,0,0);`	Set stroke to reddish
`arc(x,y+mouthYoffset,mouthWidth,mouthHeight,` `QUARTER_PI,3*QUARTER_PI);`	Draw the mouth
`}`	

Your next step is to modify my sketch by putting in more calls to **daddy**, with different sets of parameters. The next step after that would be to modify the daddy function. Then make it totally your own by defining your own function for a simple cartoon-type drawing. Put in calls to your function using different sets of parameters.

Implementing Fearless Girls vs. the Bull

The Fearless Girls vs. the Bull is what I call a coin-toss program. I make use of the **random** function to make one or the other picture appear with the location in the window based on the position of the mouse. The action is triggered using the mouseReleased function, and the figure appears where the mouse was on the window when the button was released (after being pressed down). Figure A-5 shows the Bull option. I made the screenshot smaller so I could point out the Hello, Jeanine on the upper right. I signed up when I started using p5js and logged on, giving me the capability to save my work.

Figure A-5. *Screenshot showing the Bull*

You will notice from the screenshot that the **draw** function is empty. This is because it is necessary to have a **draw** function, even if the action of the sketch is not specified in **draw** but in another function, in this case, **mouseReleased**.

The sketch makes use of the two images. Neither one is very big, but each takes up some amount of time to be loaded into the computer working memory. In order that this be accomplished before each is used, I make use of a function named **preload**. This is like **setup** and **draw** and **mouseReleased**. The underlying program "knows" to call **preload** when any and all media files are loaded. As you can see from the code in the table, the action in the **preload** function I have written is to load each image file and assign it to one of the variables. Remember: Names of variables and functions (and classes) are strictly up to us, the programmer. Do make them something meaningful for you. Do not assume the p5js system will interpret your names. I think of one as being like the head of a coin and the other like the tail.

let imgH;	Variable to hold one image
let imgT;	Variable to hold the other image
function preload(){	Header preload
imgH = loadImage("annikaFearless.jpg");	Load and set imgH
imgT = loadImage("bull.jpg");	Load and set imgT
}	
function setup() {	Header for setup
createCanvas(600,400);	Create a canvas 600 by 400
textSize(32);	Set the size of the text
text("click on the screen",10,50);	Display the text "click on the screen" at the indicated location
}	

(*continued*)

function draw() {	Header for draw function
}	Draw function is empty
function mouseReleased() {	Header for mouseReleased
background(255);	Set the background. This has the effect of erasing anything drawn previously in the window
if (.5<random(1)) {	The random function is invoked. It returns a number (fraction) between 0 and 1. The mechanics of the if statement checks if the value is greater than .5
image(imgH,mouseX,mouseY,200,200);	In this case, the imgH is drawn at the location of the mouse action
}	
else {	else
image(imgT,mouseX,mouseY,200,200);	Draw the imgT at the location of the mouse action
}	
}	

Okay, you have seen the code, but I need to tell you how to get image files when the code can access them. Look back to Figure A-1. Notice the > at the left. If you click on this, you see Figure A-6. Now click on the downward pointing arrow next to Sketch Files.

Figure A-6. *Screenshot showing panel with files*

A small window appears giving some options as shown in Figure A-7.

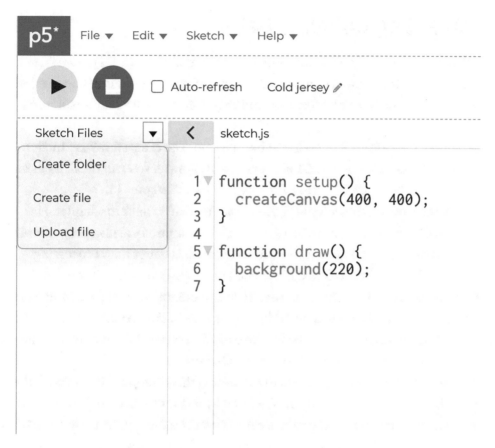

Figure A-7. *Small window showing options for adding files*

Click on Upload file and follow the instructions for all the image files needed for the sketch. I am showing this starting from the initial template. It can be done during or after writing the code. After I did this, the screen looked like Figure A-3. The Web editor maintains a folder holding the files. This includes any media files, such as the two image files, and sketch.js, which holds the code created with the Web editor. The index.html file is standard for all the p5js sketches. You can examine it. It does reference the Processing Library, mainly a collection of JavaScript functions. The style.css is another standard file for all the p5js sketches.

With this introduction and using what you learned for Processing, you can try to make other p5.js examples. The last example features 3D and definition of a class.

Implementing Rainbow Helix

The rainbow helix in my sketch is made up of a sequence of flat (2-D) pieces—I call them wedges—in 3D. I wanted to incorporate some user/player interactions, so I use **mouseDragged** to set two variables: **rotx** and **roty**. These are used for positioning each wedge.

The coding differs from Processing in two aspects. The **createCanvas** function has a third parameter, and it is WEBGL. This refers to a 3D library. You will recall that size also used a 3rd parameter when doing 3D. I refer you back to Chapter 10.

The second aspect is the definition of a class. You can go back to Chapter 4 for the definition of a class using Processing, which is the same as the Java programming language. I must admit that I like the terminology of p5.js better than Processing and Java. Broadly speaking, a class defines code and data (variables). There can be exceptions, but standard practice is to use, that is, reference, and set (read and write) the variables only with the code defined in the class definition. A class is used to create objects. The term **constructor** is used for the code that constructs an object. Other code is defined like functions. These functions are called *methods*.

Let's leave the theory and get down to explaining this example. One piece of the helix is an object in the Wedge class. It is defined by its four vertices and its color. The four vertices are specified by three values each. These are the x, y, and z positions in space (3D). The x and the y are horizontal and vertical, and the z is perpendicular to the x and y. Think of it as coming toward you out of the screen. This sketch does make use of a general, mathematical technique called parameterized curves as well as standard trigonometry. In a parameterized curve, a single value, the parameter, is used to calculate the positions in space. The value often can be viewed as time, but in this situation, it is an angle.

The fact that the **Wedge** objects fit together and take on the sequence of rainbow colors over and over is accomplished by how the constructor is invoked. It is an important programming skill to divide the work. The constructor function in the **Wedge** class definition creates a **Wedge** object based on two angles, the start and stop positions, and one color. The invocation of the constructor calculates the parameters so as to position the object along two helical spirals: one outer and one inner. The invocation also cycles through the array of colors, **rainbowColors**. The construction of what I have named **strip**, an array of **Wedge** objects, is accomplished by nested for-loops.

The Wedge class only has two methods: **constructor** and **display**. The **display** code uses **beginShape()** and **endShape(CLOSE)** to form the Wedge object, a flat shape in space. The new Wedge object is assigned to the variable **newWedge**. It is displayed by invoking **display**, and it is added to the array **strip** using an expression with the **push** function adding an item to the **strip** array.

With these general ideas in mind, please look at the table for the commented code.

let multiples = 28;	Multiples of rainbow segments
let rainbowColors = [];	Initialize rainbowColors as an array
let strip = [];	Initialize strip as an array
let rotx = 2.85;	Used to support mouse dragging changing orientation. I experimented to get these values
let roty = 0.55;	Used to support mouse dragging
let a = 190;	Radius of inner helix
let b = -6;	Step up vertically for 1 turn
let WedgeWidth;	Set in setup. It could be set now
let tDelta;	Will be set to hold difference in radians between start and end of a Wedge
let orad;	Outer radius. That is, radius of outer helix
let irad;	Inner radius

function setup() {
  createCanvas(700,600,WEBGL);
  WedgeWidth = a*PI/(3*7);
	Three complete rainbows per half turn. This looked good to me

tDelta = PI/21;	Set so three complete rainbows fit in a half turn
irad = a;	Radius of inner helix
orad = a+WedgeWidth;	Calculated radius of outer helix

(continued)

`rainbowColors[0] = color(148,0,211);`	Rainbow colors
`rainbowColors[1] = color(75,0,130);`	"
`rainbowColors[2] = color(0,0,255);`	"
`rainbowColors[3] = color(0,255,0);`	"
`rainbowColors[4] = color(255,255,0);`	"
`rainbowColors[5] = color(255,127,0);`	"
`rainbowColors[6] = color(255,0,0);`	"
`let t= 0;`	Initial value of t
	t used for parameterized curves representing the two helix coordinates
`background(200);`	Set background
	Nested for loops
`for(let i = 0;i<multiples;i++){`	Go through multiples of rainbows
`  for(let j=0;j<rainbowColors.length;j++) {`	In each case, go through seven Wedges
`    let t1 = t;`	Set t1 to the current value of t
`    let t2 = t1+tDelta;`	Calculate t2
`    newWedge = new Wedge(t1,t2,rainbowColors[j]);`	Create a Wedge going from t1 to t2 and using the jth color
`    newWedge.display();`	Display that Wedge
`    strip.push(newWedge);`	Add to the strip array
`    t = t2;`	Set new t value by advancing t to now be t2
`  }`	
`}`	
`}`	
`function draw() {`	Header for draw
`  background(180);`	Set background (erase everything)

(*continued*)

`rotateX(rotx);`	Use current value of rotx (set in mouseDragged)
`rotateY(roty);`	Use current value of roty (set in mouseDragged)
`for(let i=0;i<strip.length;i++) {`	Display each element of strip
`strip[i].display();`	
`}`	
`}`	
`class Wedge {`	Header for Wedge class definition
`constructor(t1a, t2a, c) {`	The constructor method computes and stores the eight vertex points for a new wedge. These values are used in the display method
`this.t1 = t1a;`	Set object variables, starting with t1. This is the t1 value for **this** object
`this.t2 = t2a;`	Set the t2 value
`this.h1x = irad*cos(this.t1);`	Calculate and set h1x. The first of three values setting the position of one corner
`this.h1y = b*this.t1;`	Calculate and set h1y
`this.h1z = irad*sin(this.t1);`	Calculate and set h1z
`this.h2x = irad*cos(this.t2);`	Now move on the next corner. Calculate and set h2x
`this.h2y = b*this.t2;`	Calculate and set h2y
`this.h2z = irad*sin(this.t2);`	Calculate and set h2z
`this.h3x = orad*cos(this.t2);`	Now move on to the next corner, the outer helix. Calculate and set h3x
`this.h3y = b*this.t2;`	Calculate and set h3y
`this.h3z = orad*sin(this.t2);`	Calculate and set h3z

(continued)

`this.h4x = orad*cos(this.t1);`	Now move on to the 4th and last corner of the wedge. Calculate and set h4x
`this.h4y = b*this.t1;`	Calculate and set h4y
`this.h4z = orad*sin(this.t1);`	Calculate and set h4z
`this.colorR = c;`	Set the color of this wedge
`}`	
`display() {`	Header for display method
`fill(this.colorR);`	Set the color
`beginShape();`	beginShape
`vertex(this.h1x,this.h1y,this.h1z);`	Vertex h1
`vertex(this.h2x,this.h2y,this.h2z);`	Vertex h2
`vertex(this.h3x,this.h3y,this.h3z);`	Vertex h3
`vertex(this.h4x,this.h4y,this.h4z);`	Vertex h4
`endShape(CLOSE);`	endShape, using the CLOSE option
`}`	
`}`	
`function mouseDragged() {`	Header for mouseDragged
`let rate = 0.01;`	Set value used in the calculation. I experimented and this seemed good
`rotx += (pmouseY-mouseY)* rate;`	Increment the rotx value
`roty += (mouseX-pmouseX)* rate;`	Increment the roty value. The difference between the statement, concerning mouseX, and the one above, concerning mouseY, makes the results correspond to user intuition. Remember the upside-down coordinate system
`}`	

I encourage you to play with this and make changes. You can use the underlying concepts to produce your own sketches.

What's Next

I hope you see from these examples that the change to p5.js from Processing is relatively minor. Please read again what I wrote about strong typing. The Web editor does produce some error messages, and they are helpful. It is okay to let the editor do work for you.

These three examples were all done using the Web editor. You may run into the limits on storage space, and/or at some point, you may want to download an editor to work on your computer, perhaps without a web connection. You may want to publish your work on the Web. The `https://p5js.org/` link has instructions on how to do this.

Work on Processing and p5js is ongoing, as is work on incorporating Processing functions into other languages. Use the websites to keep in touch. Join the community. Keep programming.

Index

A

Animation
    bouncing ball sketch, 59, 61–63
    bouncing polygon, 64
    definition, 59, 65
answer variable, 133
ArrayList, 136
Arrays, 58, 65

B

Ballistic motion, 130
Binary system, 137
Bouncing ball
    code, 73
    example, 70
    pentagon, 76
    planning, 71, 72, 74
    polygons, 78, 79
    program, 74
byte data type, 136

C

Callbacks, 210
Camel casing, 5
Card maker, 207
    callbacks, 210
    feedback to users, 210
    files, 208, 209
    fonts, 209

input/output library, 212, 213
libraries, 209
saving, 211
sound library, 210, 211
subclasses, 213, 214
char value, 137
Classes
    bouncing objects, 92, 94
        planning, 94–96
        program, 96
        types, 94
    definition, 85, 86
    jigsaw puzzle, 109
    make path/travel path, 100,
        101, 103–106
    ok-so-far testing, 127
    PApplet, 125
    phases of operations, 87
    tolerance of margin, 88
Codec, 236
Coin-toss sketch
    planning, 52, 54
    program, 49–52
Color Selector tool, 29
Comma-separated value (CSV) table,
    129, 261, 263, 287
Compound statement, 66
Computer application, 262
Constructor methods, 89, 238, 336,
    337, 339
createCanvas function, 324, 336

J. Meyer, *Programming 101*, https://doi.org/10.1007/978-1-4842-8194-9

Printed in the United States
by Baker & Taylor Publisher Services